POSTCARD HISTORY SERIES

The Catskills

IN VINTAGE POSTCARDS

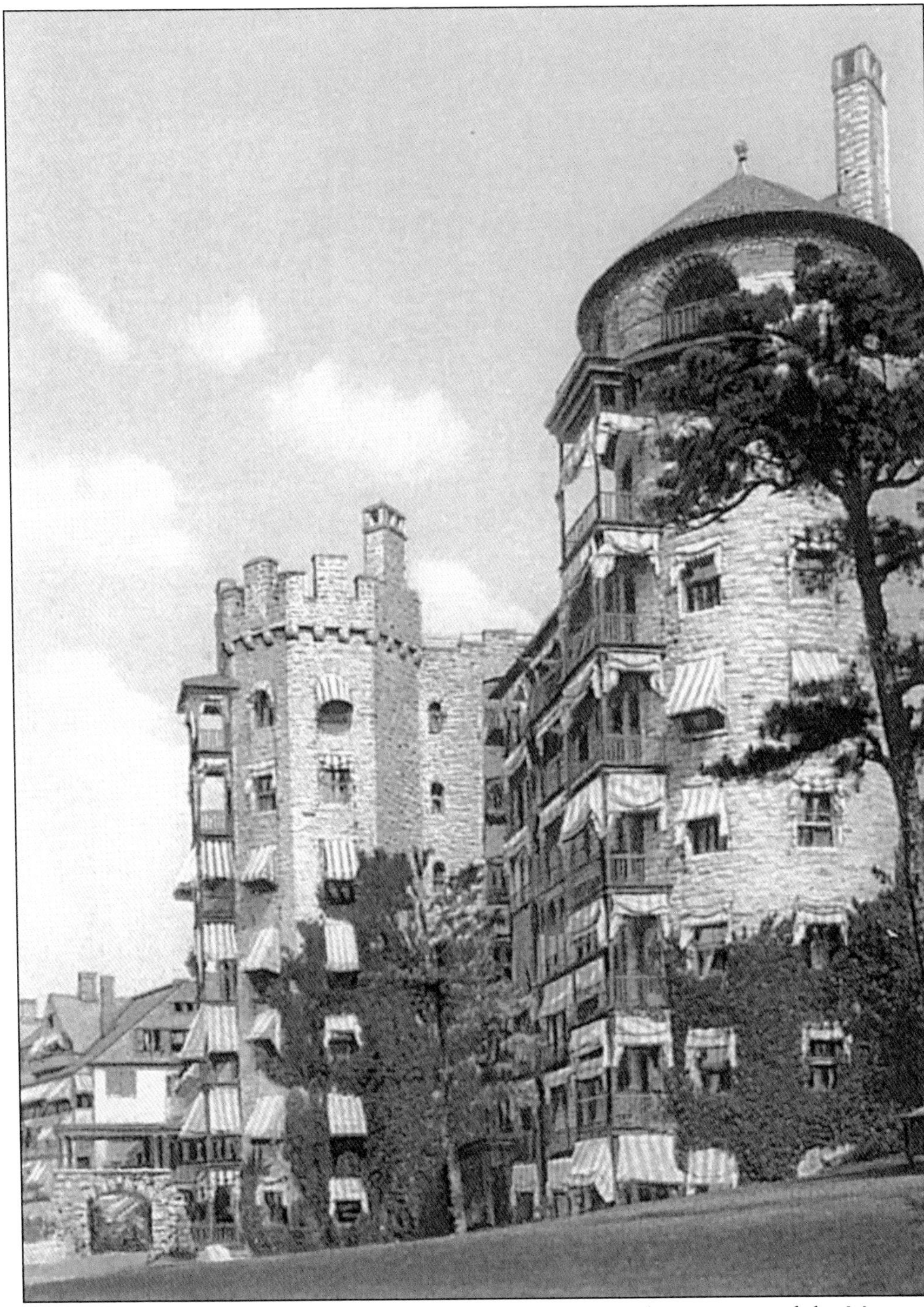

The Catskills has its castles. The scene is the newly completed stone wing of the Mountain House at Lake Mohonk. Added in 1902, it was the last substantial addition to the glorious resort that, except for the awnings, looks very much the same today. Another Catskill castle, not illustrated, was the home of photographer and postcard maker Otto Hillig (1877–1956), which still overlooks Liberty, New York, from its hilltop.

POSTCARD HISTORY SERIES

The Catskills

IN VINTAGE POSTCARDS

Irwin Richman

ARCADIA
PUBLISHING

ISBN 978-0-7385-0308-0

Published by Arcadia Publishing
Charleston, South Carolina

Printed in the United States of America

Library of Congress Catalog Card Number: 2008908785

For all general information contact Arcadia Publishing at:
Telephone 843-853-2070
Fax 843-853-0044
E-mail sales@arcadiapublishing.com
For customer service and orders:
Toll-Free 1-888-313-2665

Visit us on the Internet at www.arcadiapublishing.com

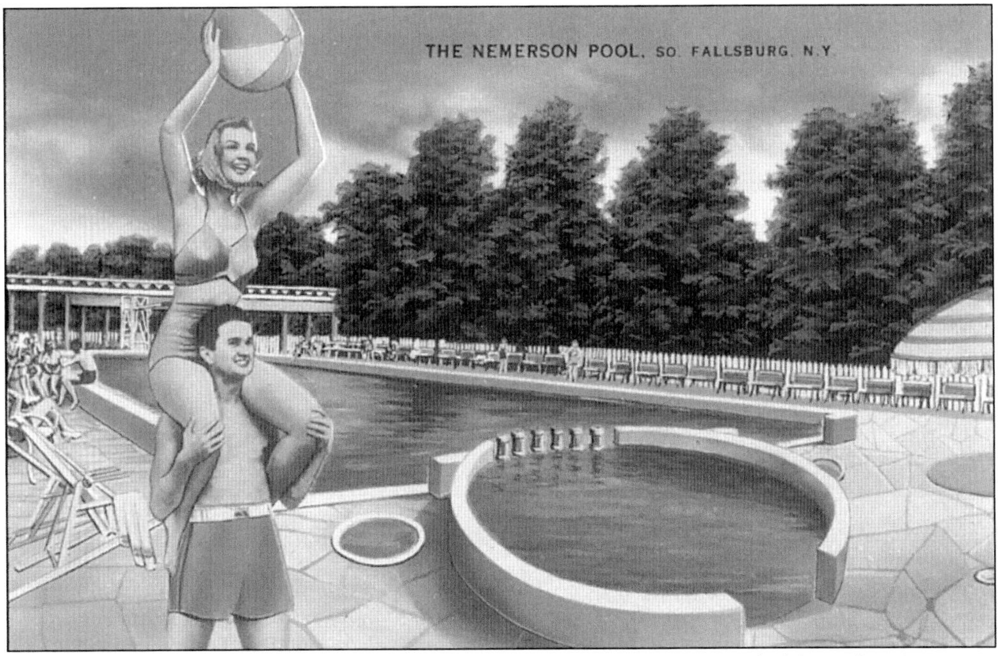

Borscht Belt resorts were at their zenith in 1955, when this card was mailed from the Nemerson Hotel in South Fallsburg. Guest Lil Cohen wrote to her friends back home, "Spending my vacation here. Perfect weather. Good Entertainment." The management boasted that "The new immense, filtered Olympic pool is fed by artesian wells," and that it was 175-by-75 feet in size.

CONTENTS

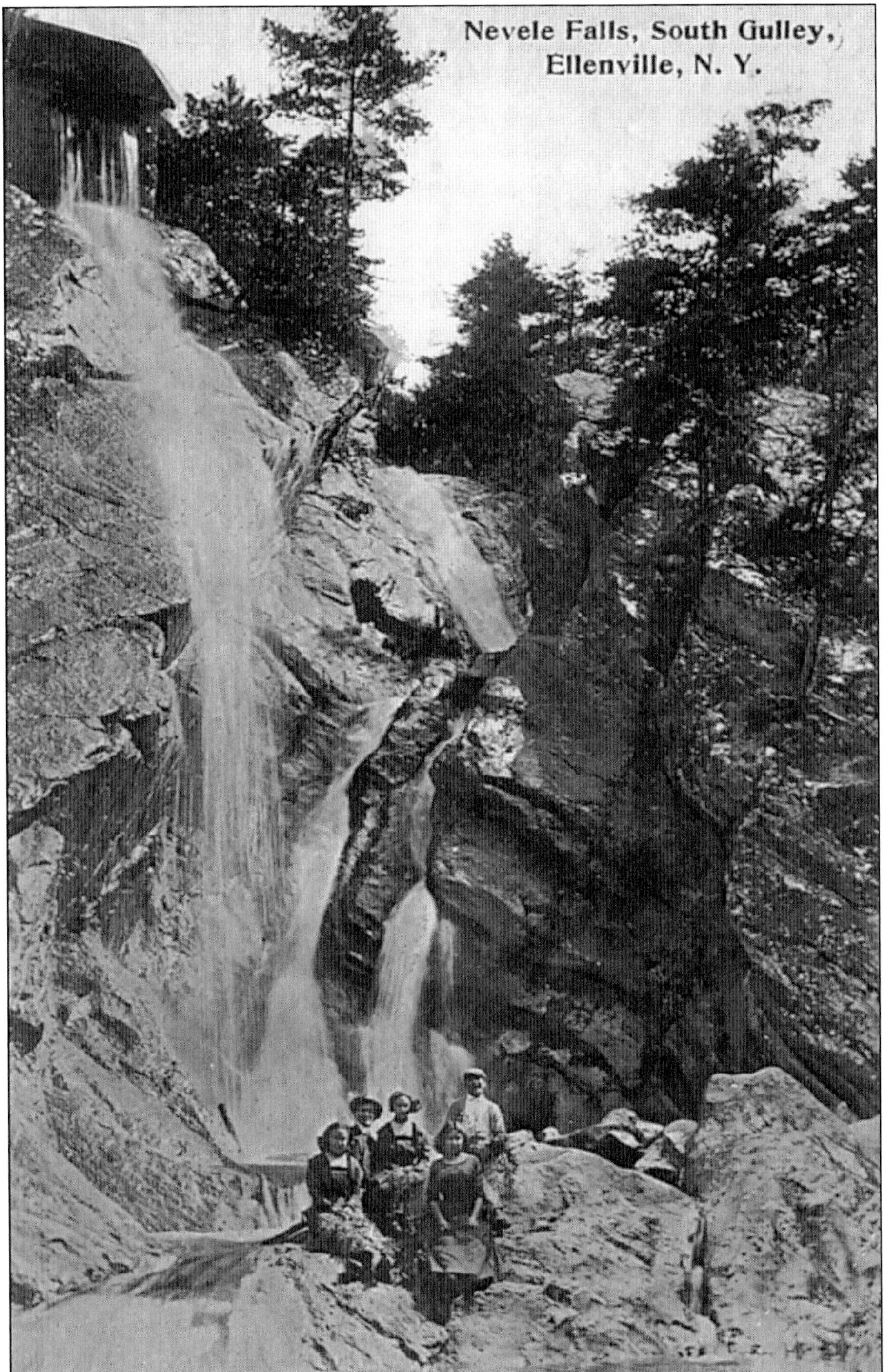

Tradition holds that the Nevele Falls was discovered by 11 picnicking schoolteachers. Nevele, of course, is "eleven" spelled backwards. A popular day-trip destination, the falls were eventually acquired by the Slutsky family as part of the large tract of land they assembled for their very successful Nevele Hotel, which remained under their ownership until 1998.

ACKNOWLEDGMENTS

Working on any book means that you rely on the kindness of others. My colleagues and the staff at Penn State–Harrisburg have, as always, been very supportive. Bill Mahar, my school director, has always done his extraordinary best on my behalf, as has Howard Sachs, our associate dean for research, whose office provided funds to help the project along and lots of free encouragement. Sue Etter, staff assistant, with help from Sue Ellen Ramer, typed and word processed the manuscript. My colleague Alison Hirsch brought T. Morris Longstreth's *The Catskills* to my attention. The reference staff at our Heindel Library proved once again that reference librarians are wonderful people. Phil Brown, my friend and the president of the Catskill Institute, has always been especially encouraging, even after I forgot to acknowledge his help in my last book. It was the wonderful reception that the book *Borscht_Belt Bungalows* received and my love for postcards that led me to compile this volume. Special friends have also helped: Joel Burcat, Pamela Moore Epstein, Henry Glassie, Gary Hagberg, Ed and Virginia LaFond, Peter Seibert, Bern Sharfman, and Elliot and Kristin Vesell. Thanks also to the Sullivan County Historical Society and to the many dealers who have supplied me with postcards. My mother, Bertha Richman, has been going to the Catskills for more than 70 years, and her encouragement is always appreciated. My wife, M. Susan Richman, reads and fixes my writing with grace, delicacy, and good humor. This displays her extraordinary talents, especially since she is a mathematician. Our children, Alexander and Joshua, and our daughter-in-law, Kristin, are our posterity.

INTRODUCTION

Jews and Gentiles at Play

A strong argument can be made that the concept of domestic tourism begins in the Catskill Mountains. The lordly Hudson River provided the first access to the picturesque region, which is, in some places, as rich in history and folklore as it is in scenery. Turnpikes, the railroads, and modern roads all affected both access and tourist populations.

> The heart, though not the full extent of the Catskills today is bounded by the Catskills State Park and embraces about 900 square miles of Greene, Ulster, Delaware, and Sullivan Counties. Measured by the foothills and the outer perimeter of today's resort areas, the Catskills include thrice that amount of land and extend from the eastern escarpment along the Hudson west to the upper reaches of the Susquehanna, and as far south as the vicinity of Liberty and Monticello.[1]

The Catskill Mountain House, the region's first important hotel, was in place by 1824, inspired by the estate movement that had been giving the banks of the Hudson a widely admired suburban caste. The Catskills were and are beautiful. "The beauty of its trees," in the words of early-20th-century travel writer T. Morris Longstreth, along with "lichened rocks [and] cascades...will repay a lengthy visit at any season." However, "There is nothing big about the Catskills." They don't awe as do the Rockies. "They are as comfortable as home. They were created, not for observation-cars, but for bungalow porches." As the 19th century blended into the 20th, the region spawned hundreds of hotels, gated residential parks, several artists' colonies, and thousands of boardinghouses, rooming houses, and bungalow colonies. While many ethnic and religious groups have or had enclaves in the region, its resort image has essentially been shaped by two groups: the old-line Protestants who first developed the region and the Jews who indelibly marked it. The relationship between these groups has not always been friendly or easy in this region, so accessible to New York City.

> And this fact [of proximity] brings me to a delicate topic; the relation of Jew and Gentile. Let me repeat two remarks: One of my friends exclaimed when I mentioned my trip [to the Catskills]; "Didn't you find it overrun with Jews?" And one day while walking through Fleischmann's, I overheard this; "Wouldn't there be too many Gentiles in Hunter?" "Oh! Not enough to hurt.[2]

To tell most of the story of the Catskills, the postcard is an ideal medium. The American picture postcard was authorized by an act of Congress on May 19, 1898, and new regulations

---

1. Roland Van Zandt, *The Catskill Mountain Hours*. New Brunswick, NJ: Rutgers University Press, 1966: 12-13.
2. T. Morris Longstreth, *The Catskills*. New York: The Century Company, 1918: 309-310.

were later passed in 1901 that standardized size and message space and led to the American postcard boom. While not present for the birth of the resort industry, the postcard was there to record many of the still lively pioneers and the changes wrought over the period from 1901 to 70, which witnessed the full flowering and the decline of the industry, as well as the establishment of an imagery widely emulated everywhere.

It was not only scenery and ethnicity, but also additional factors that led to the development of the postcard image of the Catskills. The artists of America's first painterly tradition, the Hudson River School, led by Catskill resident Thomas Cole (1801–1848), created a vocabulary of the American landscape. They interpreted not only the wilderness but the improved landscape as well. Many of these artists, for example, painted the Catskill Mountain House, and while, for the elite, the Hudson River School painters were passé by the postcard age, their popular imagery was not. Their art defined how the mountain range and its towns should be portrayed and framed. It was an appreciation of landscape that, in part, led to the success of the great 19th-century resorts that emulated the Catskill Mountain House, such as the Kaaterskill Mountain House and the Laurel House, all now vanished. Superb scenery, gracious service, and nostalgia nourish the only survivor of this age, the Mountain House at Lake Mohonk.

As America industrialized, genre painting, which often glorified the rural past, became especially popular. Among the artists involved here was Eastman Johnson (1824–1906), whose recordings and re-creations of rural American were especially in demand. Paintings by other genre artists were often adapted into the inexpensive prints widely circulated by Currier and Ives and Louis Prang and Company. Like the images of the Hudson River School painters, these compositions and themes were avidly adapted to postcards; they appealed to a nation increasingly looking backward to a simpler, purer America—one insulated from the new immigrants. This was the age when Americans of old stock wanted to separate themselves from the later arrivals. Nature was widely celebrated. Catskills-born naturalist John Burroughs was universally praised as the region's sage. Similarly, the area's Dutch heritage, with its colonial associations, was widely emphasized. Washington Irving's characters Ichabod Crane of the mid-Hudson region and Rip Van Winkle of the Catskills proper became icons that every schoolchild knew. One wag observed, "God made the Catskills; [Washington] Irving put them on the map; but it is John Burroughs who brought them home to us."

The region's subsistence farmers, many too poor to modernize, and its dirt roads were widely pictured as images of the good old days for city dwellers who had been leaving rural areas in record numbers as the new century dawned. Attracted by the antique image of the Catskills, as well as by its scenery, successful artists created rustic colonies in which to practice their art during the summer. Edward Lamson Henry (1841–1919) and his friends created, at Cragsmoor, a retreat from the ugly urban realities of an industrialized New York City. Here, Henry painted his country neighbors at their simple pastimes, and his friend Charles Courtney Curran (1861–1942) recorded the colonists glorying in nature.

The White City at the World Columbian Exhibition in Chicago in 1893 had a riveting effect on America. It sparked an escalation of civic pride throughout America and spawned the City Beautiful movement. On a more modest level, it sparked boomlets of civic pride in thousands of communities. Coming at the same time as the rise of the postcard (Congress had even authorized special World's Fair postcards.) and the subsequent collecting frenzy, there was a great demand for cards that showed local vistas, public buildings and monuments, and the homes of the local elite. These were sent and collected by natives as well as tourists. From a historian's perspective, the most important of these views are of the same town or vista published ten or more years apart, which often show the dramatic changes a growing tourist industry wrought on the landscape.

The late 19th century also witnessed the emergence of vacations for the masses. Mostly, this phenomenon was made possible by improved transportation, beginning with the railroad and nourished especially by the prosperity of the 1920s and the widespread availability of the automobile. After the 1930s and wartime, the booming postwar years fixed vacations into the

American mainstream. This was also the era characterized as the golden age of illustration. The commercial imagery of J.C. Leyendecker (1874–1951), Howard Chandler Christy (1875–1952), James Montgomery Flagg (1877–1960), and others was adapted and reflected in the cards of the period.

As the 1800s ended, a new era emerged as millions of immigrants poured into an increasingly crowded New York City. When summer came, these city dwellers craved relief from the heat and the concrete environment. The Irish and the Germans and the Italians all preceded the Jews into the Catskills, and today there are still enclaves that reflect these and many other immigrant groups. The area's farmhouses, boardinghouses, hotels, and even exclusive residential parks often changed ethnic complexion to serve the new groups. The Jewish influx began in the northern Catskills, but it became especially important with the development of the Neversink River Valley of Sullivan County starting in the late 19th century. There, the Borscht Belt of legend was born.

As the automobile became more common, new categories of resorts developed to serve the traveler. Motor camps later became trailer parks, and tourist cabins became motels. The revivalism of the mid to late 19th century gave rise to church camps, and the birth of the Scout movement led to the development of the children's camps. However, the bungalow colonies and the more than 900 hotels were among the most distinctive resorts of the Catskill region. The bungalow colonies enabled almost anyone to rent the modest equivalent of a summer home.* Meanwhile, the hotels of southern Ulster and Sullivan Counties evolved a style of excess—too much food, too much glitz—which came to characterize the Catskill image.

Standing head and shoulders above most of these hundreds of hotels listed in Phil Brown's *Catskill Culture* (Temple University Press, 1999), were a handful of elite resorts, including the Flagler, Grossinger's, the Concord, and the Nevele. They were more expensive, if not more exclusive, and offered more entertainment and better facilities than their peers, many of which went into bankruptcy trying to emulate them. The elites were the climax of Jewish resorts, although two were founded by gentiles. But, alas, none still exist in their original form.

As tourism matured, there were increasing desires to enhance the concept of reality and to interject extra fun and whimsy into vacation imagery. Many cards were sold that purported to show local scenery but actually showed more spectacular areas, sometimes outside of the Catskills. There were also the myriad comic cards that offered insight into the mind-set of a time now past.

The Catskills, today, is a resort area in flux. Modern-Orthodox Jews and Hasidim have become more and more important to the region, and in many areas, they are the dominant groups. As the resorts have changed, the interest in the region where millions of people have vacationed has grown. Books about the Catskills are becoming more common, and a Borscht Belt bungalow colony of 1969 is the setting for the 1999 motion picture *A Walk on the Moon*. The 1969 festival known as Woodstock, actually held in Bethel in Sullivan County, was a watershed in America's culture and, by extension, the culture of "the Mountains," as generations of New Yorkers have called the Catskills. My time period is mostly earlier. Join me on a trip back in time to the Catskills of yesterday: an unequal mixture of fact, fantasy, reality, and the unbelievable.

—Irwin Richman
The Cottage, 1999

* I chronicled this phenomenon in *Borscht Belt Bungalows* (Temple University Press, 1998).

One

The Lordly Hudson: Gateway to the Catskills

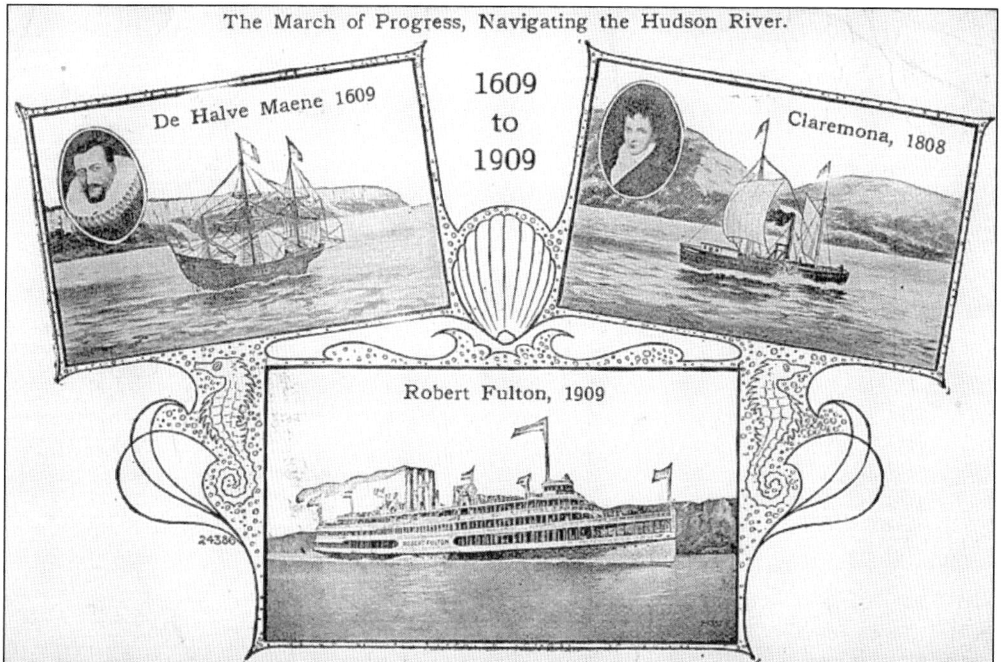

From the time Henry Hudson sailed his ship the *Half Moon* into the North River, later to be named in his honor, that river has provided a navigable route to the Catskill region. Robert Fulton's development of the steamship, beginning with the *Claremont* in 1808, made the trip up the Hudson easier, and fleets of excursion boats followed.

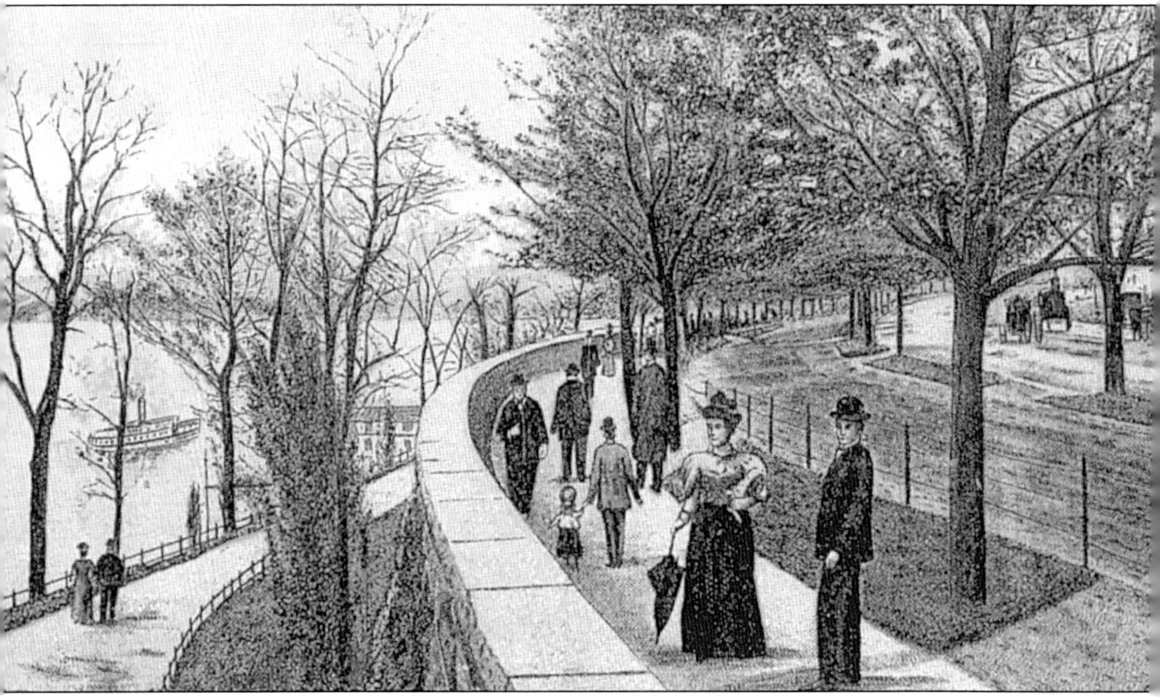

At the end of the 19th century, New York City's Riverside Park was a fashionable promenade, and Riverside Drive was becoming a stylish neighborhood. As the elegant people strolled the walkways, they were usually in sight of excursion boats going to, or coming from, the Catskills.

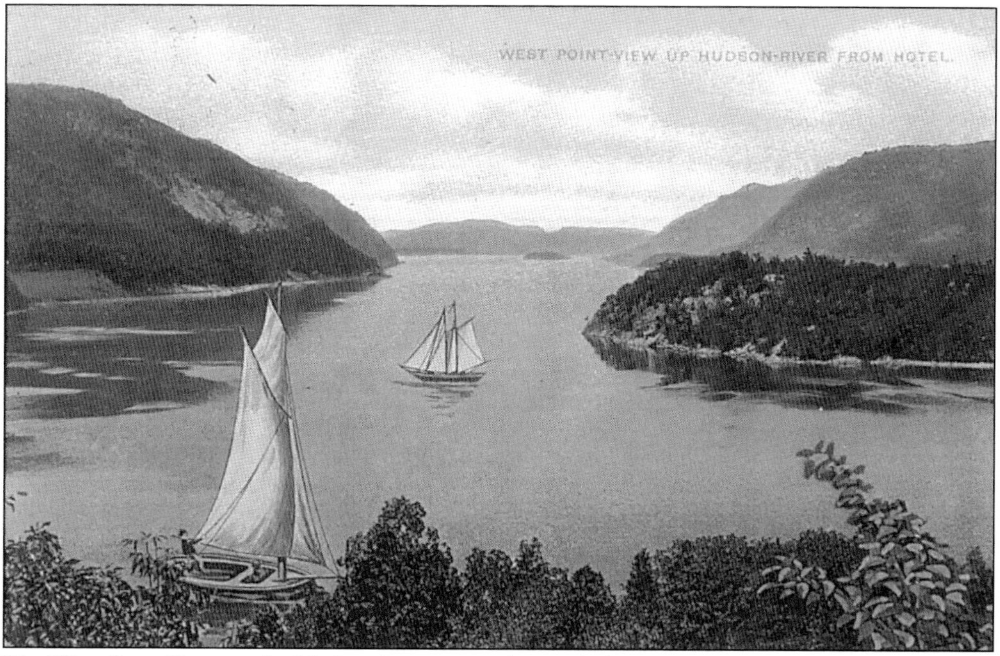

The West Point View up the Hudson River, an enhanced photograph, is remarkably similar to a watercolor by little-known artist A. Van Zandt that is owned by the Hudson River Museum in Yonkers. Inclusion of sailboats is almost mandatory in views of the river by Hudson River School painters.

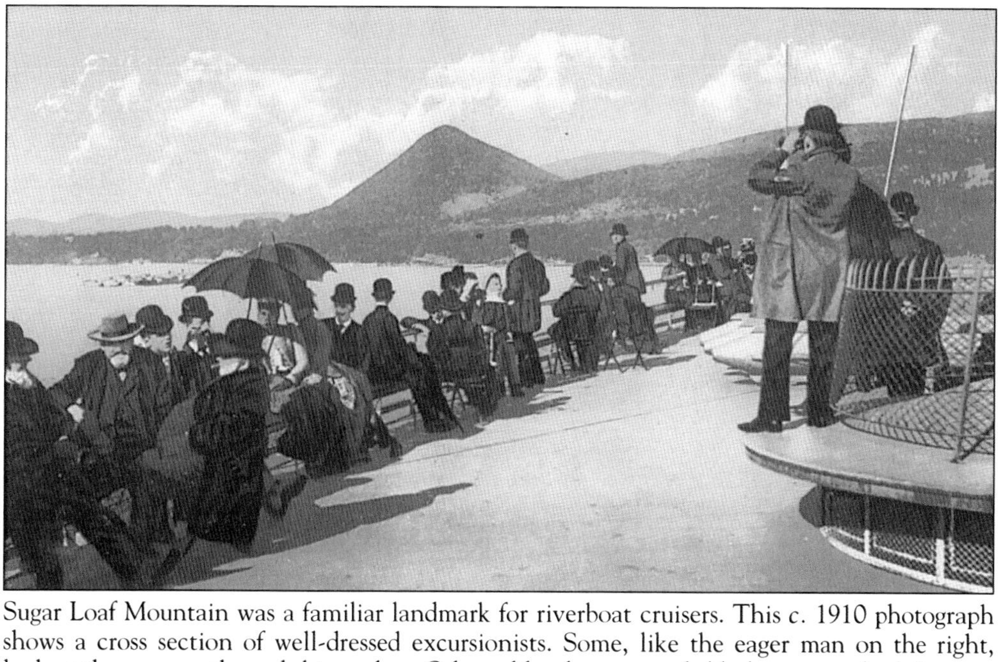

Sugar Loaf Mountain was a familiar landmark for riverboat cruisers. This c. 1910 photograph shows a cross section of well-dressed excursionists. Some, like the eager man on the right, look at the scenery through binoculars. Others, like the group of elderly men at the left, seem indifferent to their glorious surroundings.

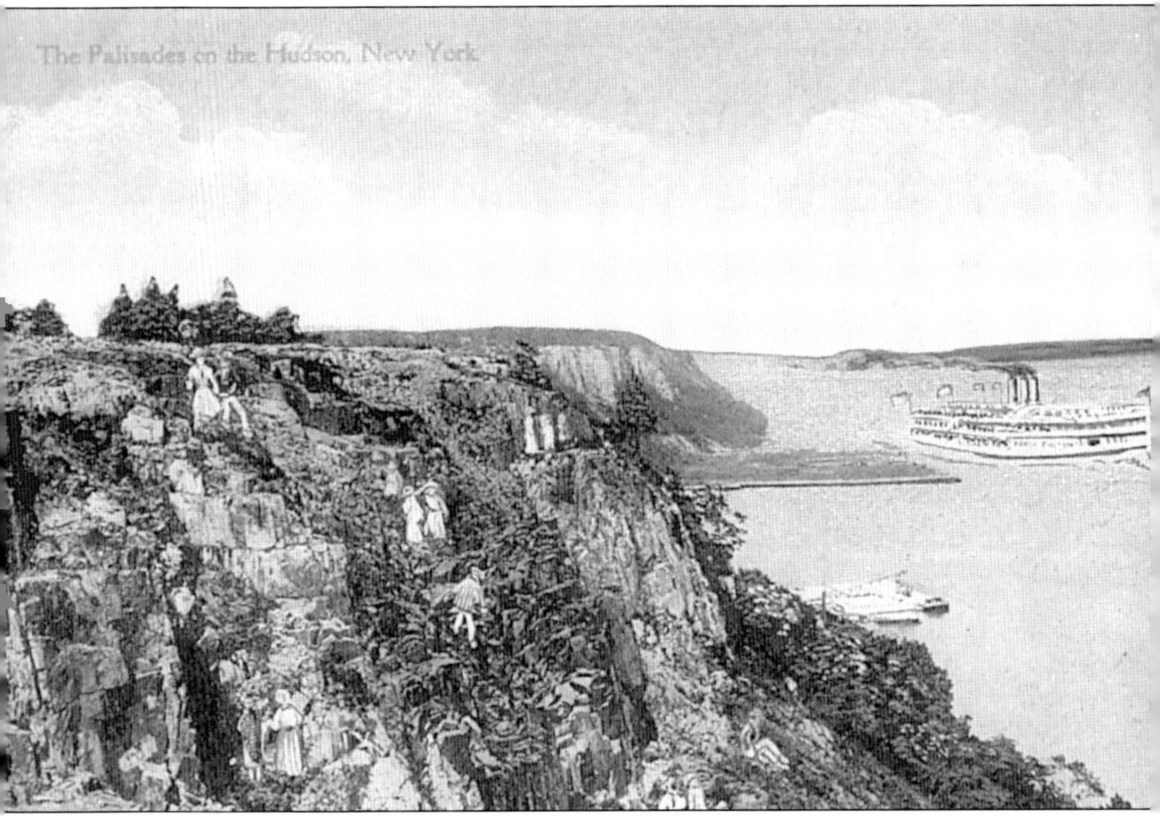

Early vacationers were mainly upper and upper-middle-class Americans. The Hudson River, alive with river craft, was their highway to the extensive Catskill region. Here, stylishly dressed day-trippers scramble over the Palisades, across the river from Hastings-on-Hudson, while their boat waits near the pier.

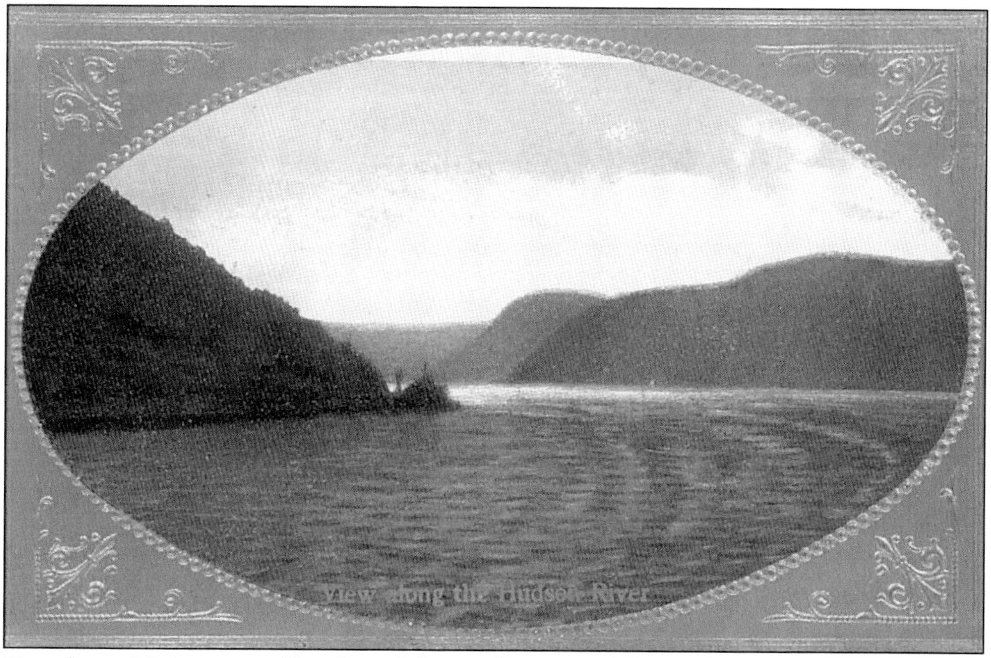

Complete with its own gold-embossed frame, this view of the Hudson near Cold Spring has been painted by many artists, including David Johnson (1817–1908). Oval paintings were popular with 19th-century landscape painters. A tiny sailboat is barely visible at the base of a distant mountain.

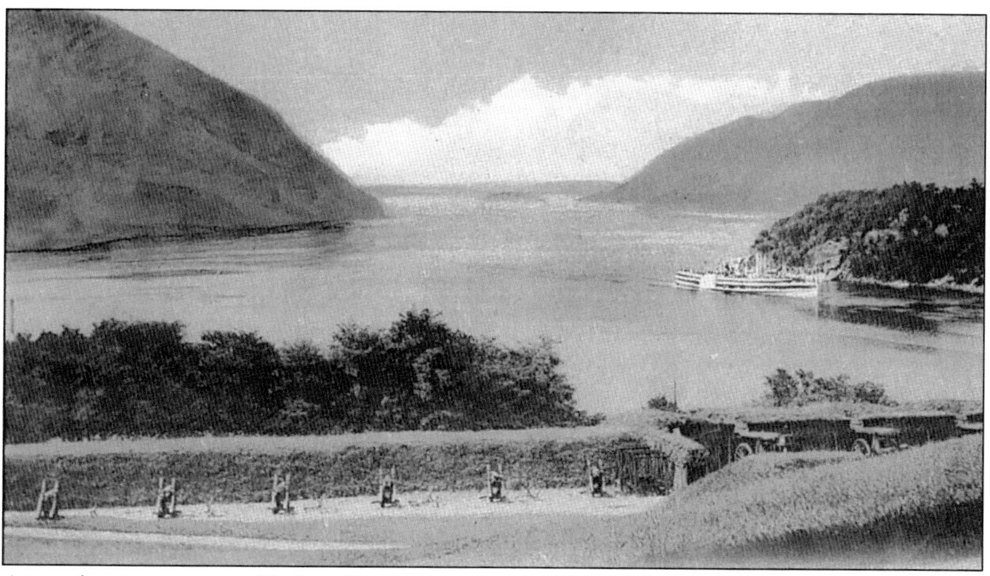

A popular stopover on a Hudson River cruise was the United States Military Academy at West Point, located at one of the most scenic spots on the river. The famed view from the Battle Monument at Trophy Point on the academy grounds was painted by many Hudson River School painters, most notably Jasper Francis Cropsey (1823–1900), whose *Gates of the Hudson* was widely known and appreciated.

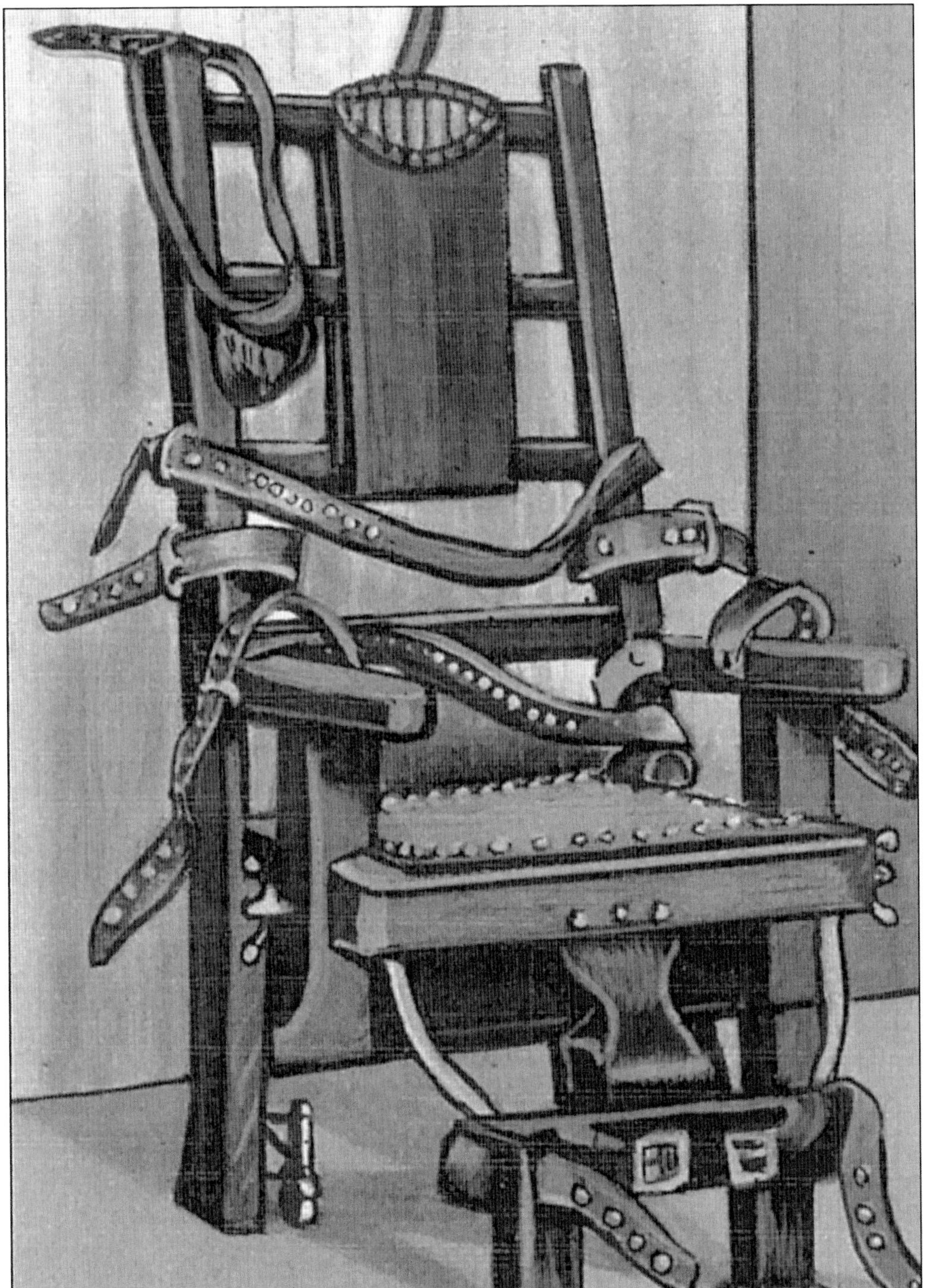

One sight, which very few excursionists ever saw but which fascinated many, was New York's "more humane modern form of execution," the electric chair housed at the infamous Sing Sing Prison in Ossining, which loomed over the Hudson. The Ruben Publishing Company in nearby Newburgh helped satisfy tourists' curiosity with this *c.* 1940s card.

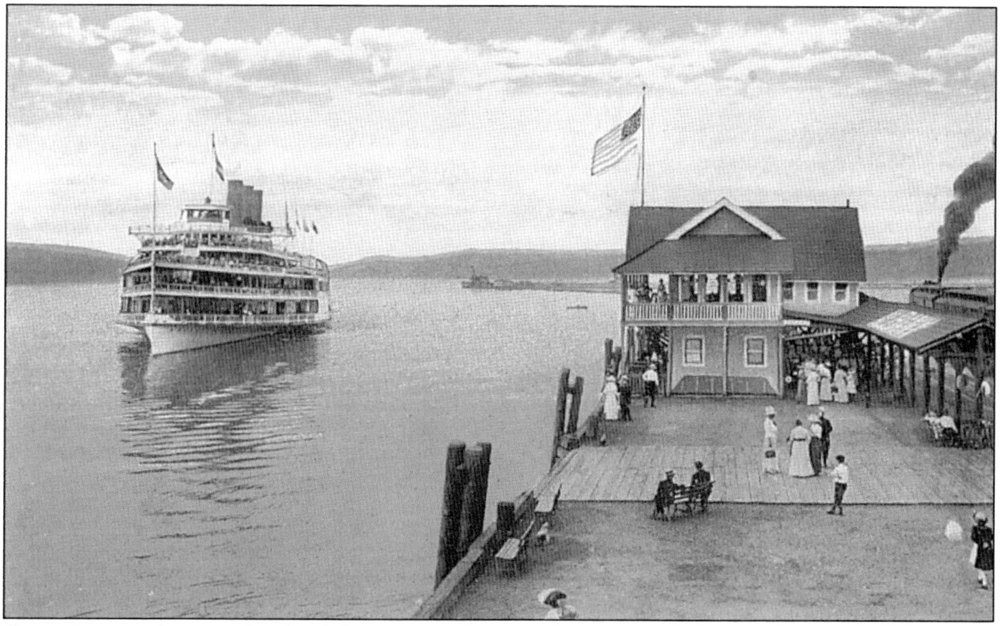

Kingston, on the west bank of the river, was an important stop for travelers who changed to a train for one of many Catskill destinations. As a boat came in, a number of people waited to greet newcomers. After the boat arrived, the dock became crowded. Trains awaited passengers. The automobiles shown here probably belonged to the various resorts, which sent drivers to meet newly arriving guests. Resort owners recount anecdotes stressing the importance of meeting their guests promptly, before a rival resort "kidnapped them away." As a young girl in the 1920s, the author's mother remembers starting her first visit to the Catskills in Kingston. Except for the clothing, the scene was probably little changed from the one in these *c.* 1910 cards.

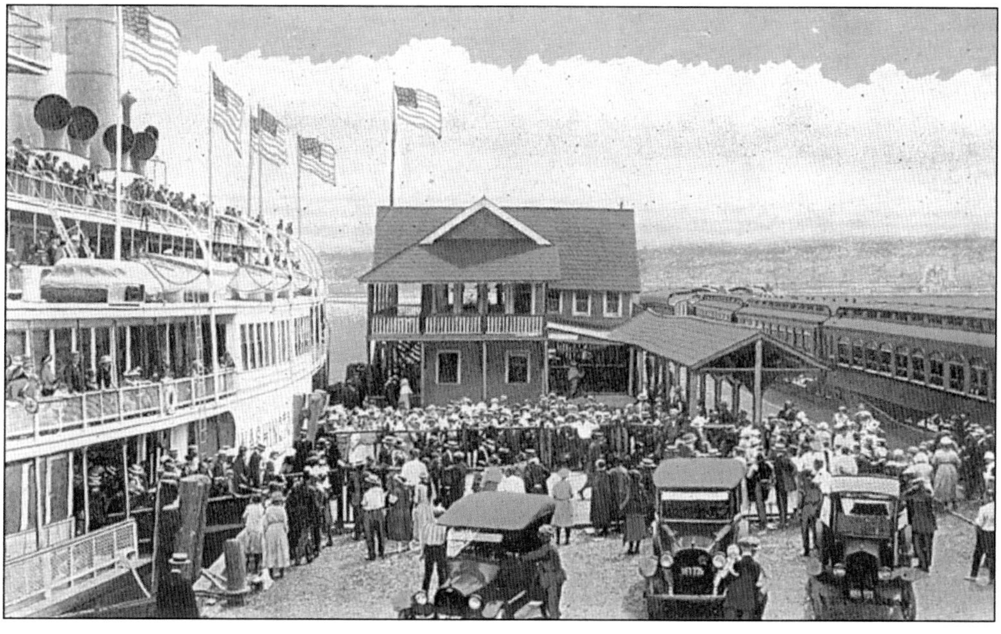

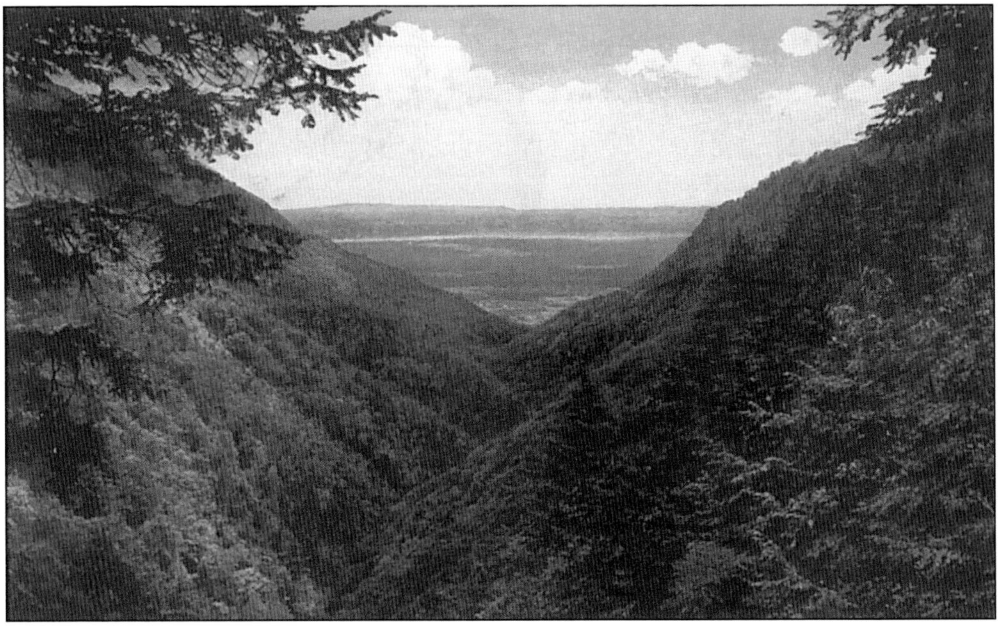

The vision of wild landscape opening to reveal agricultural possibilities beyond is a technique favored by many Hudson River School painters, including Asher Brown Durand (1796–1886), who often used the theme in his work. It is seen in his *Catskill Clove* and numerous other paintings. For many, this landscape vision was the ultimate Catskill experience.

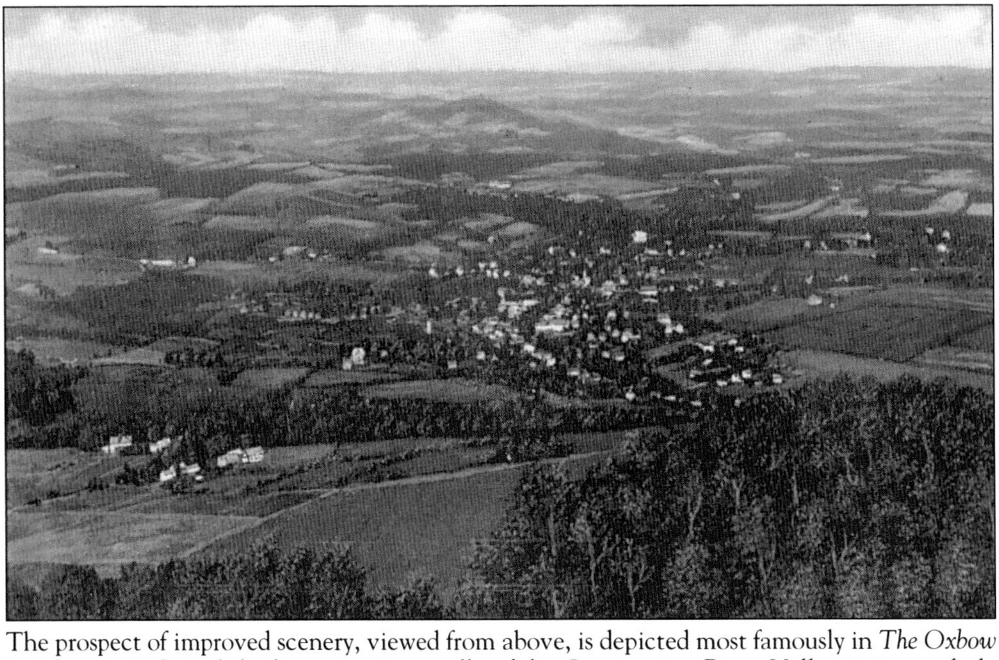

The prospect of improved scenery, viewed from above, is depicted most famously in *The Oxbow* by Thomas Cole. While that scene is actually of the Connecticut River Valley, it is popularly associated with the Hudson. Compositionally, *Stamford, NY, from Mt. Ut-Say-Au-Tha Observatory* owes a great deal to the work of both Cole and his student Frederick Edwin Church (1826–1900), whose great estate Olana overlooks the Catskills near Hudson, New York.

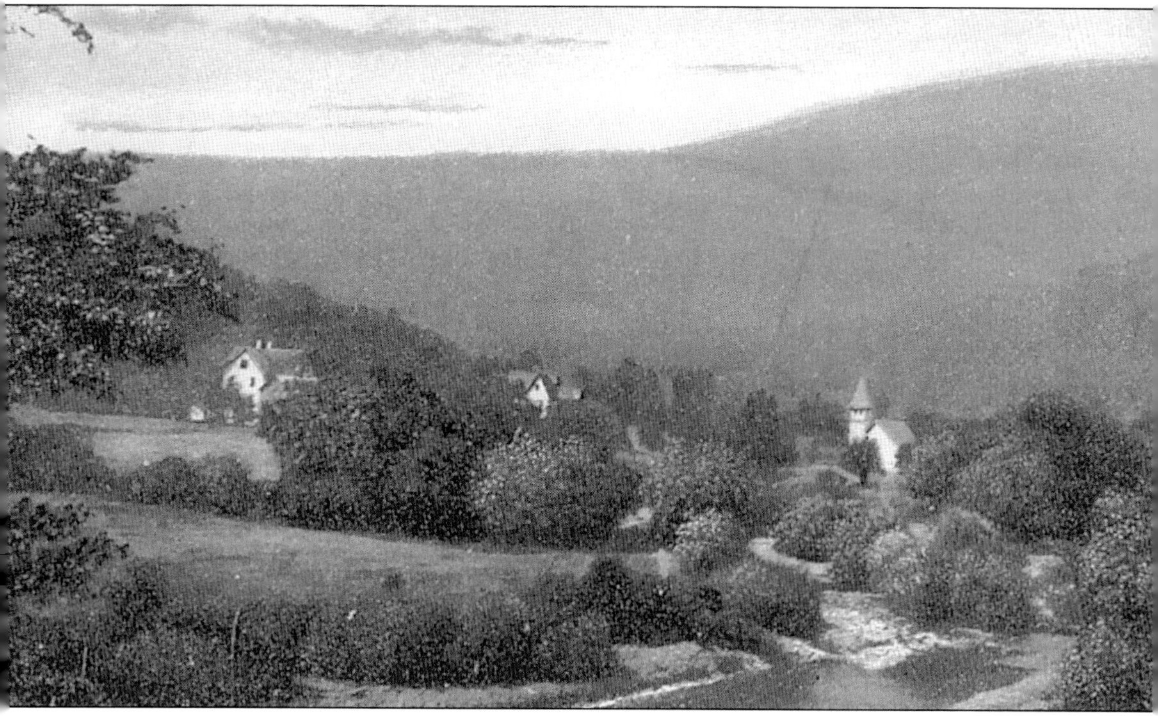

The name *Big Indian* is redolent with the wild romance of the Catskills, but, of course, Native Americans were long gone from the mountains before the great tourist era began. This scene, with the stream in the foreground, the houses and the church in the middle, and the mountains in the distance, is a classic Hudson River School composition.

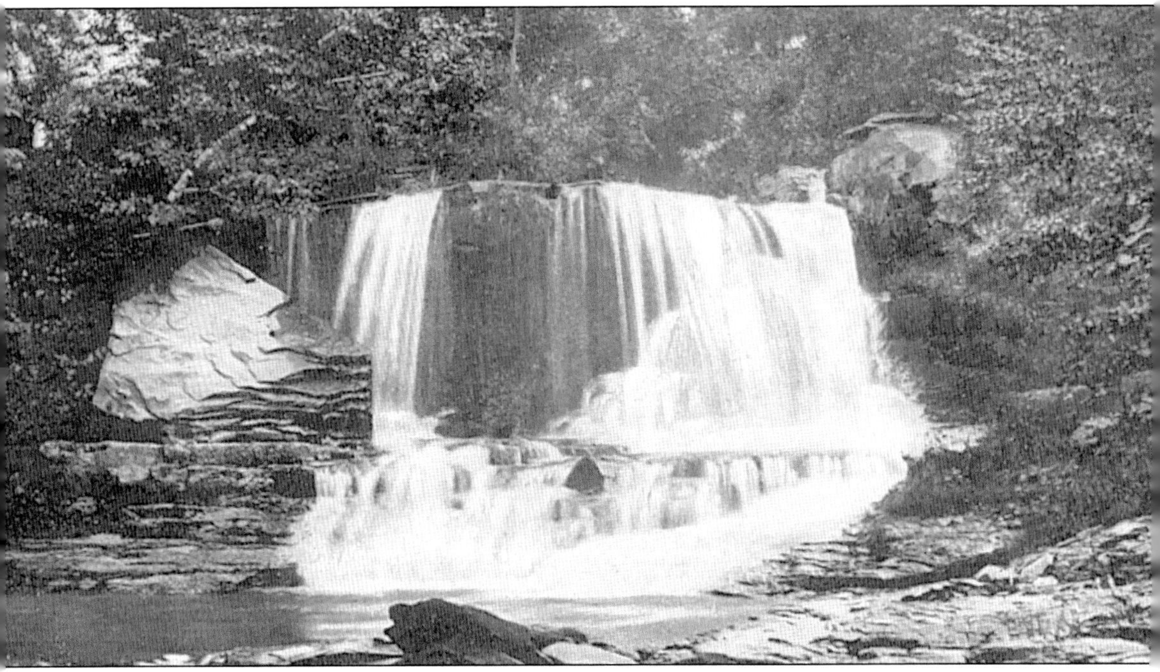

The many waterfalls of the Catskills were a major tourist attraction and were often linked with the name of a resort. Hence, Lock's Falls is located in relation to the Maple Laurel House. Visiting the falls was an important pastime for guests, who often toured from cascade to cascade.

Two

THE GREAT RESORTS: AMERICA'S FIRST TOURIST DESTINATION

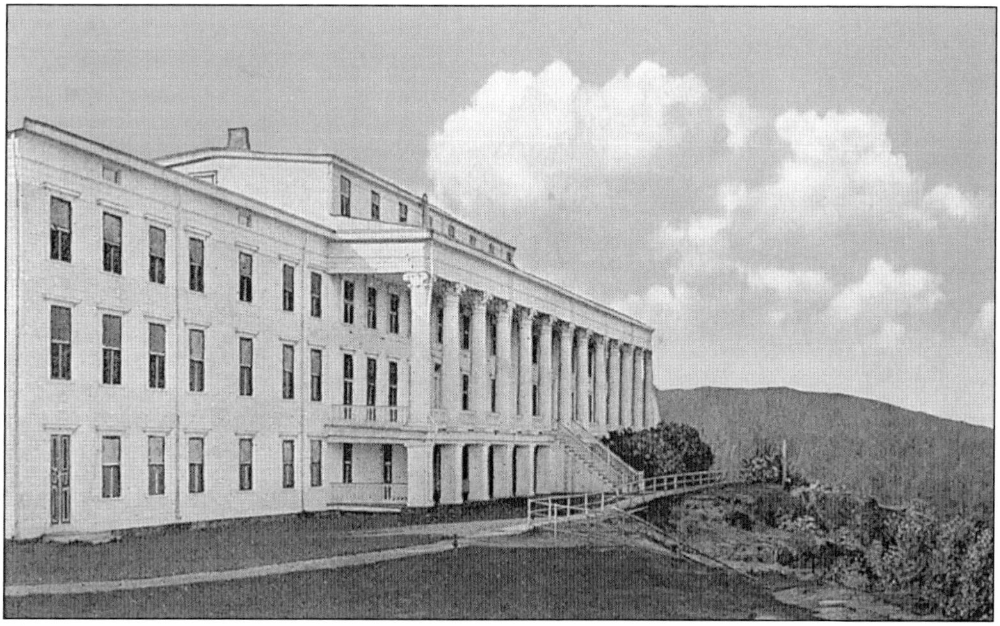

The Catskill Mountain House was the subject of numerous paintings by Hudson River School artists, including Thomas Cole, Sanford Robinson Gifford (1823–1880), and Jasper Francis Cropsey. A pioneer, grand, Christian-only hotel in the Catskills, it remained dominant for 100 years and was the inspiration for scenically located hotels throughout the country. It became a Jewish resort in 1930. Later acquired by the State of New York, it was burned to the ground, ironically, by the New York State Conservation Department on January 24, 1962.

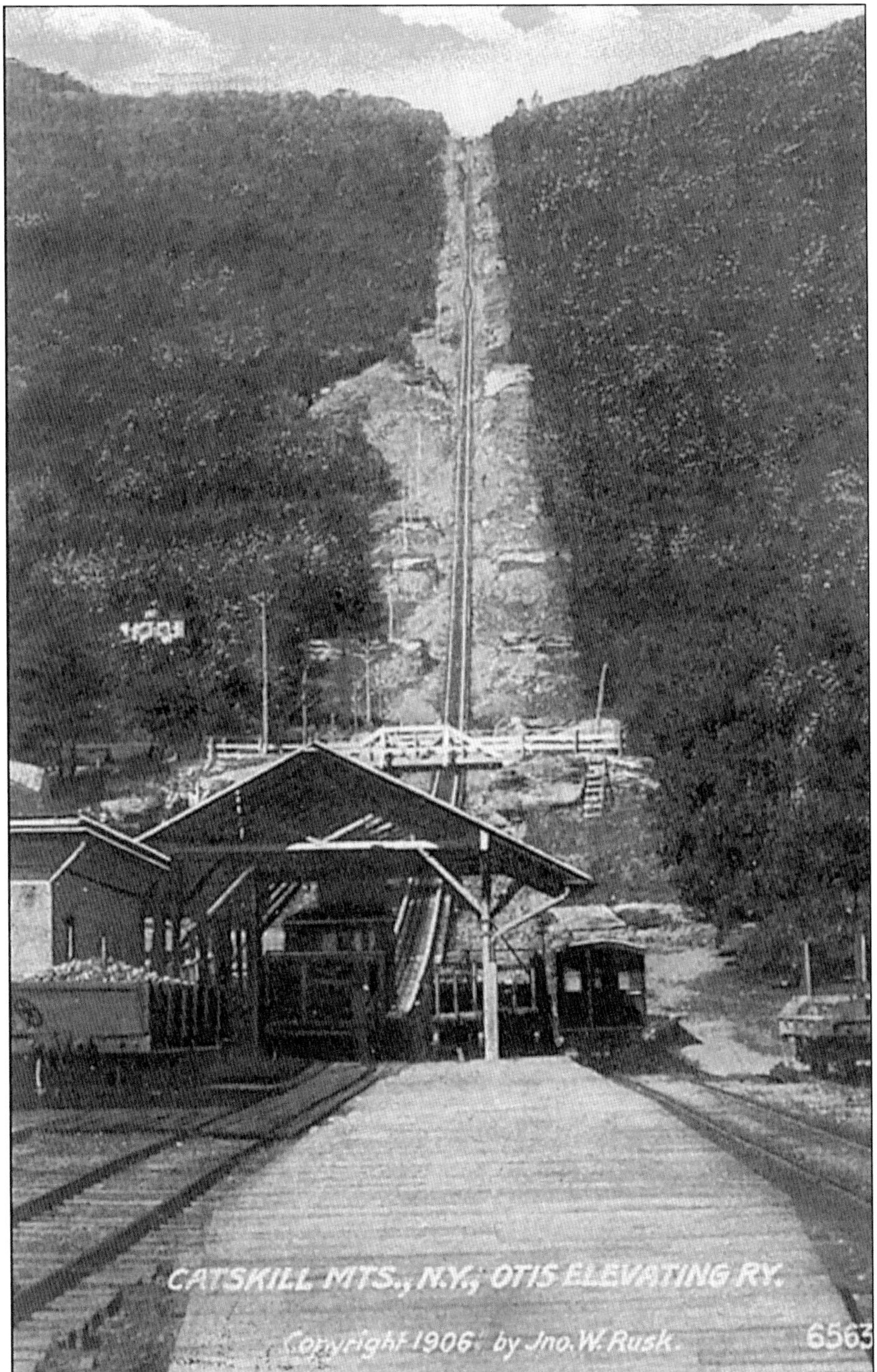

In the early years, the trip to the Catskill Mountain House was long. It involved taking a steamer to Catskill and then a stage to the Mountain House. That changed in the 1880s when the Catskill Mountain Railway was built, with a stop at the foot of the mountain. In 1892, the Otis Elevated Railroad was built up the mountainside directly to the hotel.

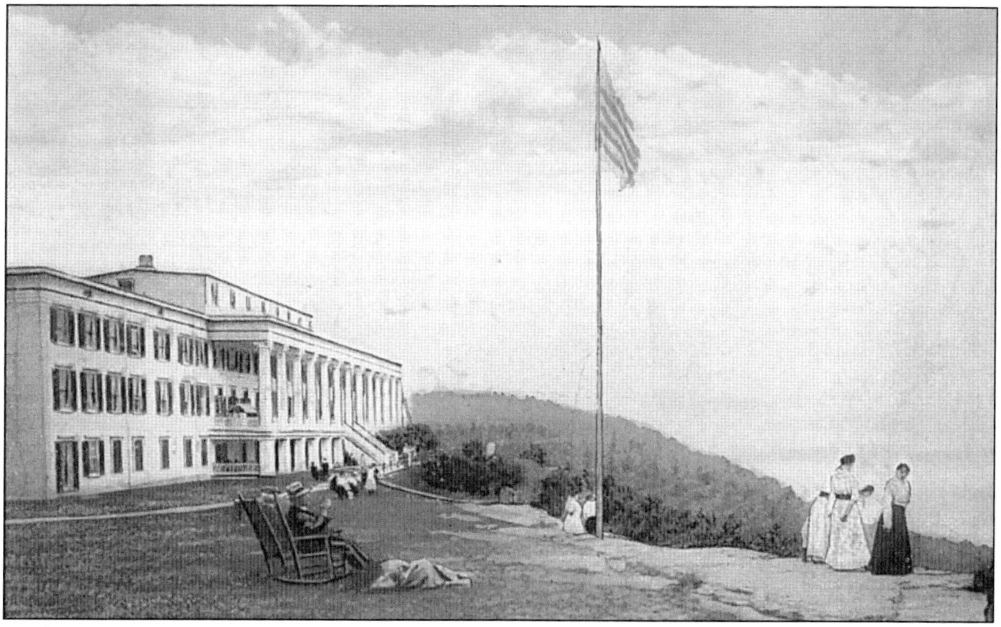

Looking at the view was a favorite pastime of visitors to the premier and very expensive Catskill Mountain House. Every guest got up before dawn at least once a season to watch the spectacular sunrise over the Hudson.

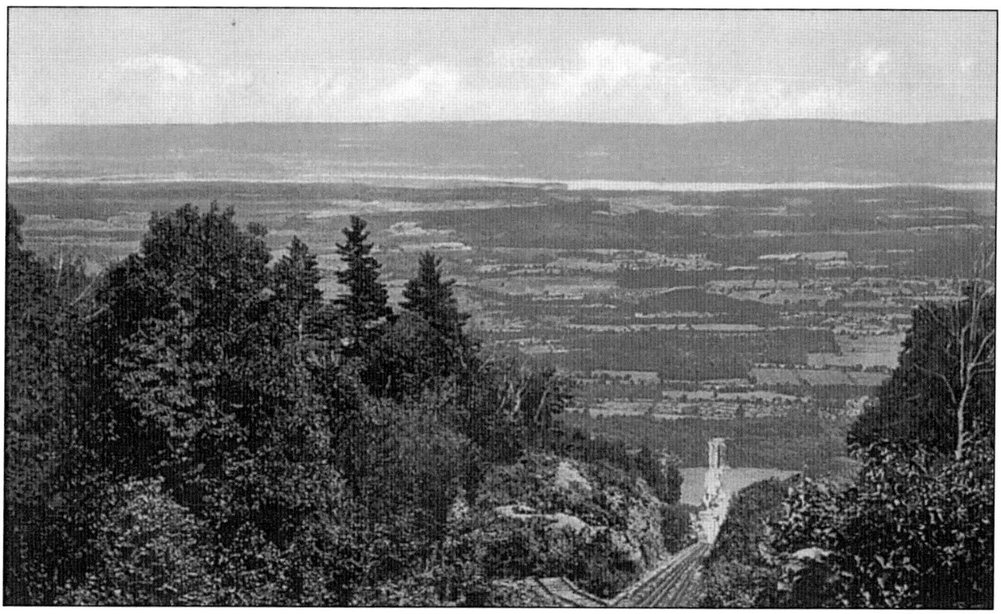

In the antebellum period, it took about 3.5 hours of stagecoach travel to cover the 12 miles from the village of Catskill to the Catskill Mountain House. By 1892, the railway from New York covered 125 miles in the same amount of time. Rail travel made it possible for day-trippers to enjoy the fabulous view.

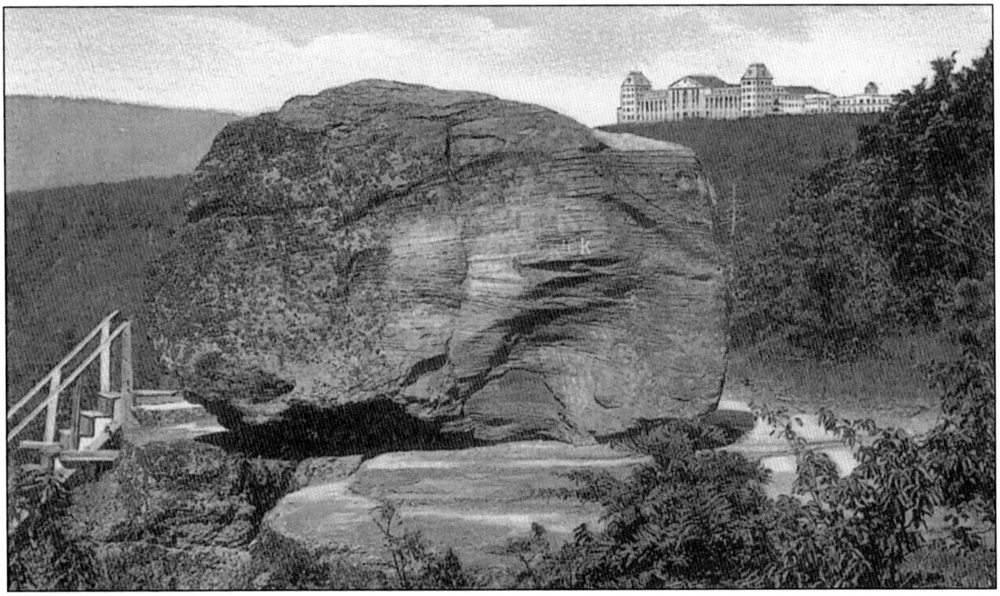

Great rocks, like waterfalls, were often destinations for hotel guests. Boulder Rock was on the grounds of the Hotel Kaaterskill. The spelling "Kaaterskill" was not Old Dutch but rather the adaptation by Mrs. George W. Harding, whose husband built the grand hotel in 1881.

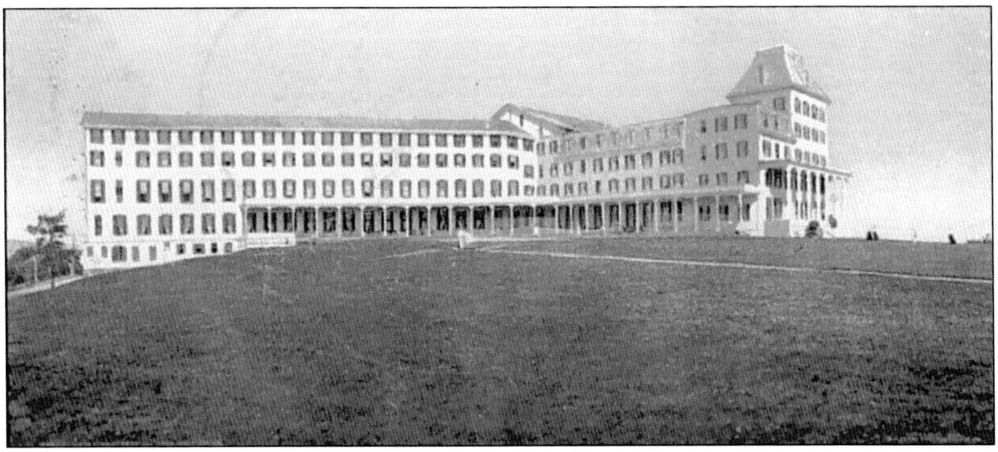

The 1,200-room Hotel Kaaterskill was built to provide direct competition to the Catskill Mountain House, but it was short-lived. When the ethnic composition of Catskills' vacationers changed, the hotel was sold, in 1920, to Harry Tannenbaum. In September 1924, it burned in a spectacular fire, which was seen all the way to Massachusetts.

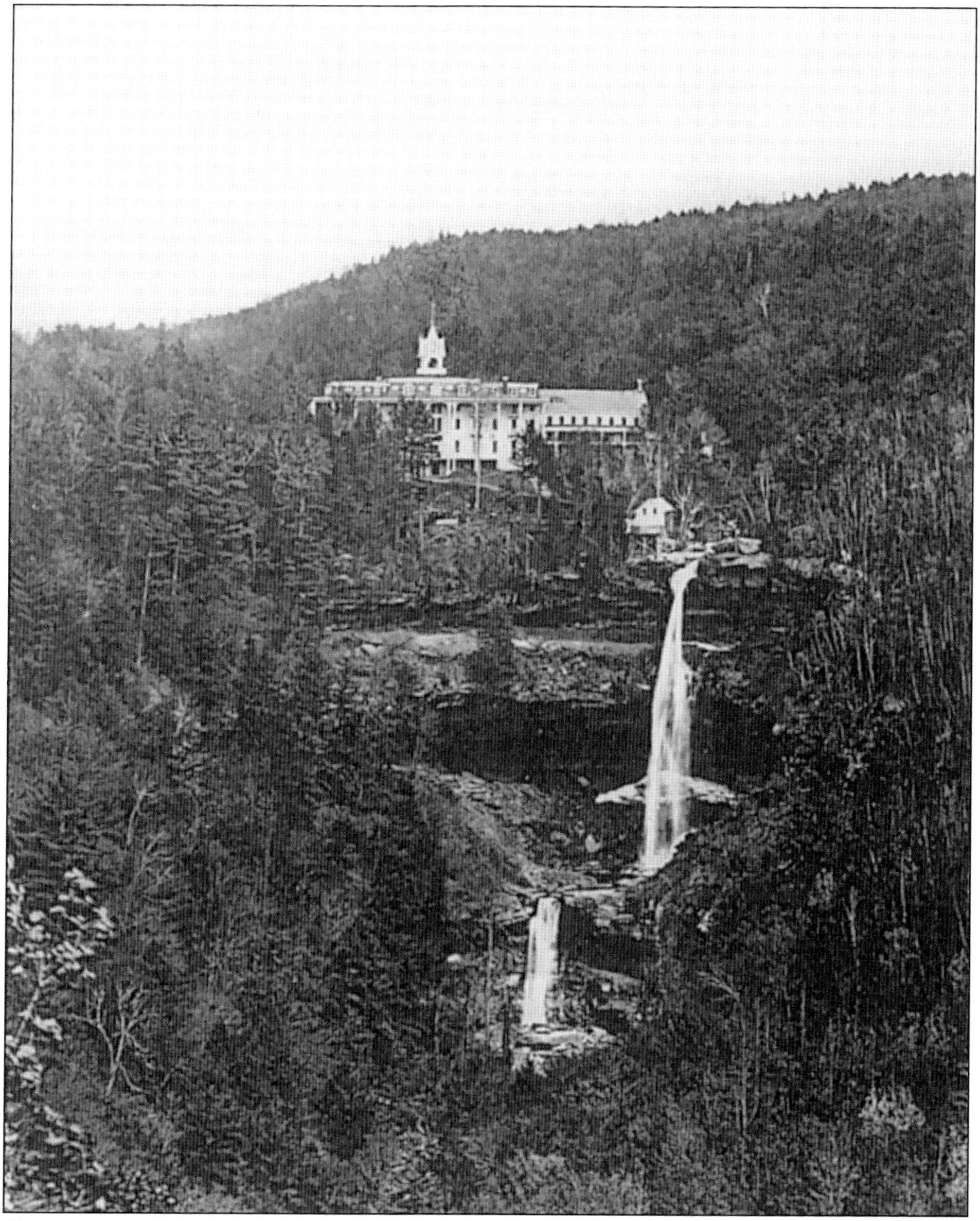

The Laurel House was situated on top of Kaaterskill Falls. Begun as a modest farm hotel, it was enlarged after the Civil War and again between 1881 and 1884. Eventually, it had 250 rooms. It was the longest-lived grand hotel in the region, surviving into the 1960s, when it was purchased by the New York State Department of Conservation.

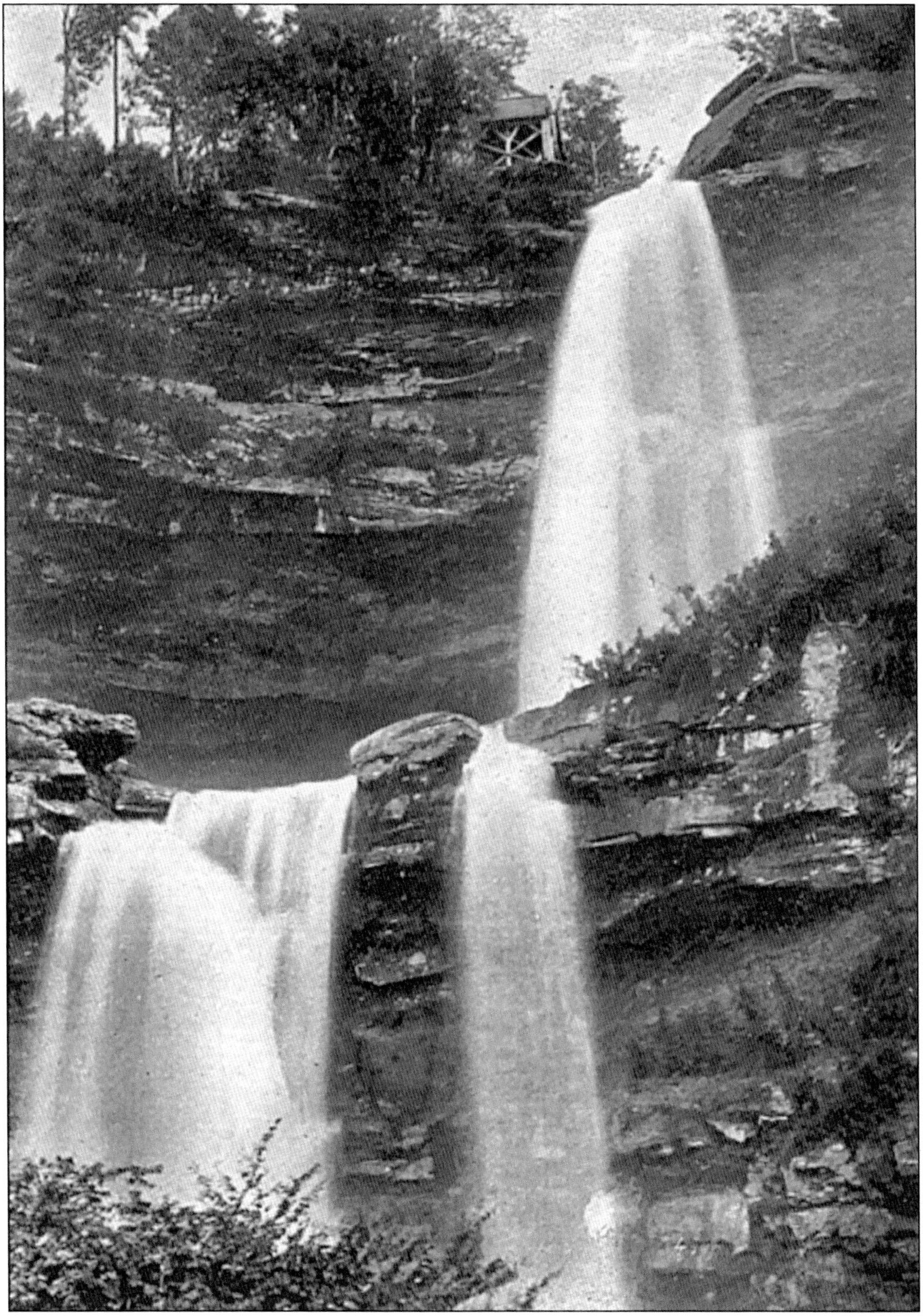

Kaaterskill Falls was especially popular with Hudson River School artists and the general public. From the 1850s, owners of the Laurel House ran refreshment pavilions at the falls for guests and for day visitors. Today, the falls are virtually unknown because there is neither road nor trail access to them.

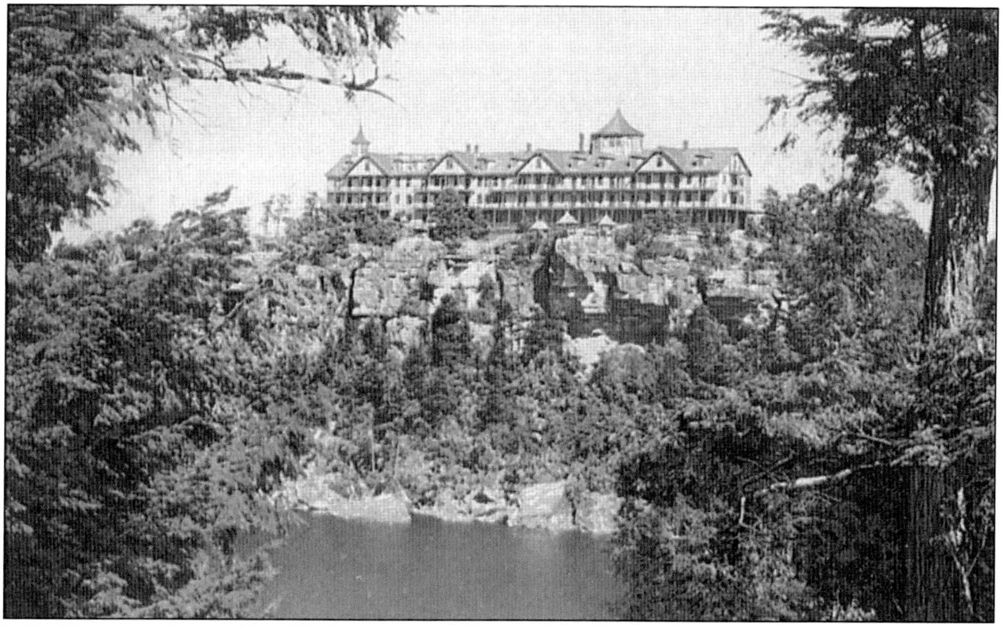

Lake Minnewaska, a glacial lake high in the Shawangunk (or Southern Catskill) Mountains, was developed by Albert Keith Smiley, whose twin brother Alfred Homans Smiley built the nearby Mohonk Mountain House. The Lake Minnewaska Mountainhouse was built in 1879 and was enlarged to the size seen in this view in 1888. The hotel's name was changed to the Cliff House in 1887.

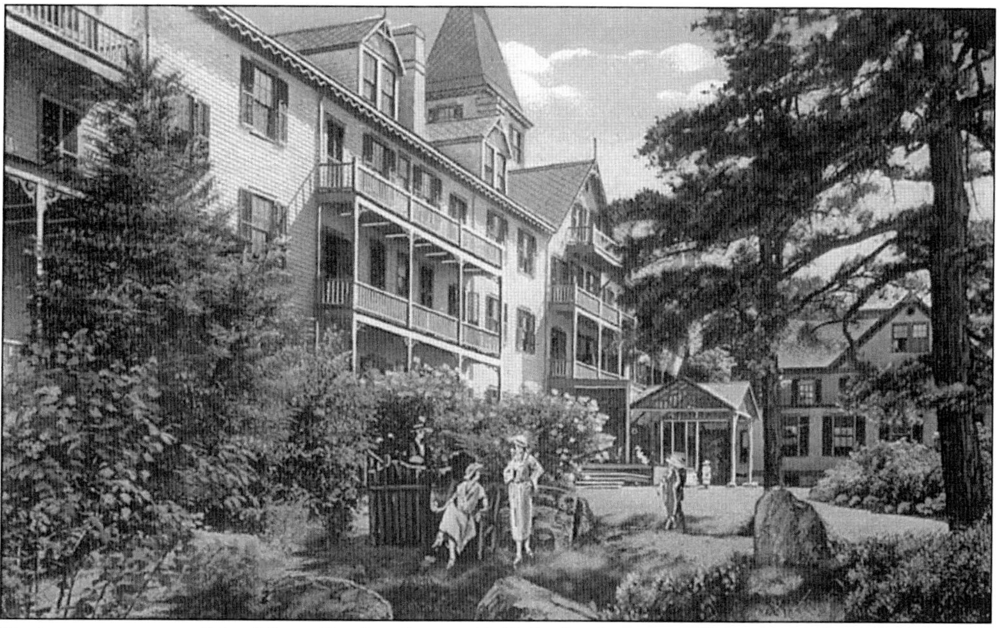

Business was so good for Albert Smiley that in 1887, he built a second hotel on Lake Minnewaska, in the midst of the 9,000-acre tract he owned. The new hotel, which he called Wildmere, was expanded to its final size in 1910. Both Wildmere and the Cliff House eventually burned. After much bitter squabbling, the State of New York acquired this peerless site for a state park in the late 1980s.

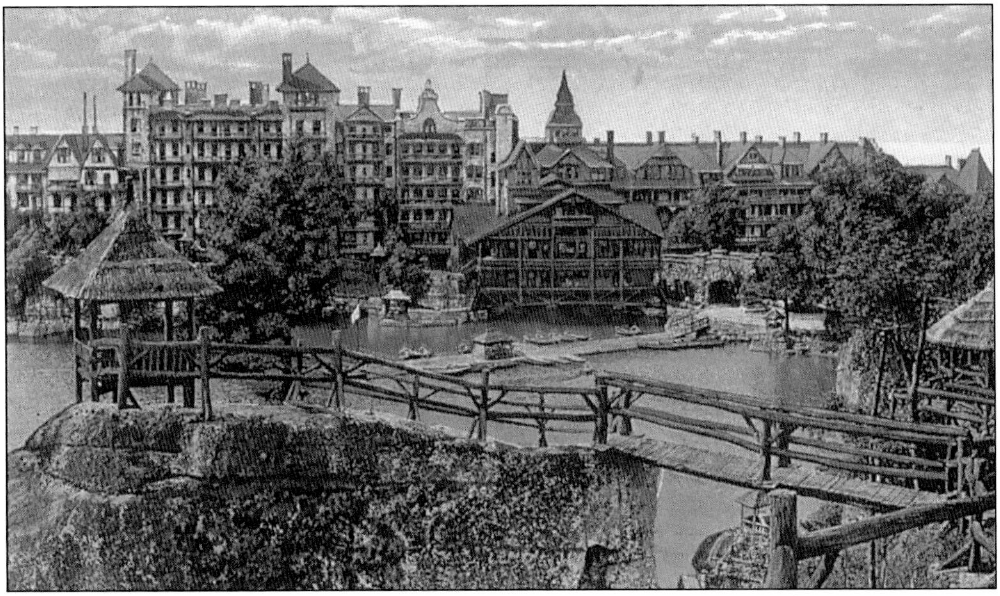

The Mountain House at Lake Mohonk was built by Alfred Homans Smiley in 1879. It was enlarged at various times, lastly when the dining room was extended in 1910. Still owned and meticulously maintained by the Smiley family, this marvelous National Historic Landmark retains all of its vintage charm.

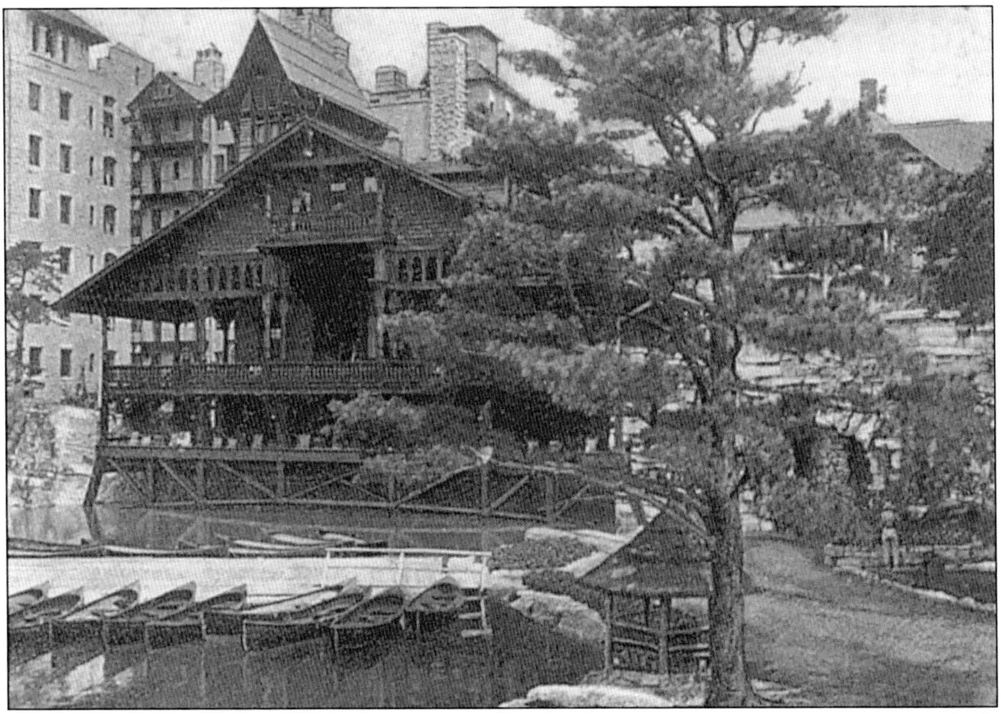

Next to the porte cochere (carriage port) are the large porches of the Mountain House, which overhang glacial Lake Mohonk. Completed in 1899, when the parlor wing was added to the resort, the double-decker porches are where guests still sit in rocking chairs to enjoy the breeze or stand to feed the trout in the lake below.

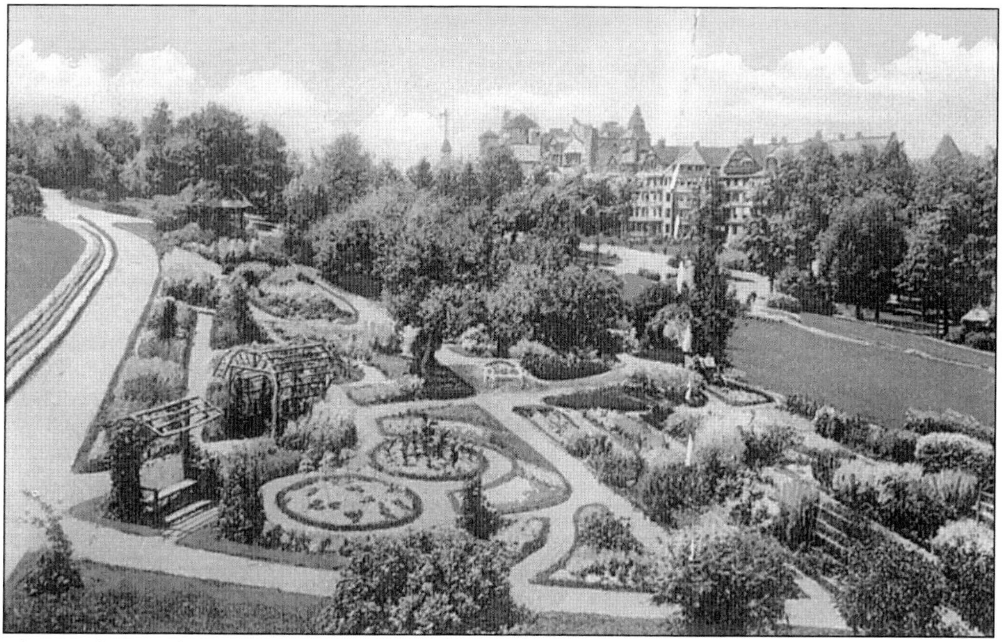

The Display Gardens at Lake Mohonk were begun by Albert Smiley in 1888 on a very unpromising site. Soil for the gardens had to be brought in from a mile away. Beautifully maintained today, as they were in this *c.* 1920 postcard, the gardens feature thousands of bedded, flowering annual plants.

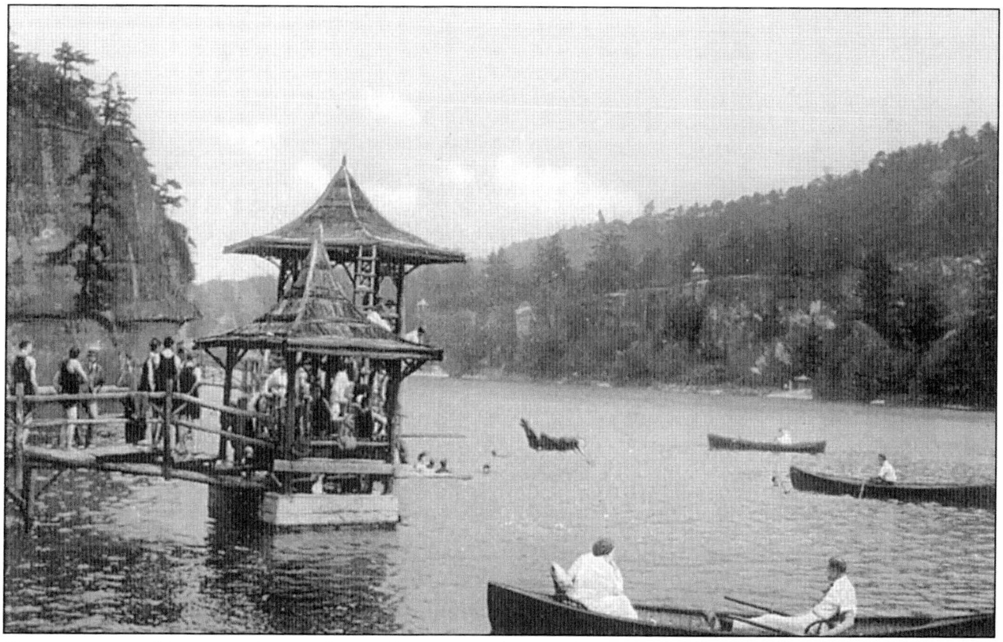

Swimming and boating have always been popular with guests of the Mountain House at Lake Mohonk. The characteristic rustic gazebos are still used at the swimming beach and as rest spots for hikers walking the miles of trails that crisscross the 3,500-acre property. Canoes still ply the lake, but bathing suits have become much briefer than those seen in this *c.* 1910 card.

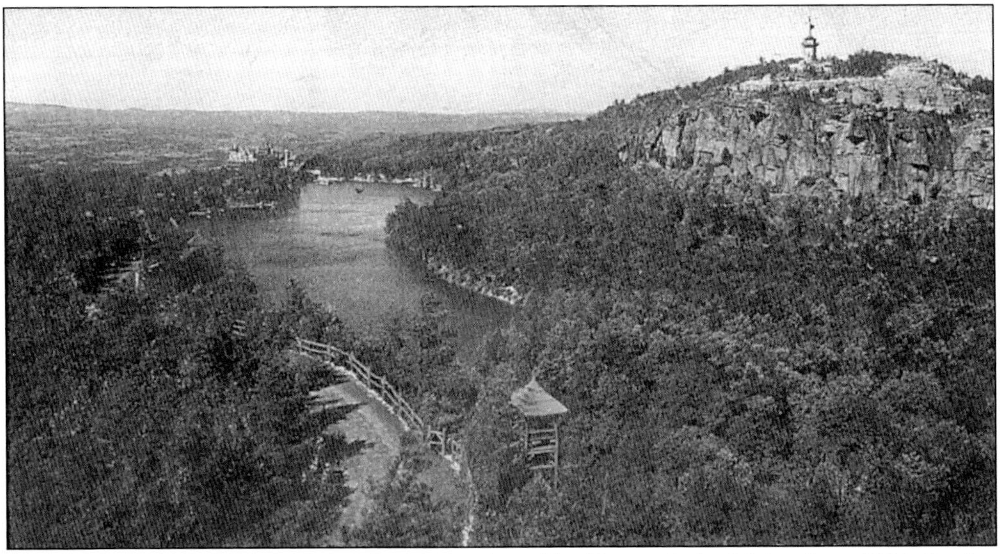

A wooden observation tower was first erected on Sky Top at Lake Mohonk in 1872. In this 1906 view, we see its replacement. In the 1920s, this structure was replaced by the present castle-like Albert K. Smiley Memorial Tower, made of conglomerate rock quarried from the site. It is claimed that six states can be seen from this vantage point.

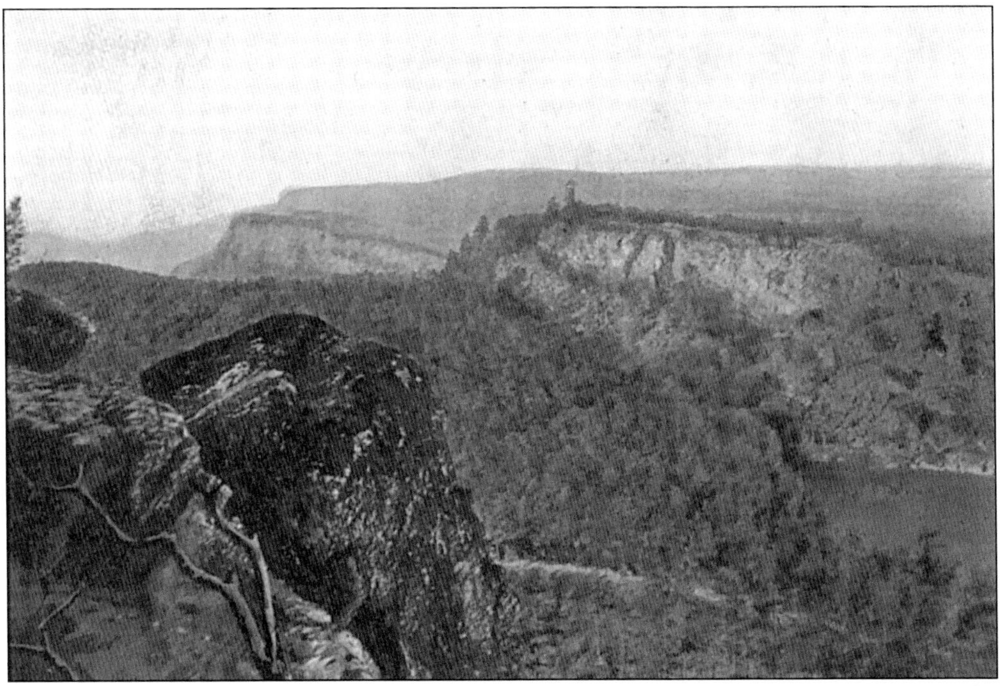

The escarpments of the Trapps and Millbrook Mountain are visible looking south from Sky Top at Lake Mohonk. The view today is as pristine as it was in this c. 1910 card, although the escarpments are now extremely popular with rock climbers, who consider them the best climbing terrain in the eastern United States.

Three

Life in the Rearview Mirror: Looking for the Good Old Days

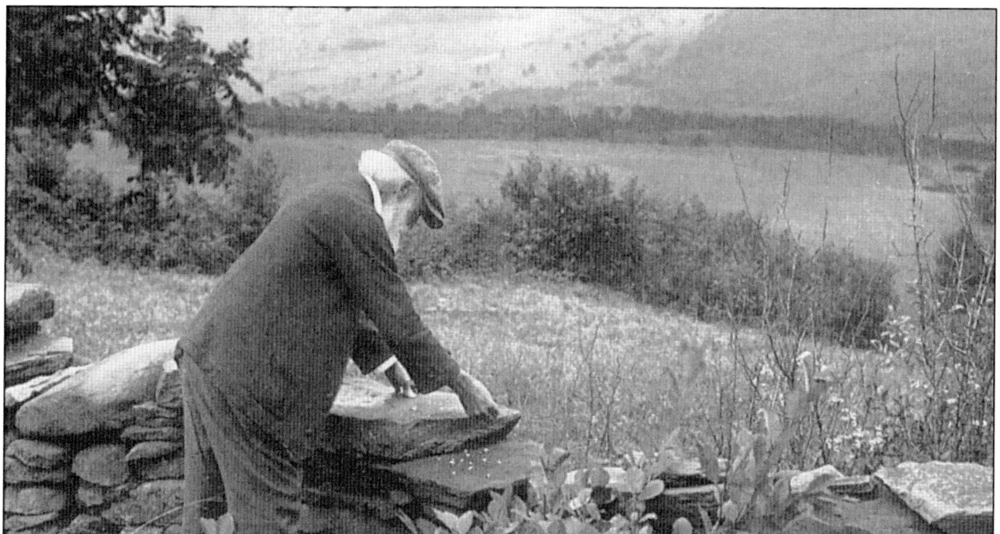

John Burroughs (1837–1921), one of America's premier naturalists, lived most of his life in the Catskills, whose virtues and terrain he widely praised and lyrically described in his very popular writings. His life is celebrated in a series of nostalgic postcards. One card shows the one-room schoolhouse near Roxbury that he attended. Others show his home, which was called Woodchuck Lodge, and his final resting place. Not a hermit, Burroughs was the friend of many of the most famous and powerful people of his era, including Thomas Alva Edison and Henry Ford.

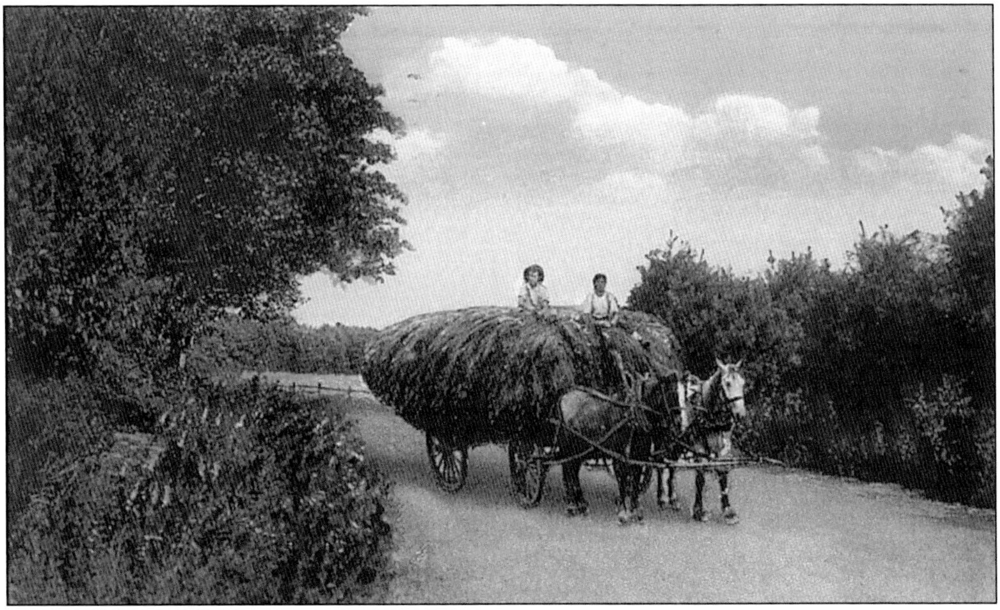

Scenes of haying and hay wagons were promoted by popular American painters as exemplars of "the good old days." In the poor farmland of much of the Catskills, including Sullivan County, scenes like this were common for a long time. This card was mailed in 1926, but the author remembers watching horse-drawn wagons being loaded with hay as late as the 1950s.

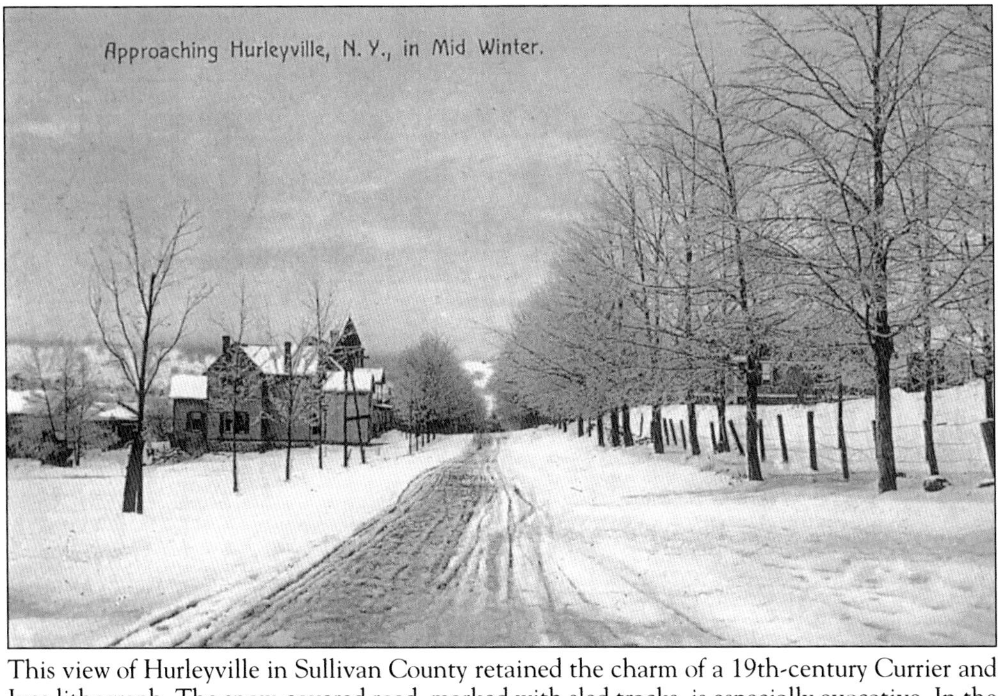

This view of Hurleyville in Sullivan County retained the charm of a 19th-century Currier and Ives lithograph. The snow-covered road, marked with sled tracks, is especially evocative. In the 1920s, Hurleyville became a bustling resort community. The postcard was sent to Ed Berman of Beverly Road in Brooklyn early in the 20th century.

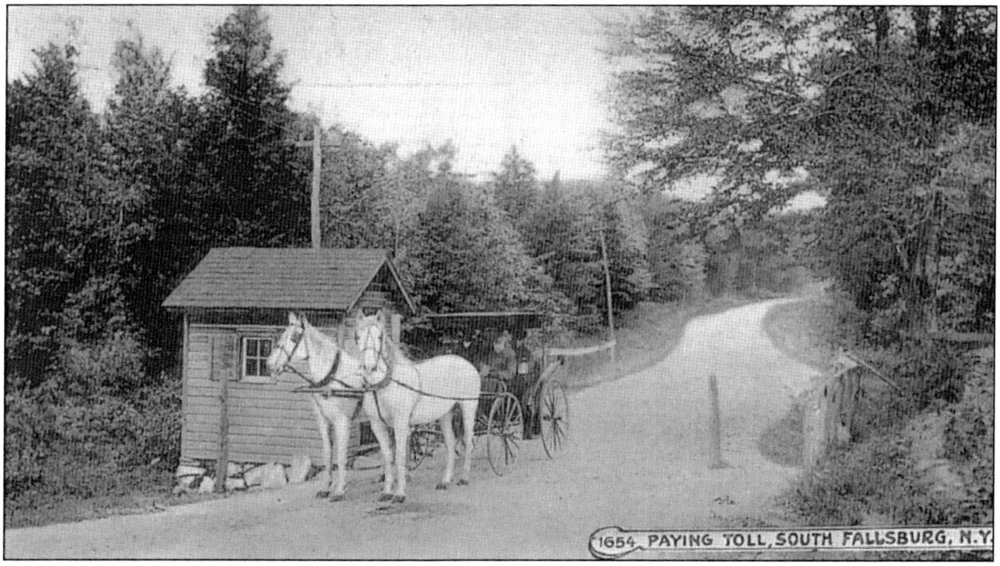

A surprising number of Catskill roads were turnpikes until the age of the automobile gave rise to the subsequent demand for public roads. Tollhouses, as seen in this 1906 view, remained a very popular image for genre painters such as John George Brown (1831–1913) and for the urban dwellers who bought and received most of these cards.

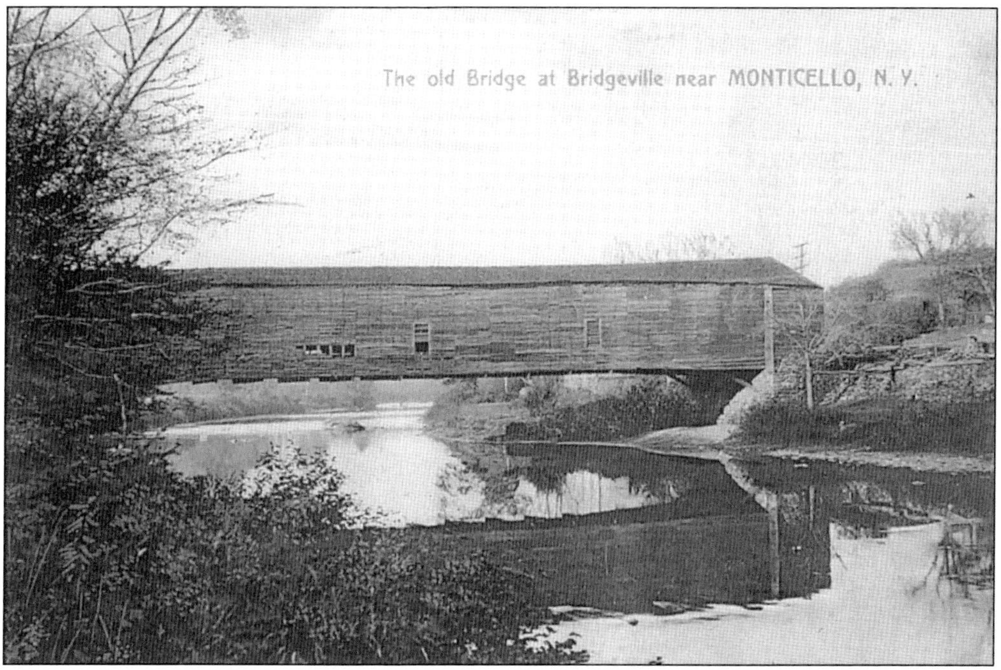

The covered bridge is an enduring recollection of old-time America. Wooden bridges were clearly archaic and nostalgic when this card was sent in 1915. This covered bridge stood right off the present Exit 106 of Route 17 in Sullivan County. Long gone, it was replaced by an iron bridge.

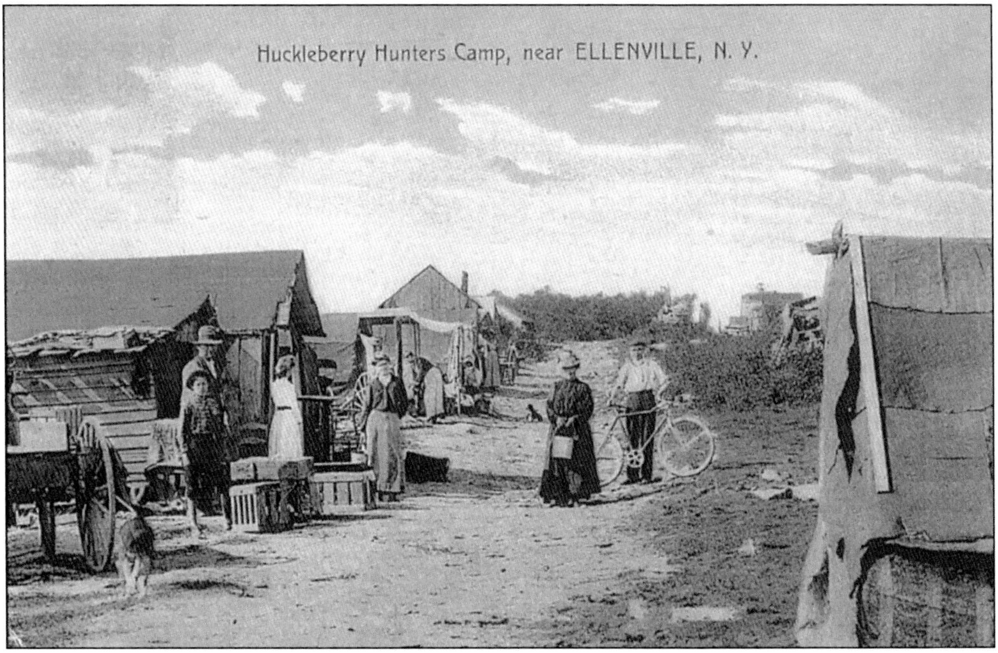

Huckleberry pickers were locals who lived a preindustrial existence well into the 20th century. Dwelling elsewhere during most of the year, they built shantytowns in the mountains where the fruit grew. Their unique lifestyle is recorded in *The Huckleberry Pickers: A Raucous History of the Shawangunk Mountains*, a recent book by Marc B. Fried.

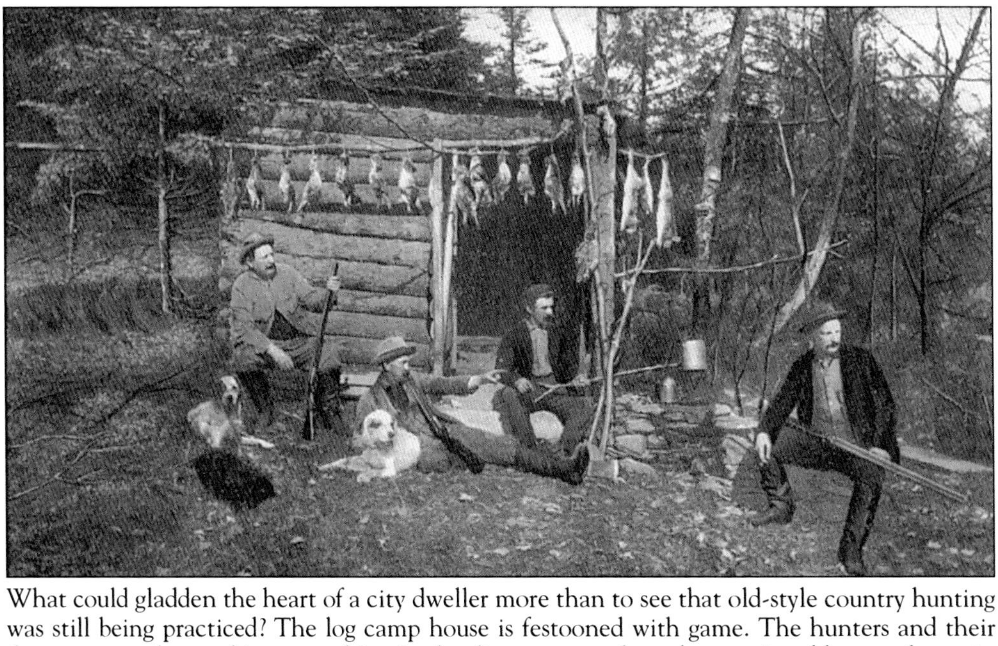

What could gladden the heart of a city dweller more than to see that old-style country hunting was still being practiced? The log camp house is festooned with game. The hunters and their dogs, apparently watching something in the distance, may have been painted by popular artist Arthur Fitzwilliam Tait (1819–1905), who often worked for Currier and Ives.

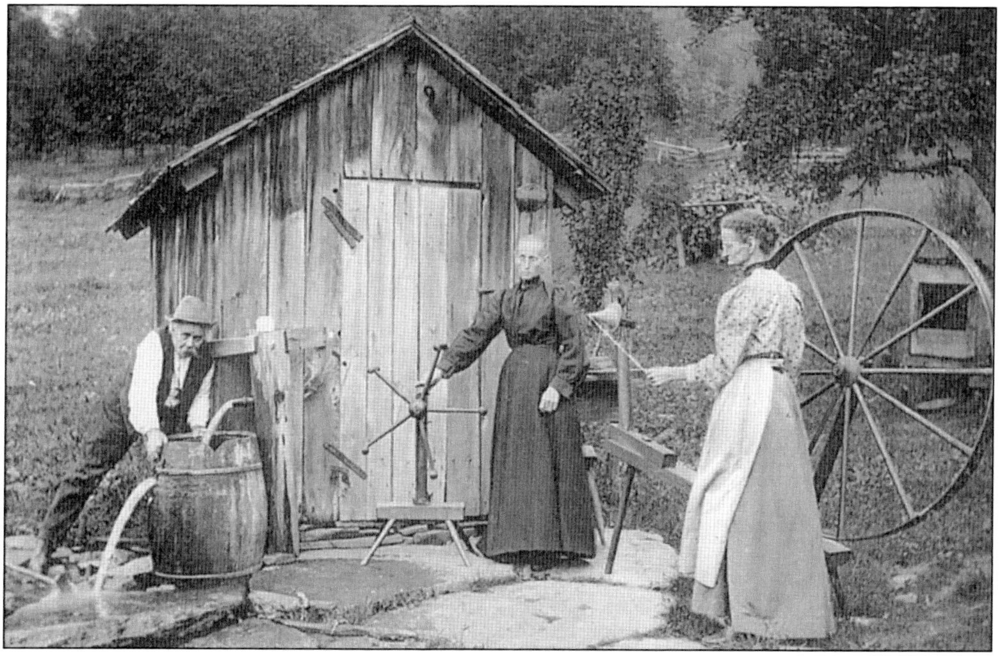

The locals in Woodbourne were really posing for the tourists during "Colonial Days," a card mailed in 1910. The imagery is amusing. The woman demonstrating spinning does not have a supply of wool to spin. Her friend has an empty wool winder, and what is the man doing with that primitive pump and gushing barrel?

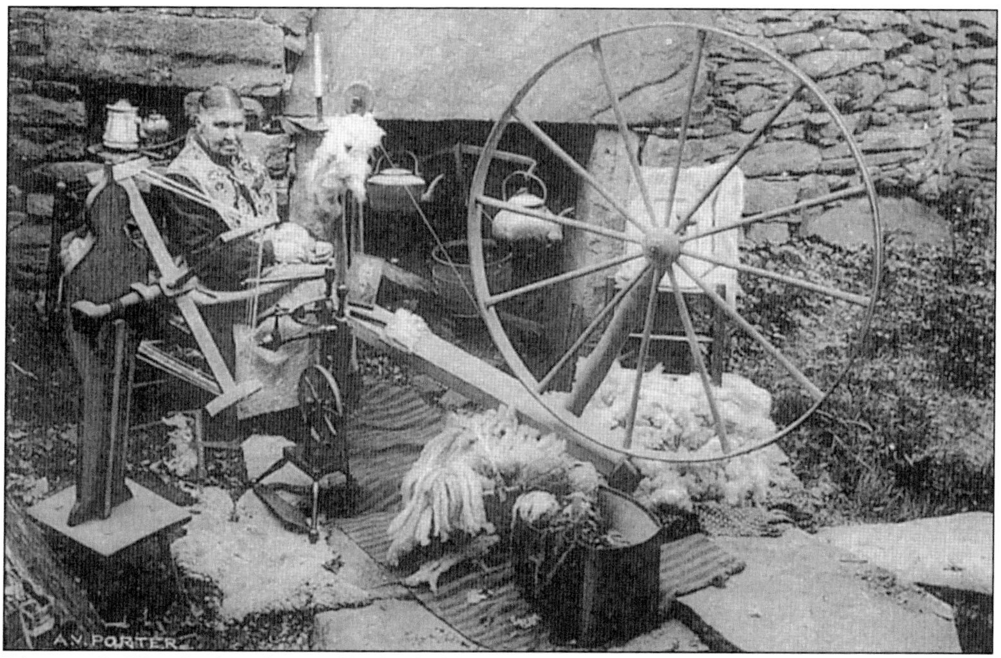

"Auntie de Witt," of Grahamsville, looks like she is ready for everything Colonial on this card, which was actually published in the Catskills. She is apparently outdoors. Is she in the ruin of an early building? In the fireplace, there are two kettles, and she is armed with two spinning wheels, as well as a wool winder and a goodly supply of wool rovings to spin.

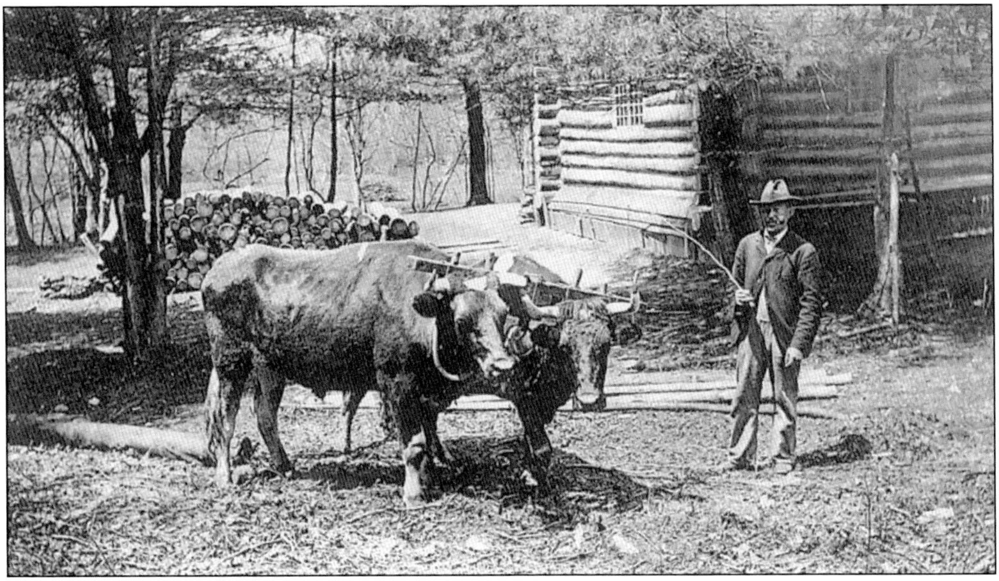

Images of teams of oxen and drovers were extremely popular with genre artists and were often featured in the inexpensive prints of Currier and Ives. These two postcards show the oxen in traditional settings. The upper one has a log building in the background and was mailed from Monticello to a friend in the same town. The lower one portrays the oxen, cart, and driver as "A Vanishing Type," and was sent to a young boy in Linfield, Pennsylvania, asking, "How would you like to have a pet like these?"

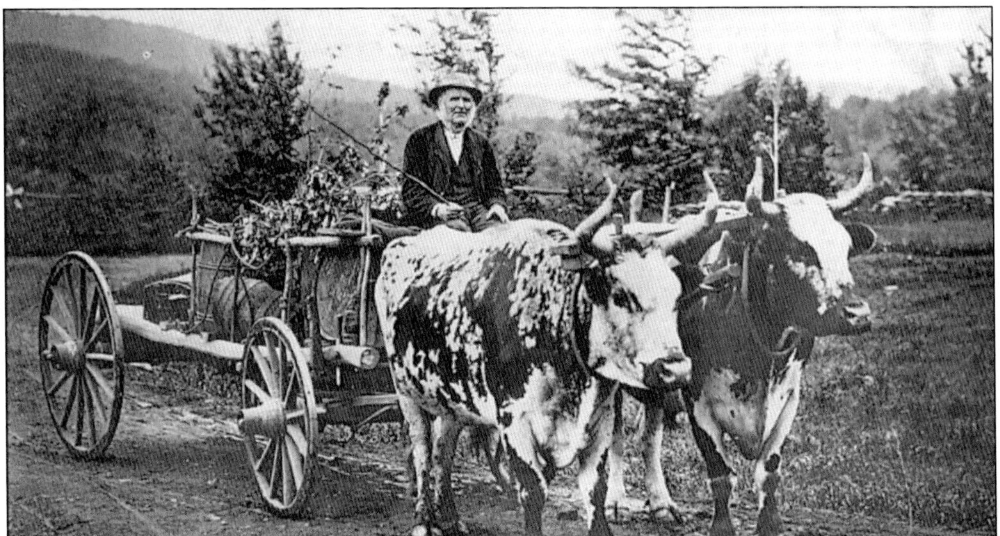

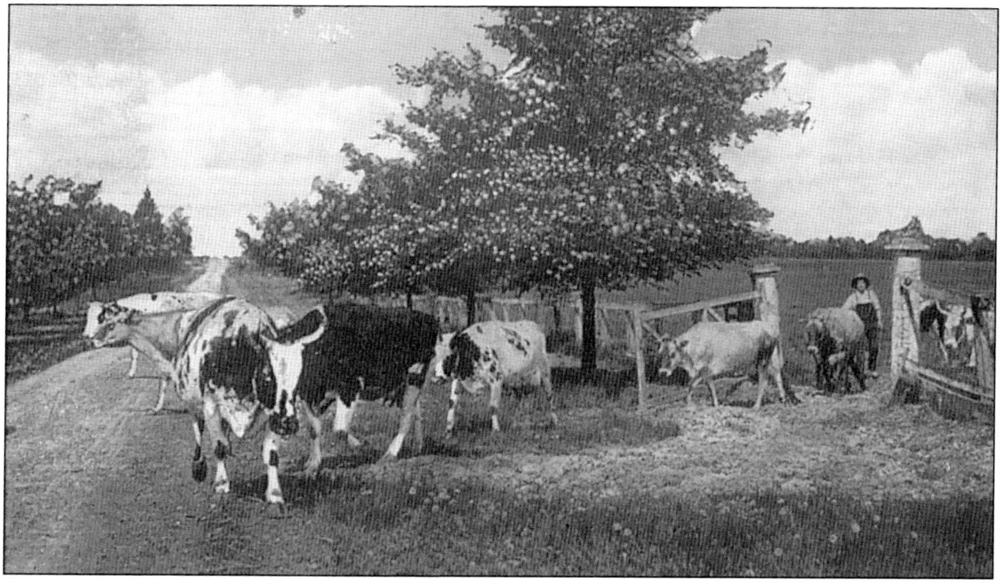

Another enduring image of the olden days was of cattle being taken to pasture, often by the "barefoot boy with cheek of tan," as immortalized in the 19th century by poet John Greenleaf Whittier. This card was mailed in 1929; however, the author remembers his friend Harold Rosenshein, a Jewish farmer's son, herding cows in Woodbourne in the late 1950s.

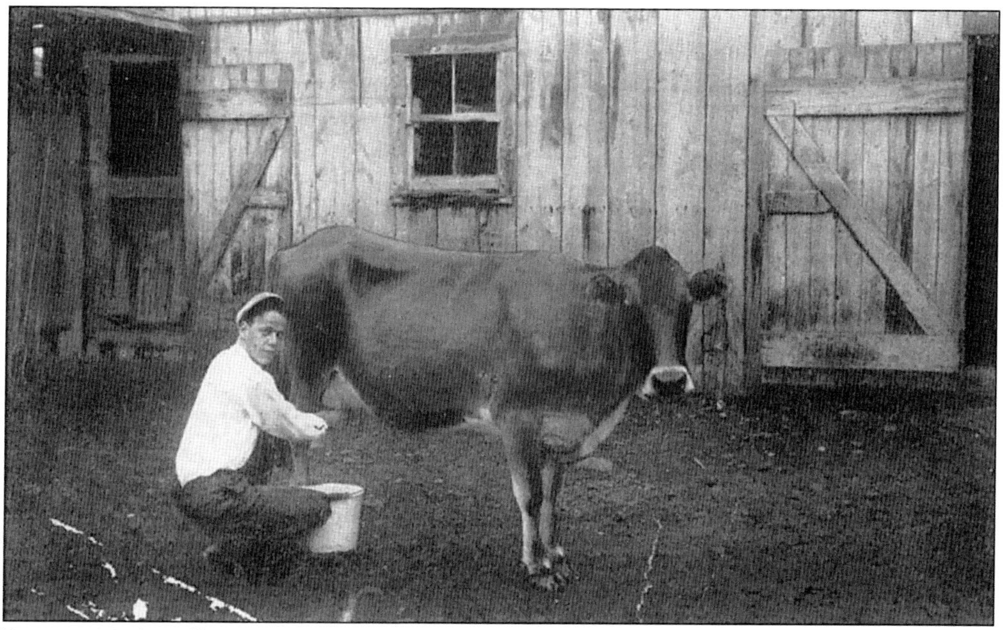

Even in Hurleyville in 1942, when this card was mailed, most people got their milk out of a bottle marked either "Crowley's" or "Dairylea." Clearly an example of tongue-in-cheek nostalgia, the card was mailed from Hurleyville to nearby Ferndale.

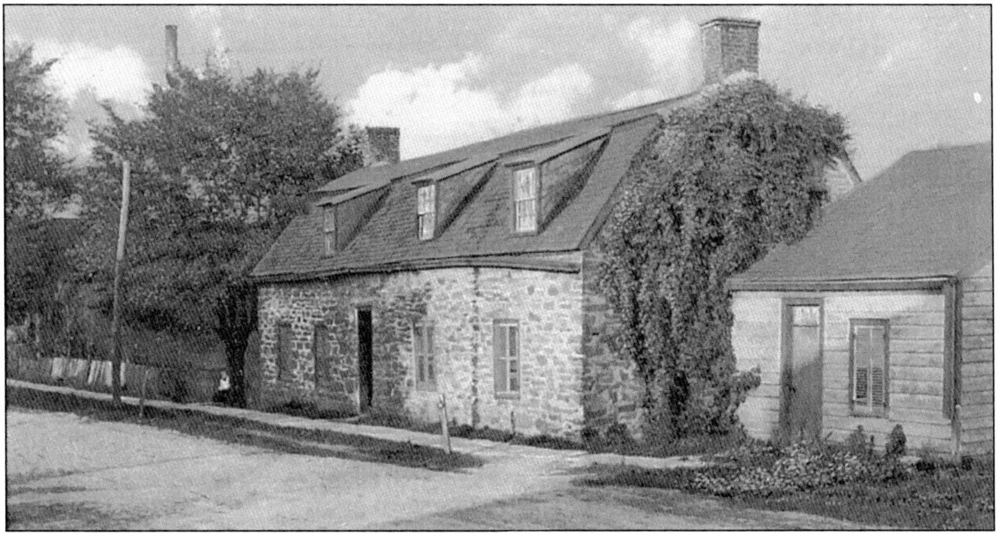

Stretching the definition of the Catskills, this card, c. 1905, claims that the "Oldest House" in the Catskills was erected in 1724 in Athens (near Albany). The house is a Dutch Colonial farmhouse, but there are much earlier stone houses in the more traditionally defined Catskill region. For example, several of the houses that line the street in Hurley date earlier, as do the houses on Huguenot Street in New Paltz.

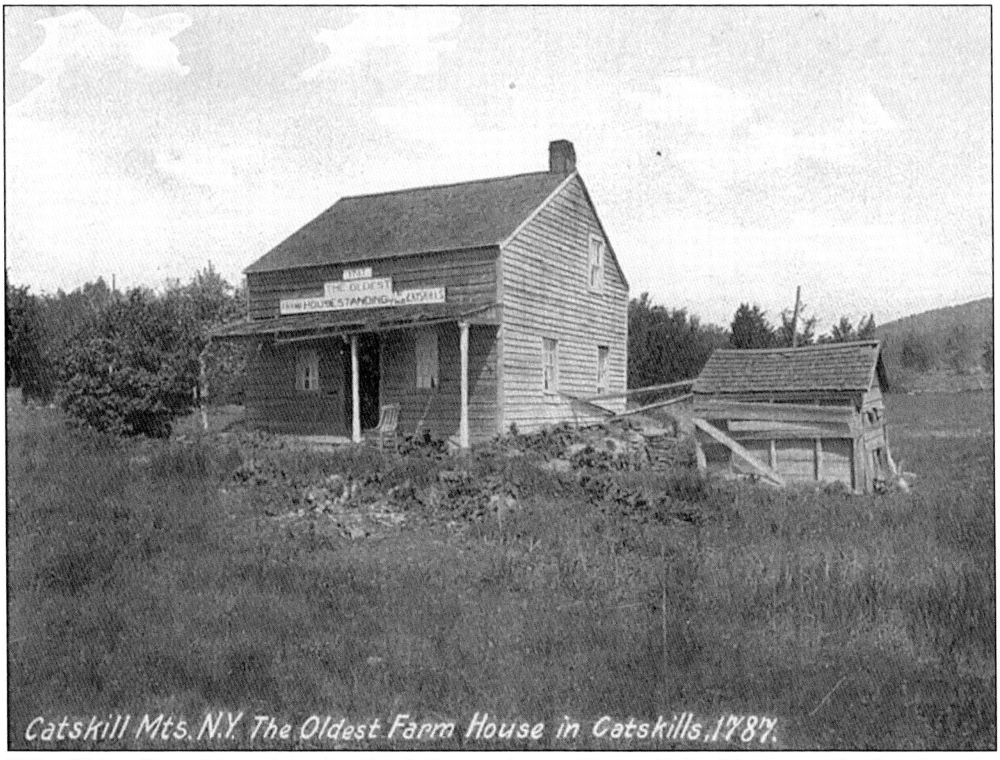

"The Oldest Farm House" in the Catskills stood near Haines Falls. Traditionally dated to the 18th century, the farmhouse was a popular image on early-20th-century postcards. Shown only in a ramshackled state amidst unkempt fields, it was always very clearly labeled.

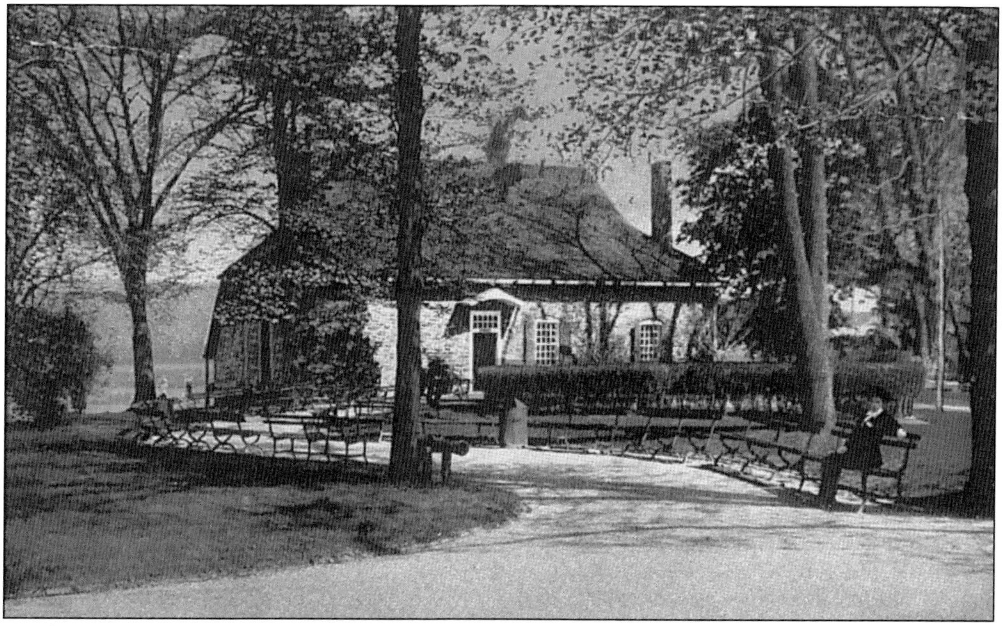

Washington's Headquarters at Newburgh is, perhaps, the first house museum in the United States. Picturesquely situated overlooking the Hudson, the building combines the image of the father of his country with a Dutch Colonial period house into an irresistible package of patriotism and nostalgia, which was widely painted before becoming the subject of many postcards.

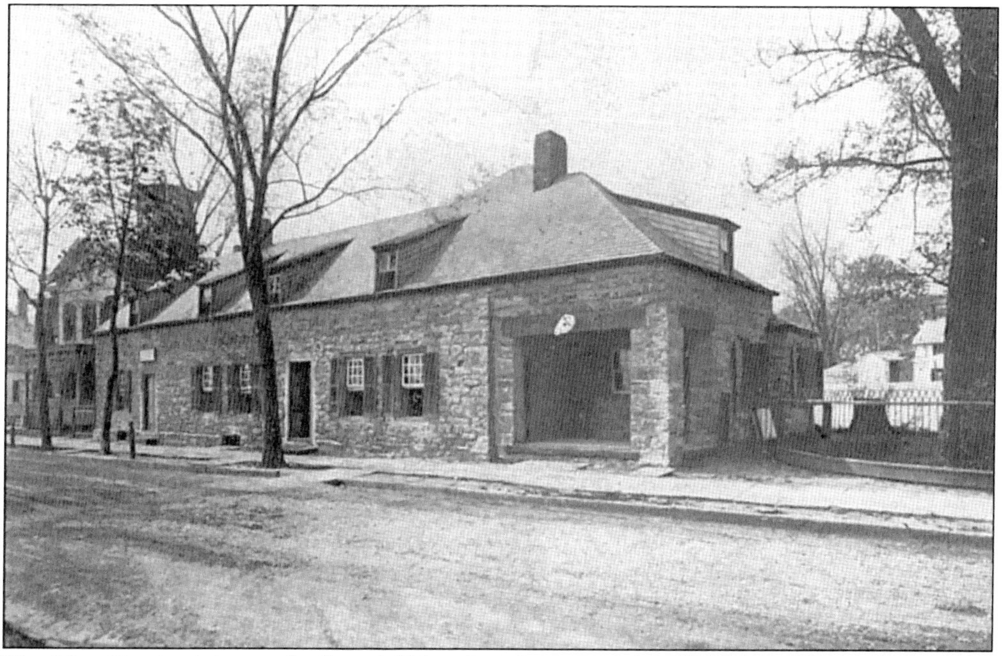

The Van Gaasbeek house, built *c.* 1676, is best known as the Old Senate House. During the Revolution, it briefly served as New York's capitol when the new state senate met in Kingston in 1777. A picturesque Dutch Colonial building, the house was a very popular postcard image. This *c.* 1905 card was addressed to a lady in Liberty, New York.

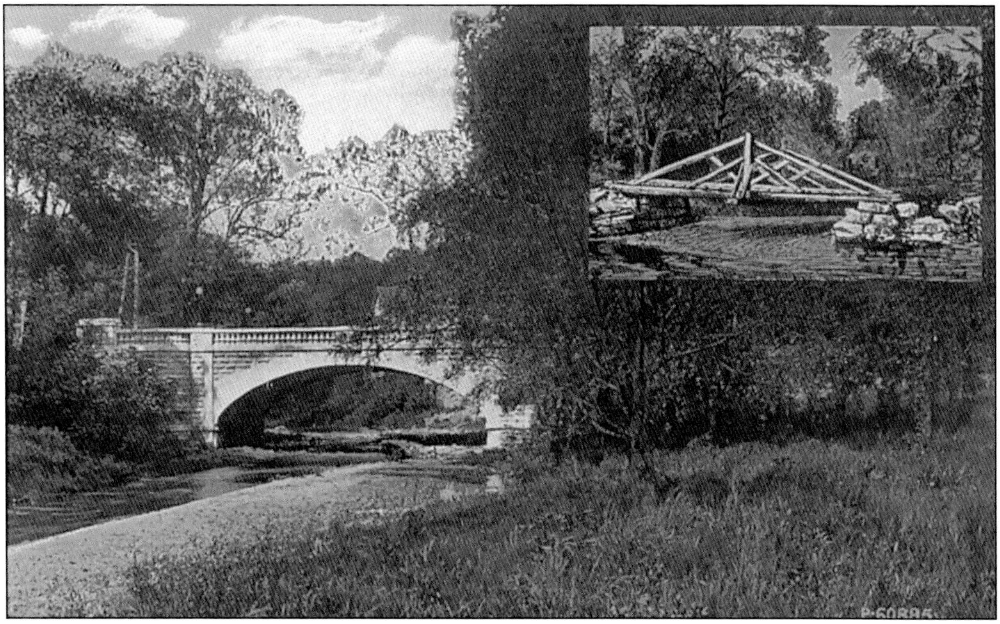

The most widely known "historic" events and characters of the Dutch era of the Hudson Valley and the Catskills are, in reality, the figments of novelist Washington Irving's imagination. Many people visit Tarrytown to see where the hapless Ichabod Crane fled from the headless horseman.

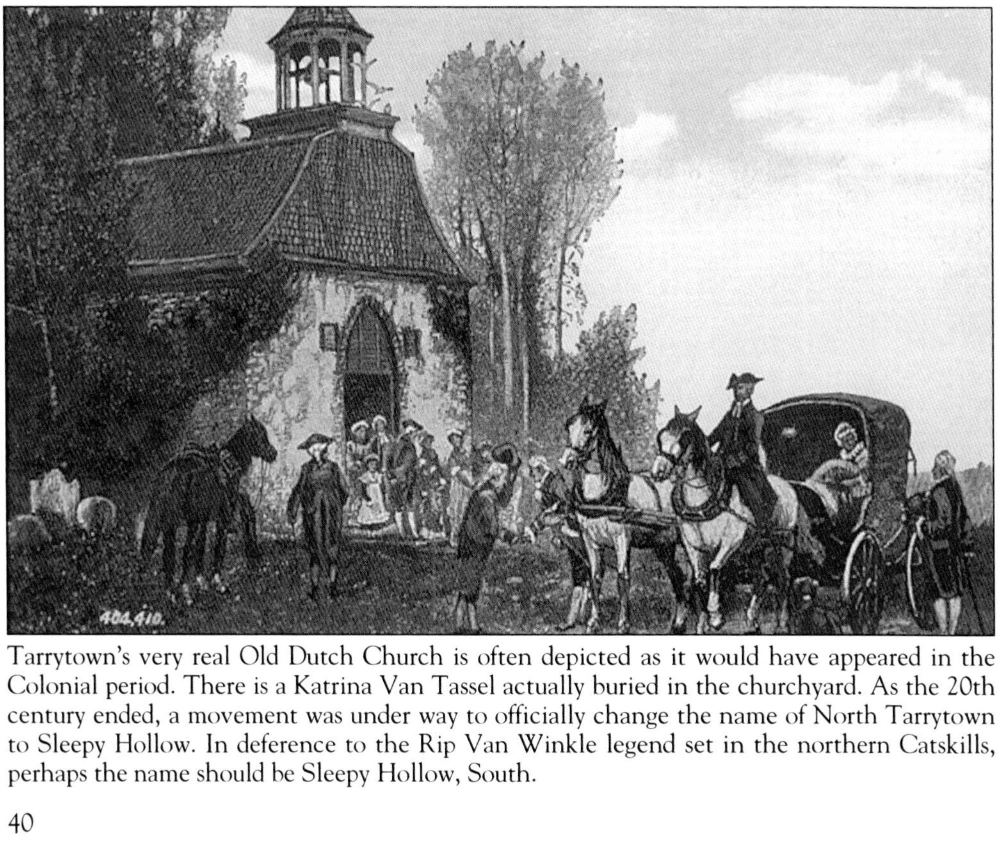

Tarrytown's very real Old Dutch Church is often depicted as it would have appeared in the Colonial period. There is a Katrina Van Tassel actually buried in the churchyard. As the 20th century ended, a movement was under way to officially change the name of North Tarrytown to Sleepy Hollow. In deference to the Rip Van Winkle legend set in the northern Catskills, perhaps the name should be Sleepy Hollow, South.

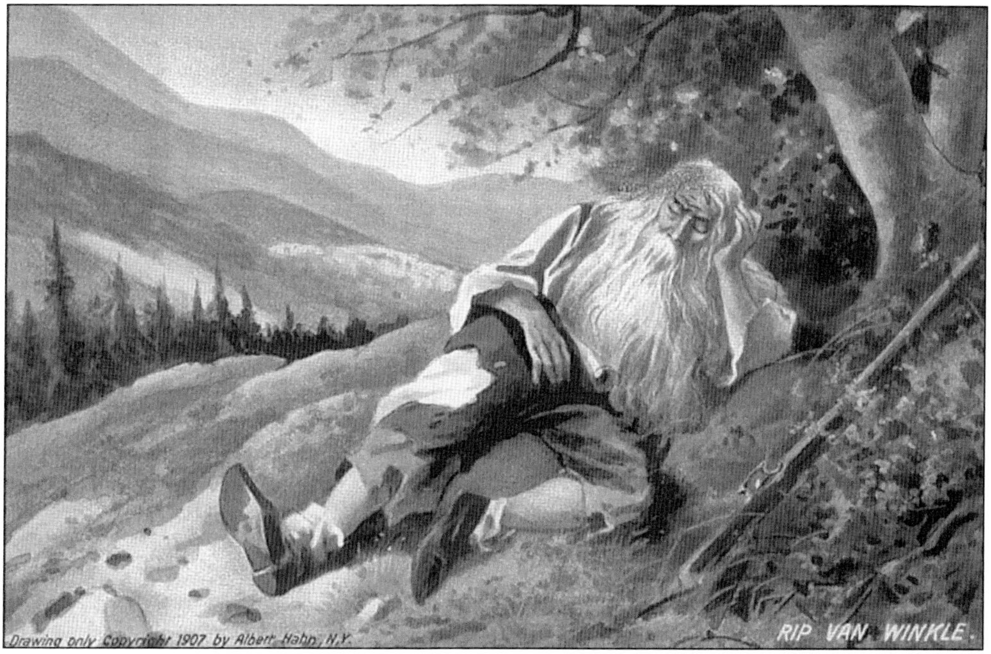

The image of Rip Van Winkle is, of course, strongly related to the Catskills. Many postcards show the elderly, bearded man. In August 1909, Lizzie sent this card to a friend in Chester, Pennsylvania, with the message "Rip Van Winkle was a lucky man. HaHa having a fine time." Washington Irving, who liked a good joke, enjoyed the fact that people believed Rip to have been real. The boulder on which Rip purportedly slept is up the ravine from "his house."

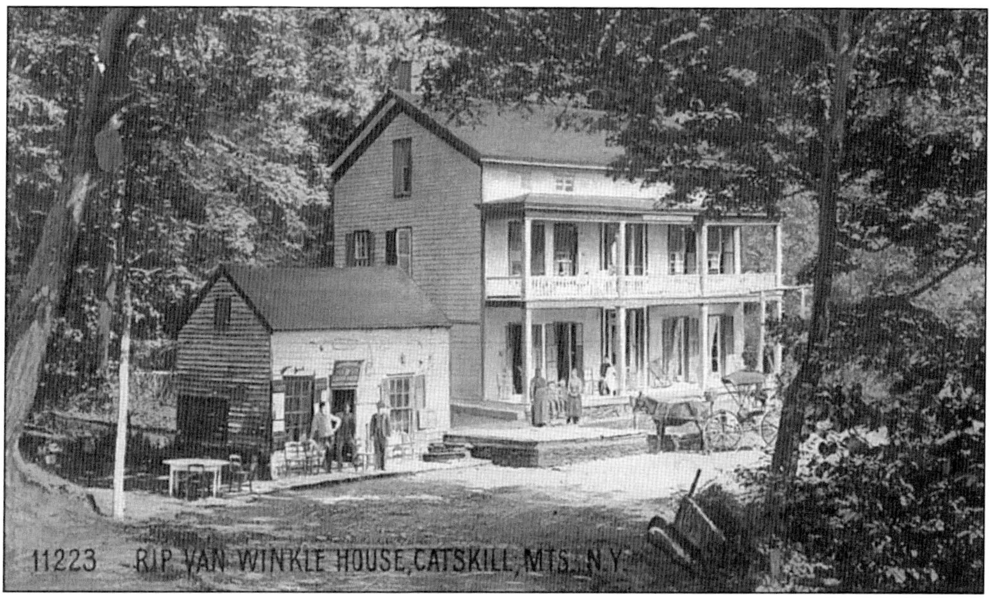

As early as 1832, the already legendary Rip Van Winkle had been given a specific geographical home, near the Catskill Mountain House. A single-room shanty existed on this site from at least 1828. By the 1860s, a "Rip Van Winkle" was living on the site, selling refreshments. Sometime between 1865 and 1870, the Rip Van Winkle House seen in this 1906 card was built. It was first a roadside tavern and then a boardinghouse, before it burned c. 1916.

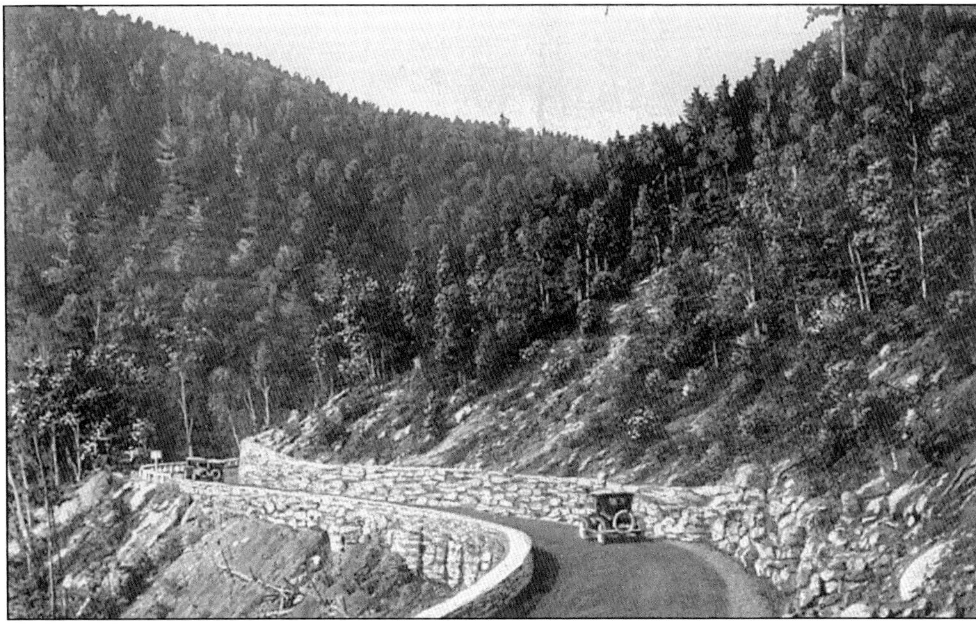

The Rip Van Winkle Trail, state Route 23A, was opened in 1924 and passes very near the site of the Catskill Mountain House, the region's first great resort. The highway replaces part of a private road controlled by the Beach family, who owned the famed hotel. Rip's Lookout Point featured an establishment that sold souvenirs and beer. Rip would have appreciated the latter.

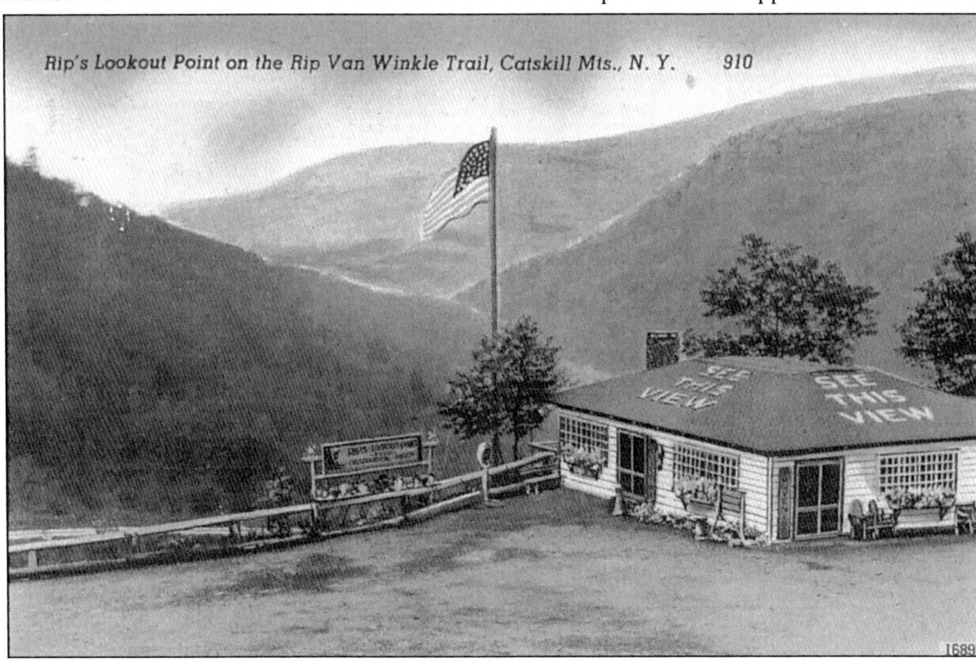

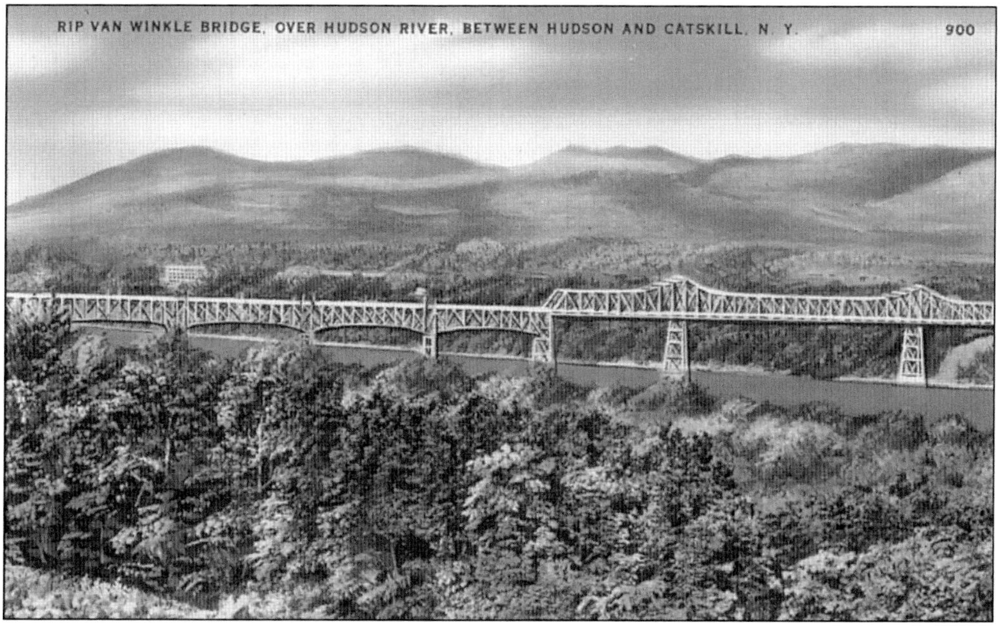

Use of the Rip Van Winkle name and legend continues unabated, in motels, shopping centers, and most spectacularly, in a bridge that spans the Hudson below Olana, the home of painter Frederick Edwin Church. The bridge connects the towns of Hudson and Catskill, the center of the traditional Catskill area. Nowhere in America does the world of literature, art, and tourism come together more completely than in the countryside near the town of Catskill.

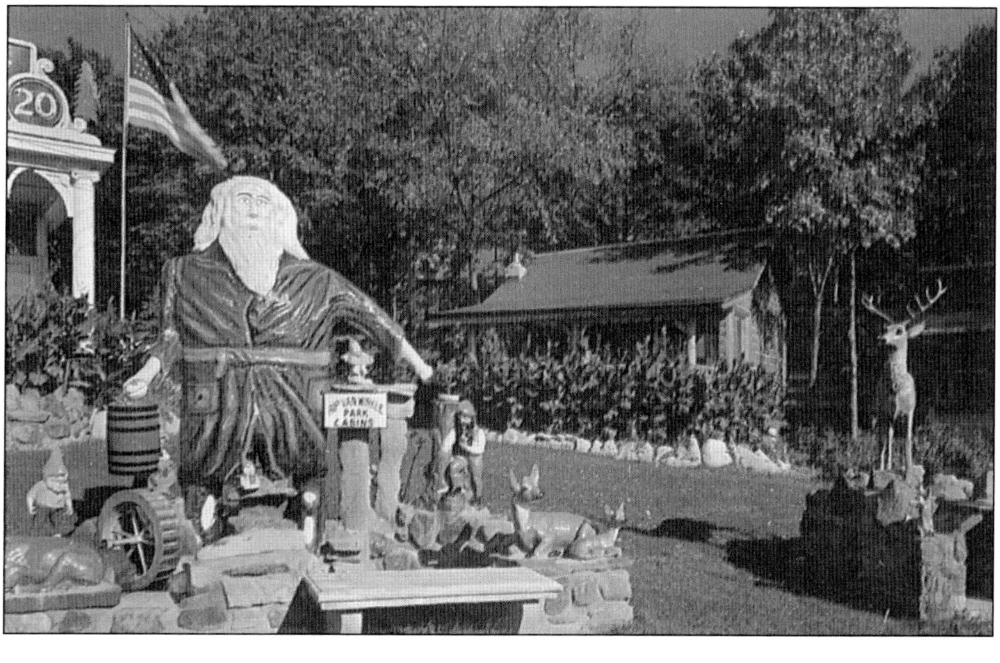

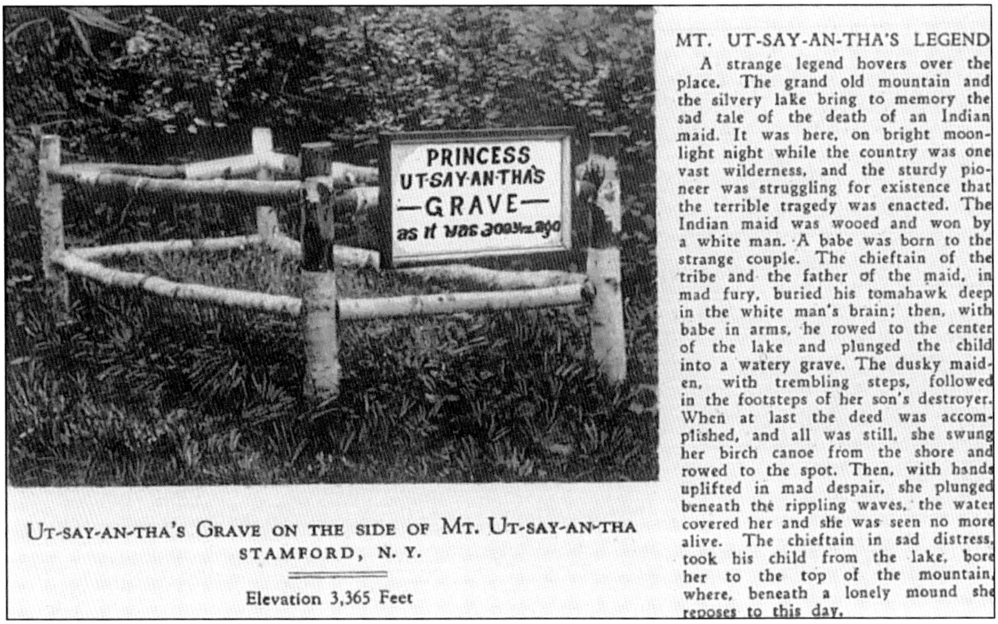

Native Americans were present in legend only during the great resort era. In the 1990s, their presence was greatly missed when, as a last ditch effort, Sullivan County tried to establish a reservation at the Monticello Raceway in order to obtain casino gambling. The romantic, if racist story of Princess Ut-Say-Au-Tha, set in the northern Catskills, is typical of regional Native American lore, which usually incorporates bloodshed and the white-red conflict. Legend is often tied to high, prominent spots, hence the choice of the very top of the mountain that later sported the scenic observatory pictured in a 1940s card printed in Chicago.

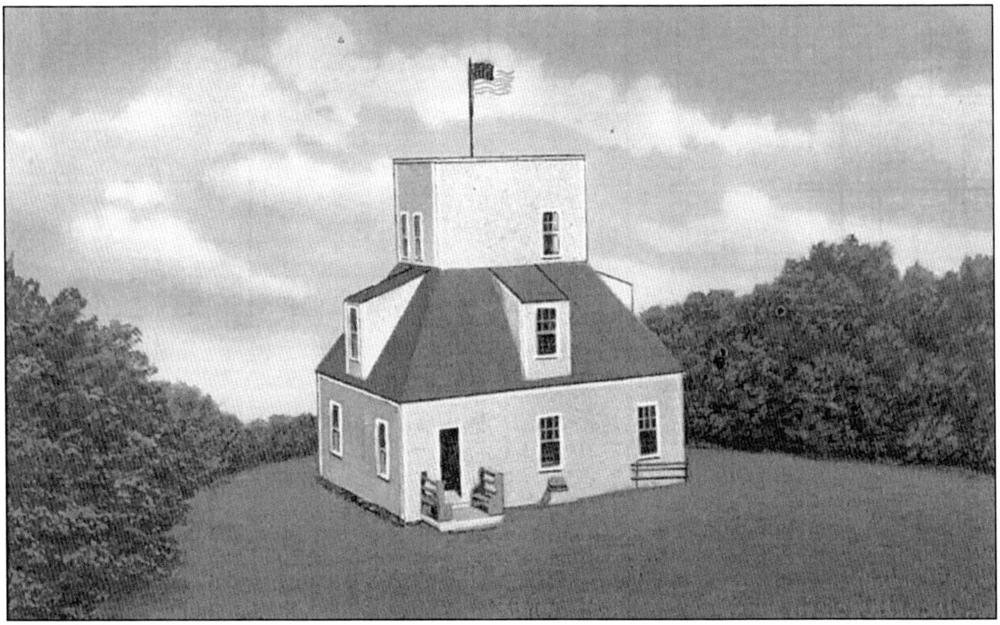

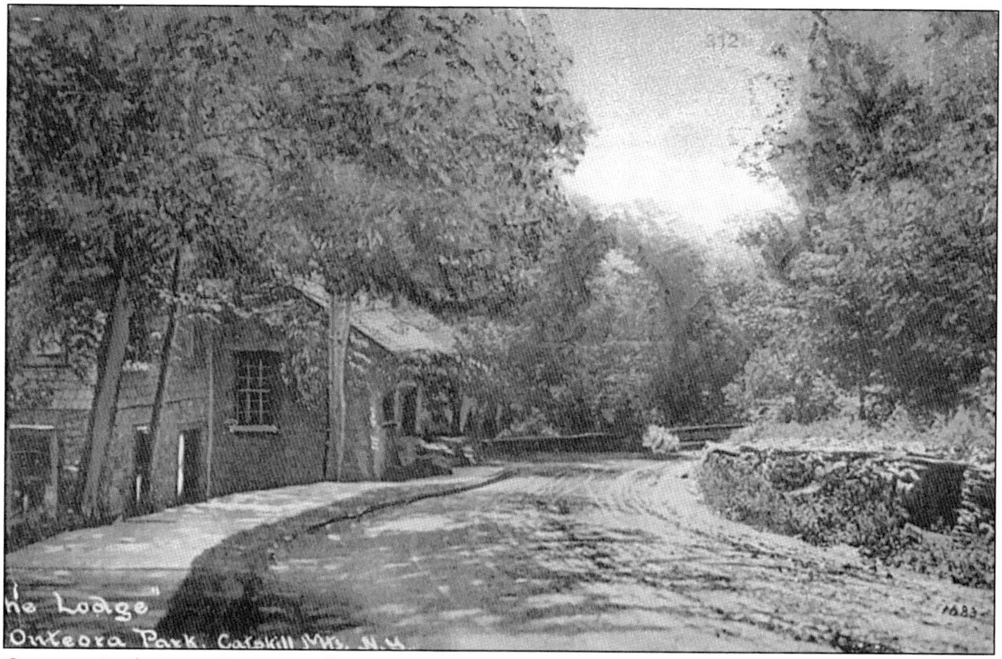

Onteora Park, near Tannersville, was founded in 1883 by Francis Thurber, one of America's leading wholesale grocers, and his sister, Candace Thurber Wheeler, design associate of Louis Comfort Tiffany. Organized as part of the park movement of the late 19th century, Onteora was designed to be exclusionary, limiting its residents to only the "best people." In other words, neither Catholics nor Jews need apply. Making it less stuffy than other Catskill cottage parks (Twilight, Elka, Sunset, Santa Cruz, etc.) was the artistic bent of many of its residents, including painter Dora Wheeler, Candace's daughter. Other artists in residence included painters Carroll Beckwith and John White Alexander. Mark Twain spent the summer of 1890 at Onteora. Actress Maud Adams (1872–1953), a leading light of the American stage, summered there for many years.

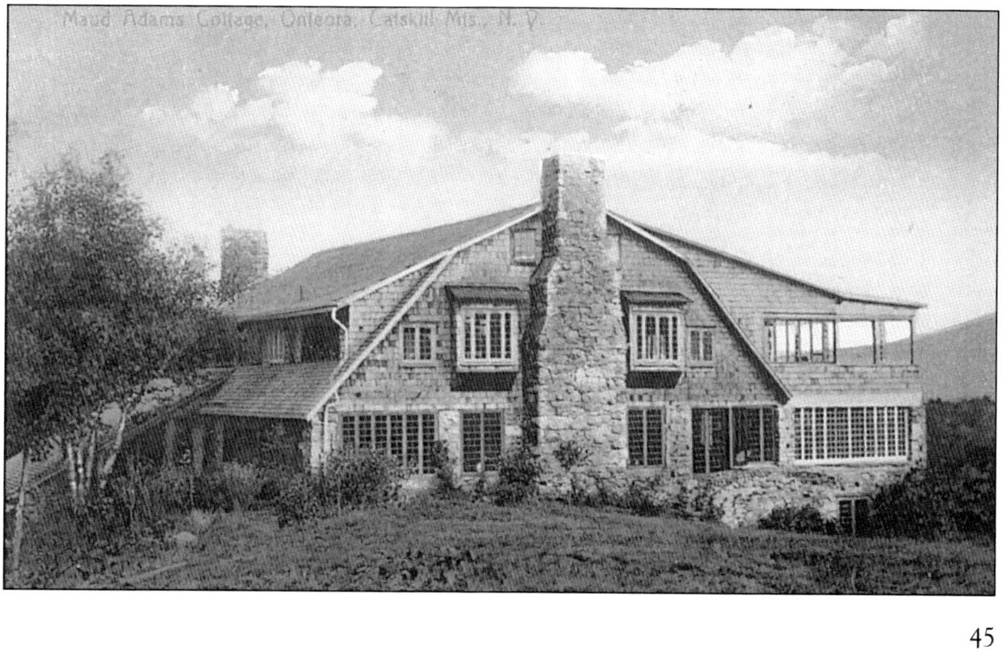

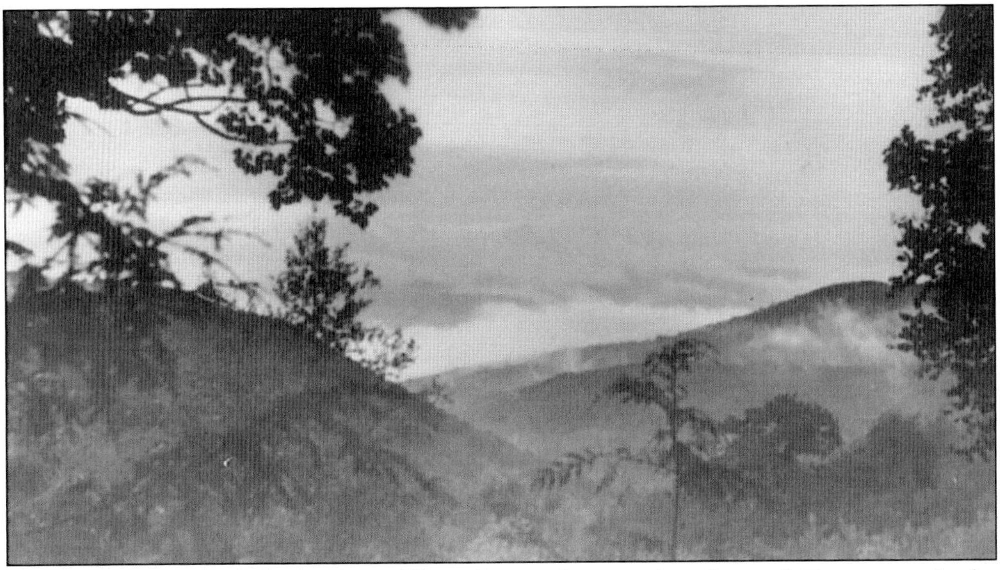

Visible from a hillside high above Ellenville, in the artist's colony of Cragsmoor, is the place where the northern Catskills end (right) and the Shawangunks, or southern Catskills, begin. In the 1880s, painter Edward Lamson Henry (1841–1919) "discovered" Cragsmoor, and soon, other artists, most notably American Impressionist Charles Cortenay Curran (1861–1942), followed.

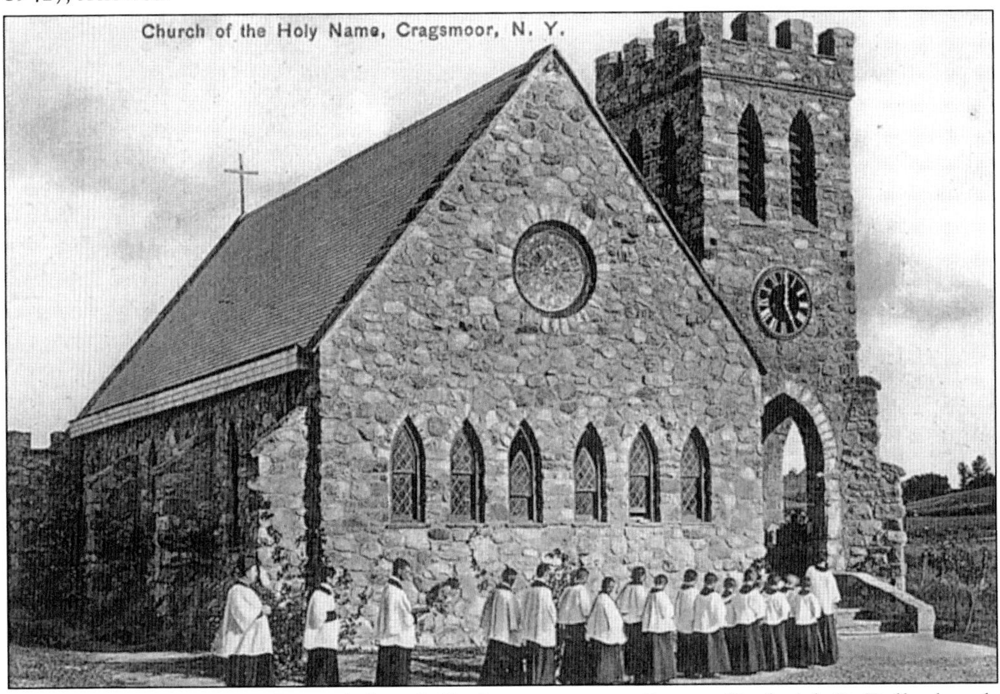

The Cragsmoor artists enhanced their hillside community. Painter Frederick S. Dellenbaugh (1854–1935) designed the picturesque Church of the Holy Name, as well as the nearby Library on the Mountain. Episcopalian, the church has never been heated and is used only in the summer. Today, it is a popular spot for weddings. The famed overlook where the Catskills and the Shawangunks come together is visible behind this unique building.

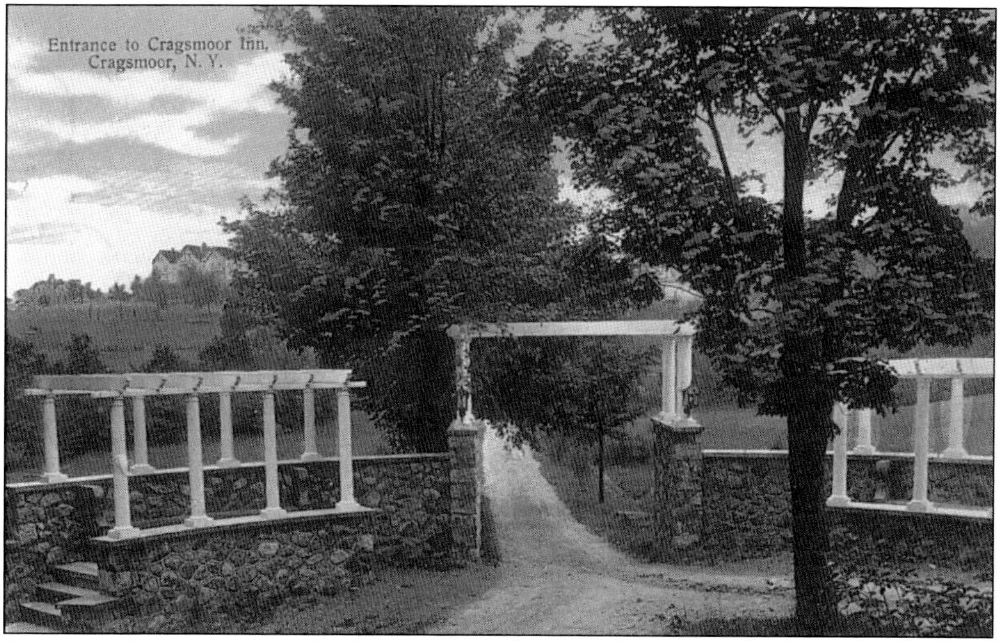

Scenery and artists attracted other summer people to Cragsmoor, which soon sported its own hotel, The Cragsmoor Inn. The resort's entrance featured the classic pergolas that were very much favored by the summer colonists, who often used them at their homes as well. Cragsmoor artists were conservative, family-oriented people, and it is no surprise that the Cragsmoor Inn's rooms were advertised as "large, airy, and arranged for the convenience of families." Additionally, the inn announced that it provided an atmosphere of "freedom with safety" for children.

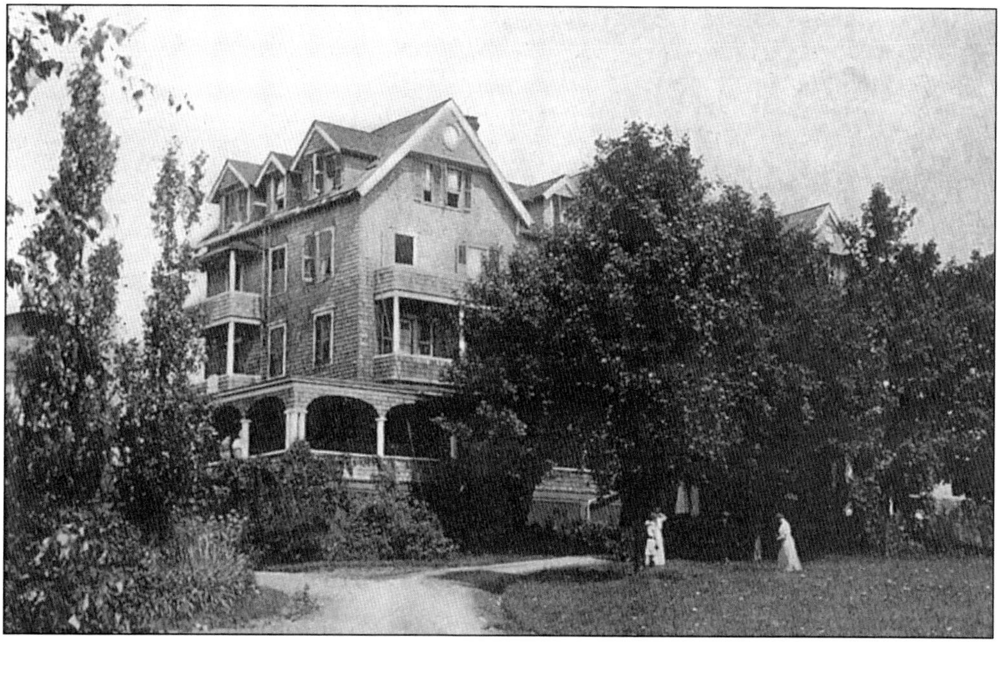

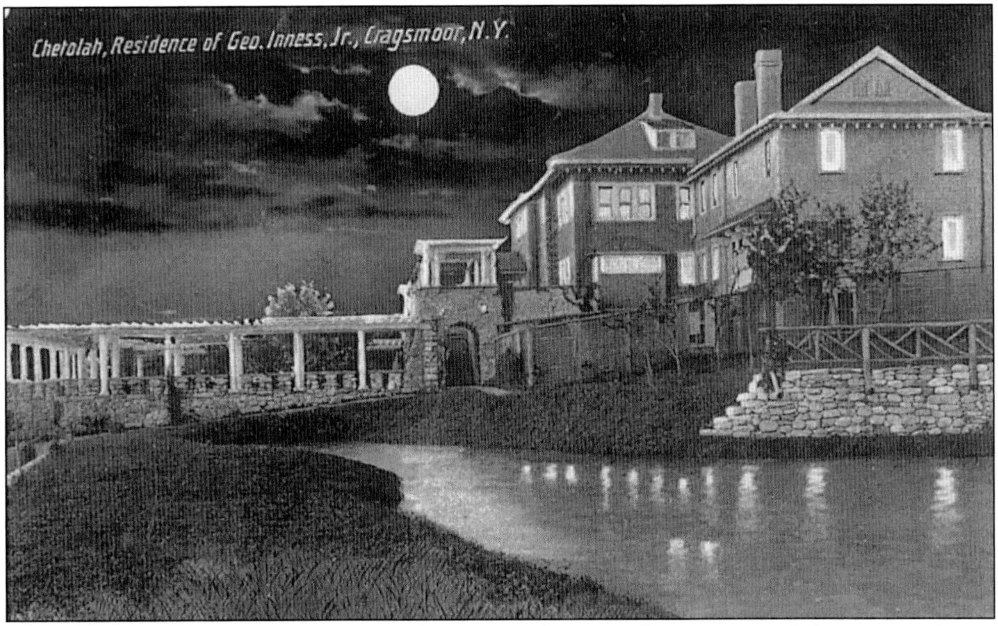

George Inness Jr. (1853–1926), the painter son of a more famous artist father, married into the wealthy Scribner publishing family. Enjoying the society of other artists and intellectuals, Inness and his wife built an impressive house called "Chetolah" at the Cragsmoor colony, which is now being restored.

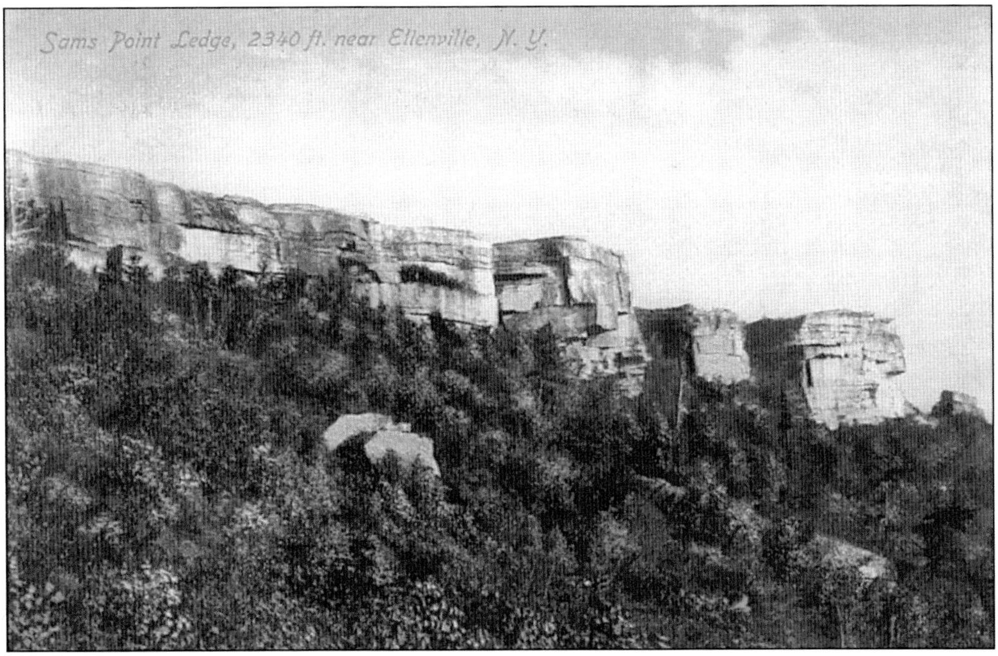

Above Cragsmoor is Sam's Point, a geologic feature named for a white trader known only as Sam. In the 18th century, Sam allegedly leaped from the far end of the ledge (Sam's Point) to escape from pursuing Native Americans. Improbably, he landed unhurt in the canopy of trees below. The promontory was a popular spot for the Cragsmoor artists, especially Charles C. Curran, who painted many works on top of the ridge.

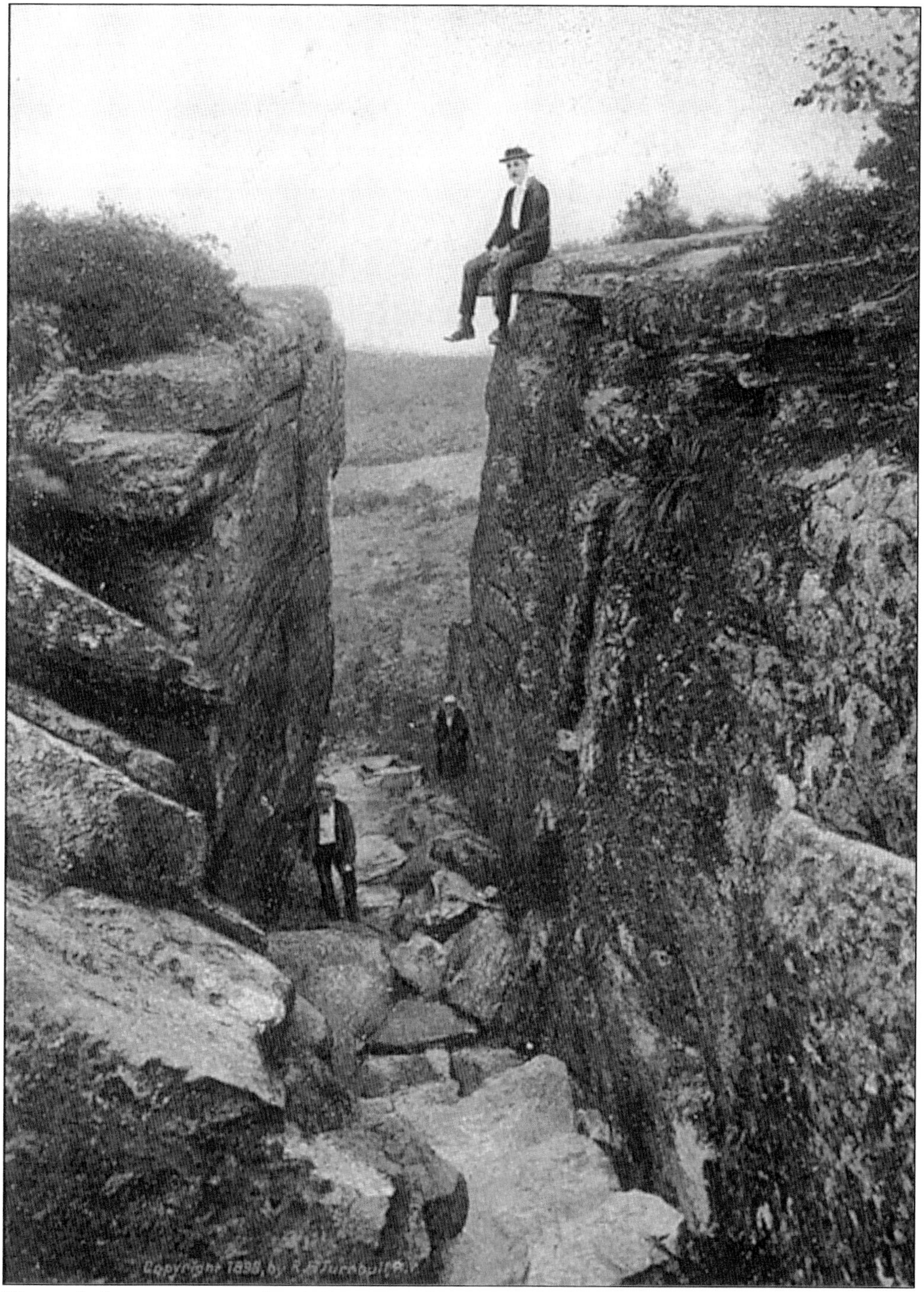

The rock formations near Sam's Point are fantastic. Climbers and tourists have always found the dangerous perches irresistible, as did this formally attired gentleman, c. 1910. Today, as part of Ice Cave Mountain Park, the stone steps are accessible, but climbing is forbidden.

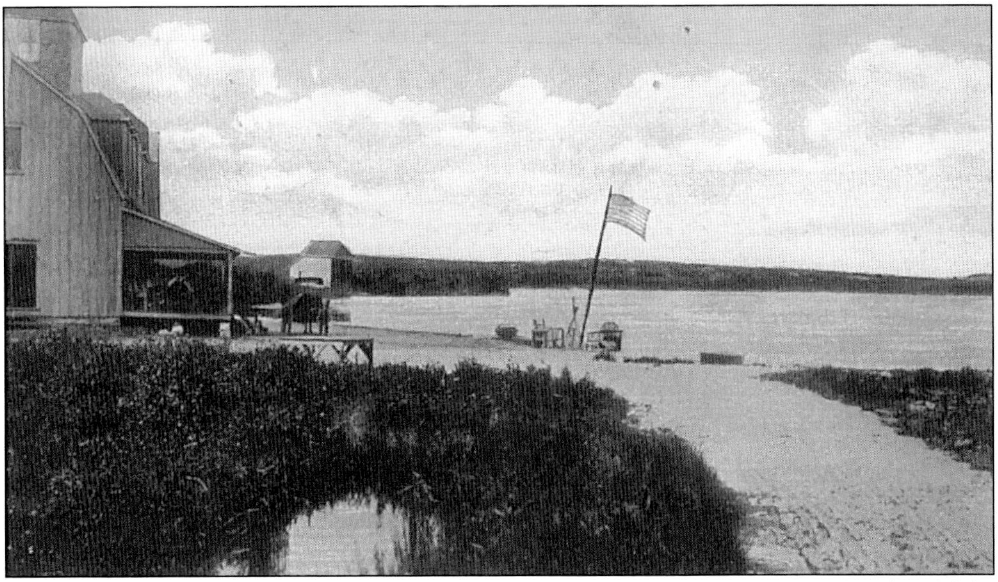

Near the top of the mountain, not far from Sam's Point, is Lake Maratanza, the glacial lake shown in this 1907 view. Maratanza, like Mohonk and Minnewaska, was embellished with a resort hotel on its shore. The grand Queen Anne Revival-style hotel called the Mount Meenahga was never as renowned as its more northerly neighbors, and it eventually burned. Lake Maratanza is acidic, and today, its crystal-clear, soft water is completely devoid of life. Owned by the town of Ellenville, the lake serves as the community's reservoir.

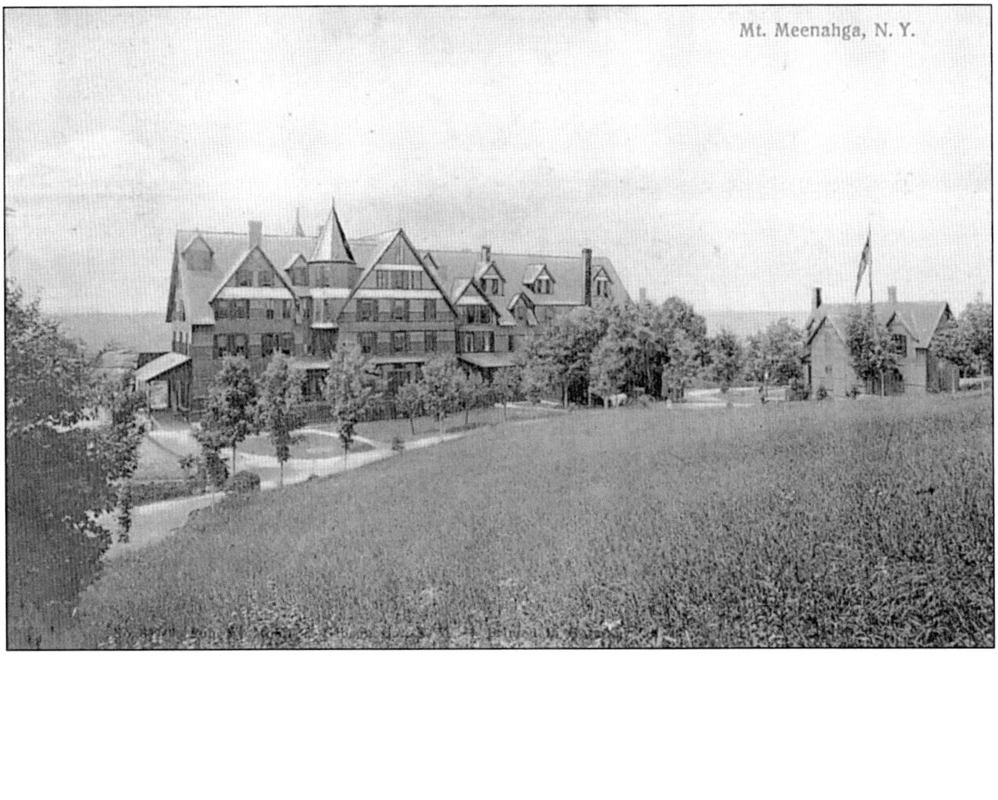

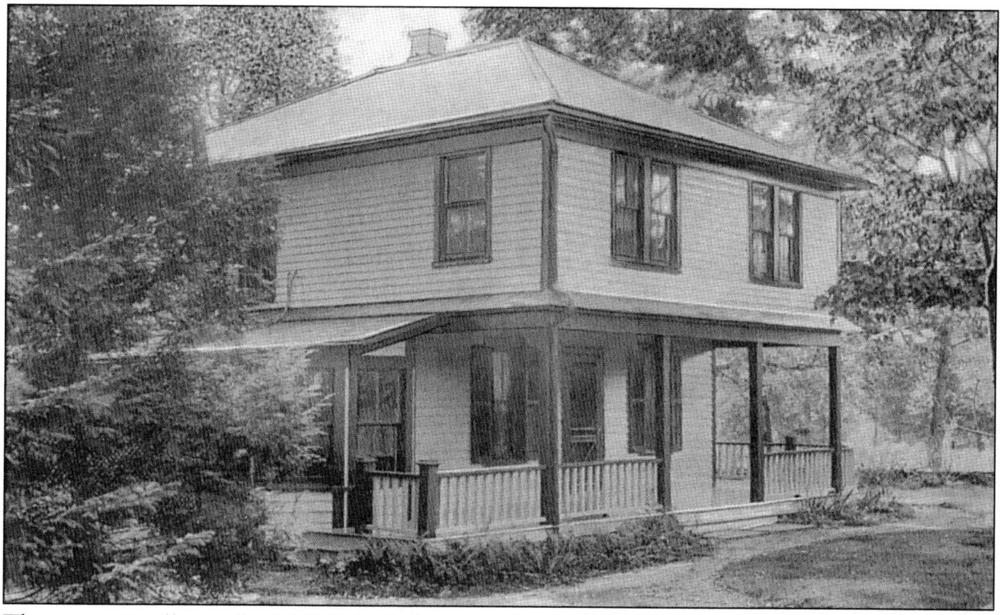

The most intellectually oriented of the private Catskill residential parks was Merriewold Park, near Monticello. The park was founded by social theorist Henry George (1839–1897), the exponent of the single-tax theory popular in late-19th-century radical circles. Most of Merriewold is very rustic, and its houses are simpler than those at the other parks. George's daughter married William C. DeMille (1878–1955), a film director with a brilliant career, although not as well remembered as his younger brother, Cecil B. DeMille, who visited at the George-DeMille house (above). William's daughter, the great choreographer Agnes DeMille, best remembered for the dances she created for "*Oklahoma!*," summered at Merriewold until her death in 1993. The Merriewold Club House is pictured below.

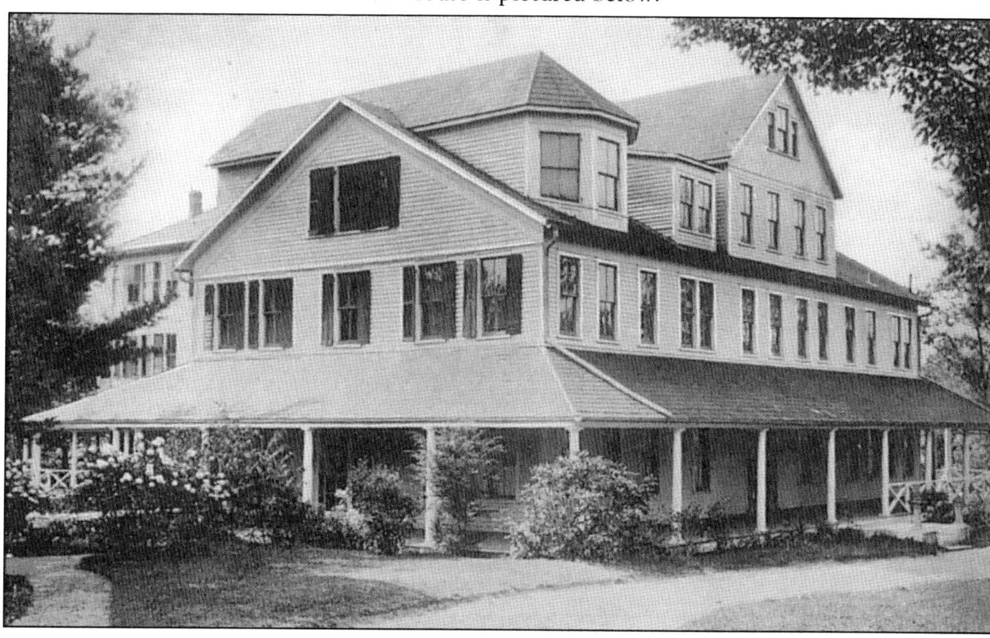

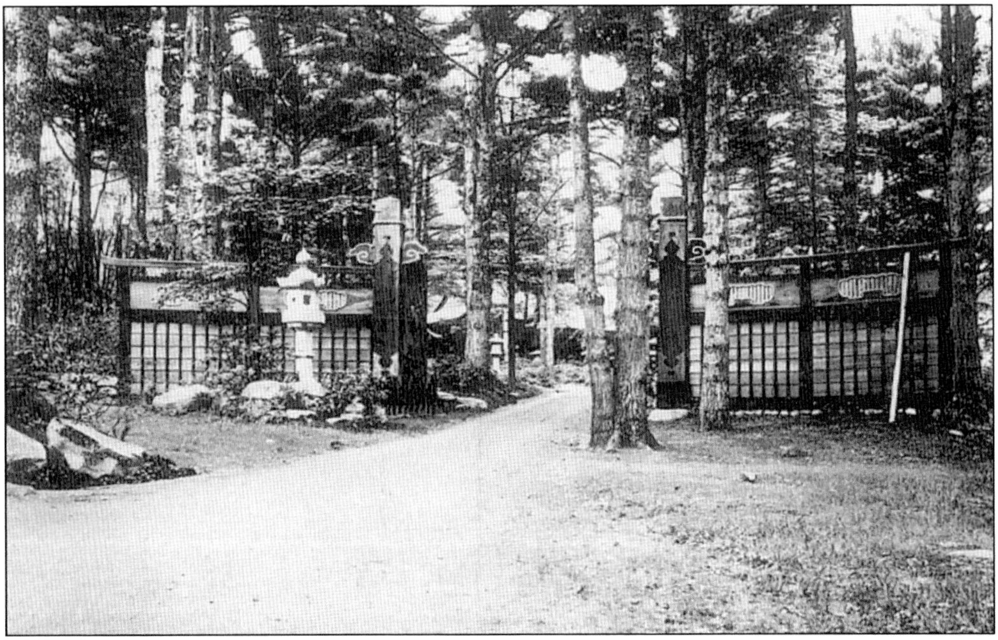

Far more exotic than the rest of Merriewold was the estate Sho-Fu-Den, developed by Dr. Jokichi Takamine (1854–1922), a Japanese-American inventor and businessman, and his American-born wife, Caroline Hitch. The main house was completely fabricated in Japan and brought to America for an international exposition. Afterward, the Takamines purchased the structure and rebuilt it at Merriewold for use as their summer home. The Takamines are generally credited with having partially financed the first planting of Japanese cherry trees at the Tidal Basin in Washington, D.C. Sho-Fu-Den is now owned by the Japanese Heritage Foundation.

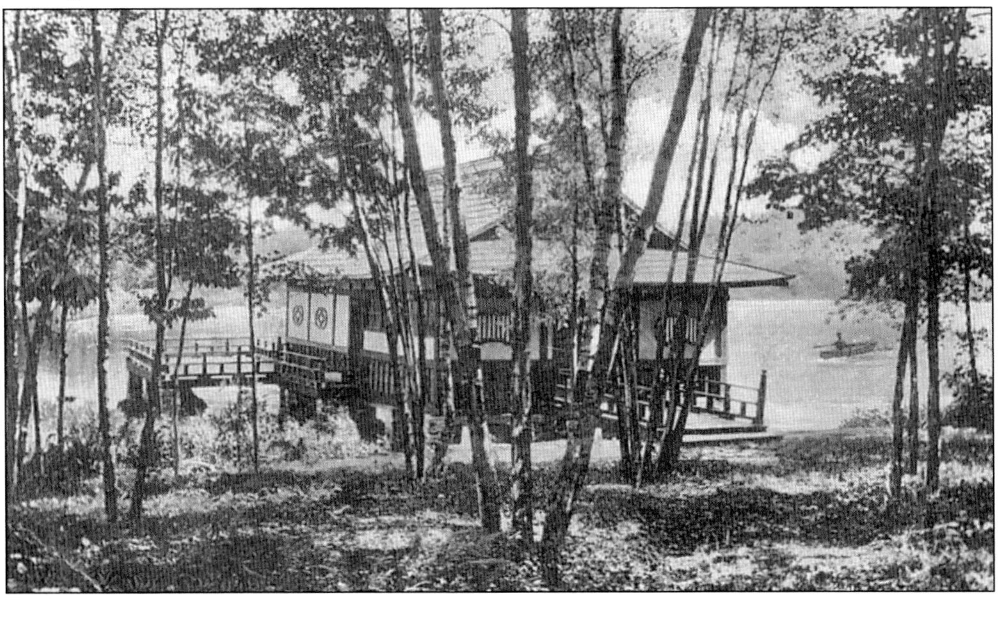

Four

The Spirit of 1893: Every Town Has Something Special

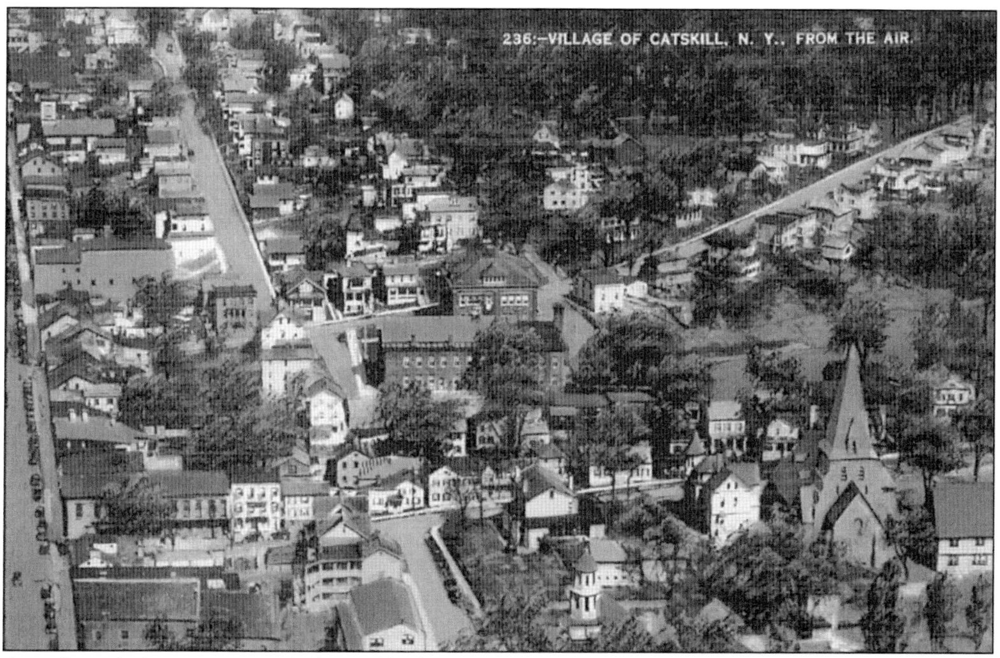

Aerial cards became very fashionable beginning in the 1920s. This view of the "Village of Catskill" shows that the town had not changed much from the post–Civil War period, its heyday when it prospered as the gateway to many of the great Catskills resorts.

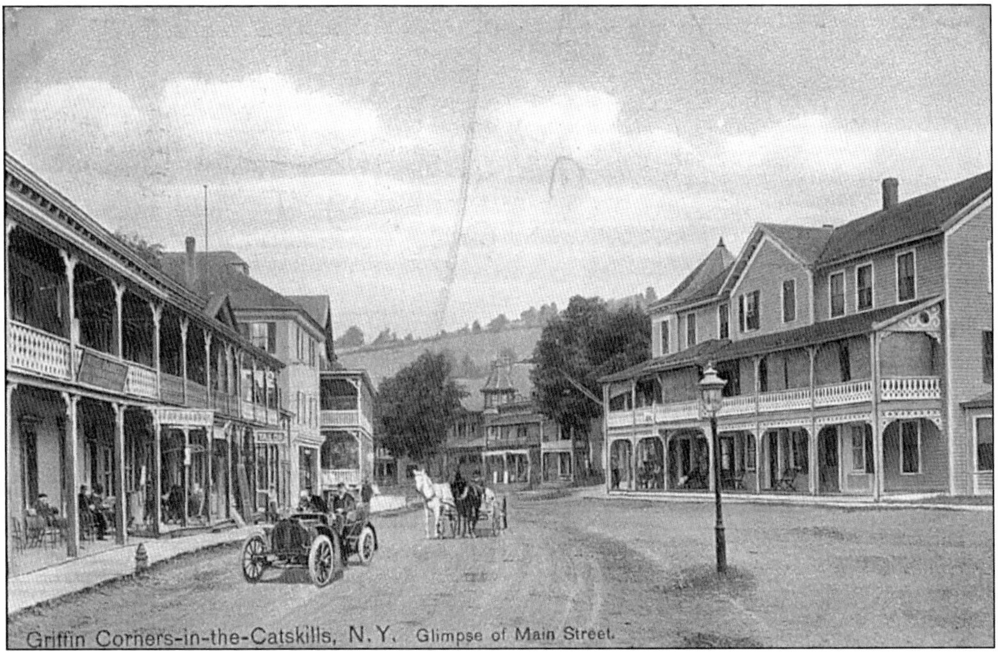

The first Jewish resort area within the Catskills was established in 1883, when the Fleischmann family, Jews of Hungarian origin, bought 60 acres of land near the town of Griffins Corner. The town soon changed its name to Fleishmanns. These cards, mailed several years after the transition, show a reluctance of many to acknowledge the change and are, perhaps, emblematic of the anti-Semitism that has been an unfortunate constant in the Catskills.

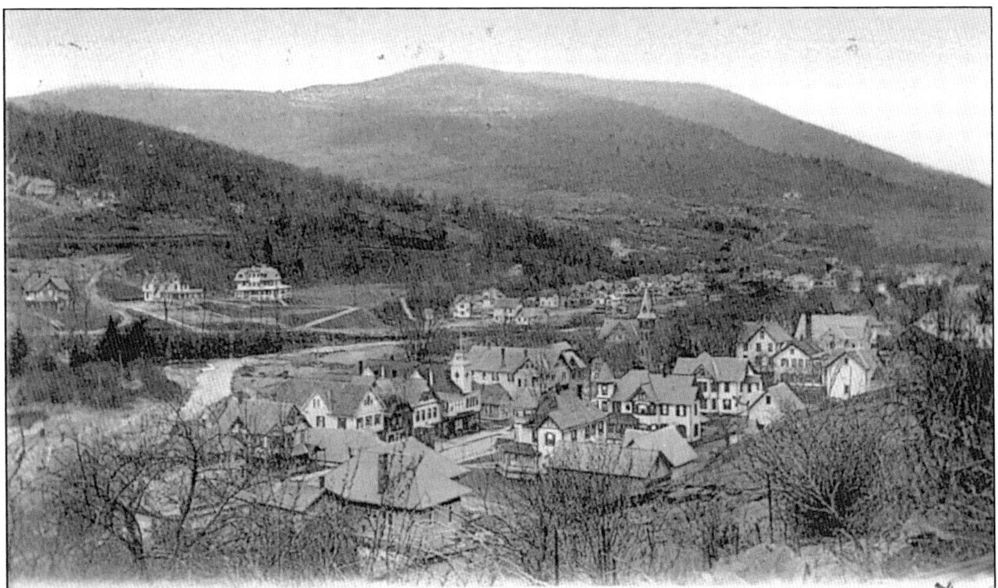

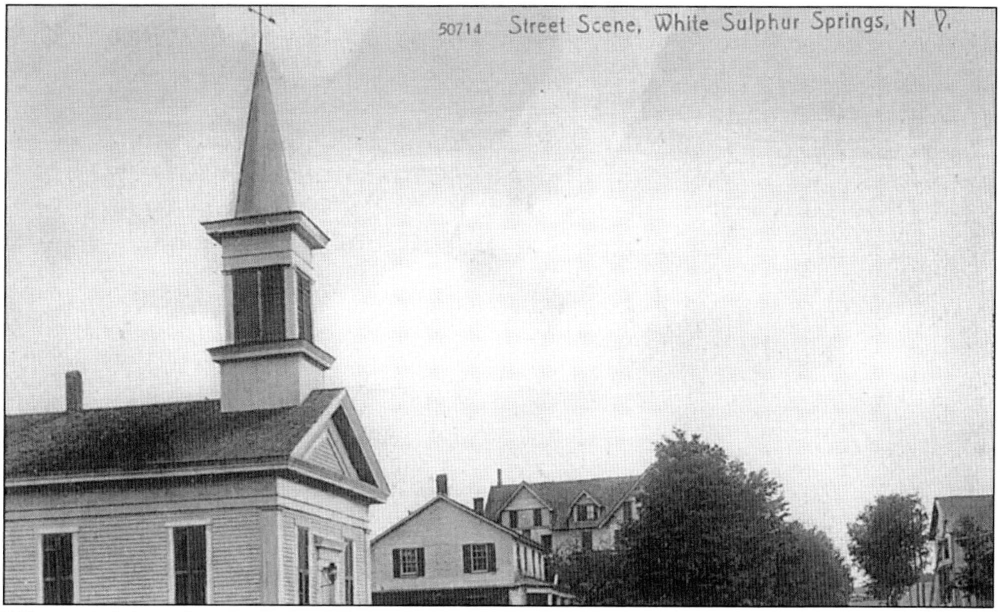

White Sulphur Springs in Sullivan County was very proud of its wholesome Christian appearance. Note the prominence given to the fine Greek Revival church. Named to emulate the famed West Virginia resort, New York's version had a number of boardinghouses and several hotels, one of which is visible in the background. Despite its well-known odorous water, the resort never amounted to very much.

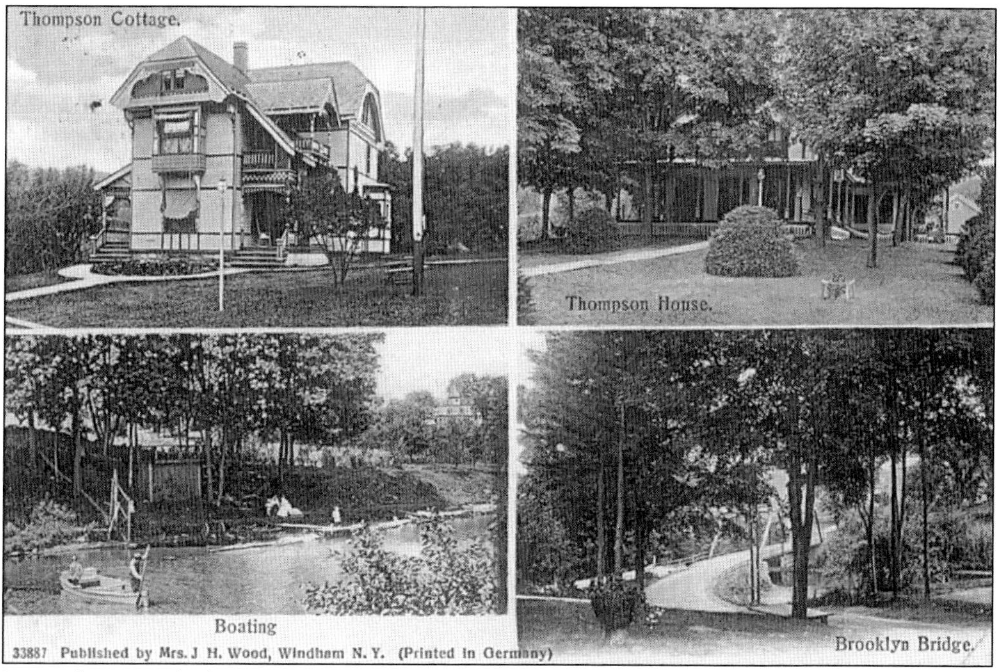

Privately printed, this 1908 card informs "This is where we are now. Having a dandy time. Beautiful place." The image is certainly one of refinement. Windham was very proud of having its very own Brooklyn Bridge built at the same time as its more famous namesake and leading towards the nearby community of Brooklyn.

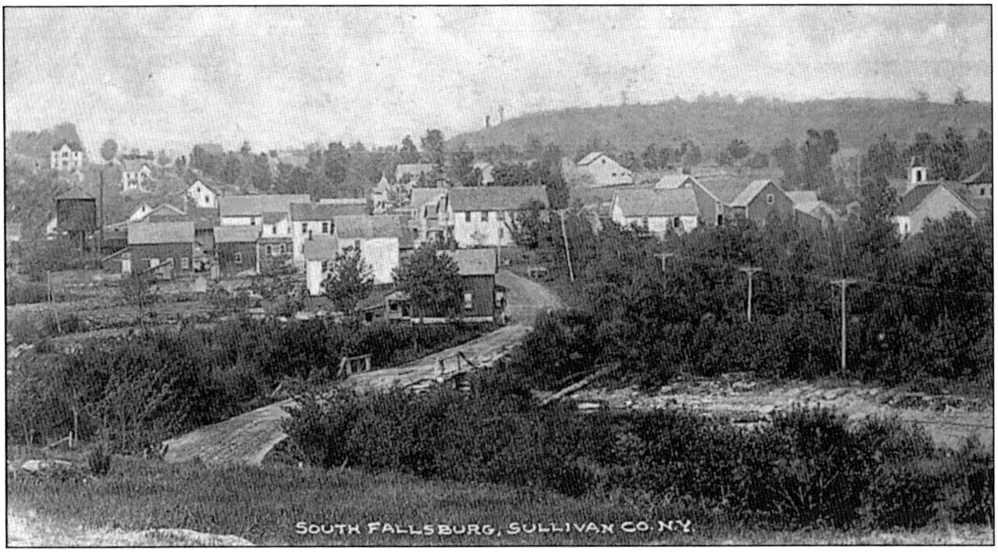

What a difference 30 years or so can make. The c. 1905 postcard of South Fallsburg is a very unsentimental and realistic view of the rural farm town, with its unpaved road. Note the barns in the backyards and the prominence of the church. The road shown above is the same Main Street seen in the 1930s card. This later view shows the street paved, sidewalks in place, and buildings that either date from the 1920s or have been extensively remodeled. At the far end of the street, on the left, is the Rivoli Theatre, which is still in operation. Why the change? South Fallsburg emerged as a boom town in the 1920s, when it become a center of the Borscht Belt.

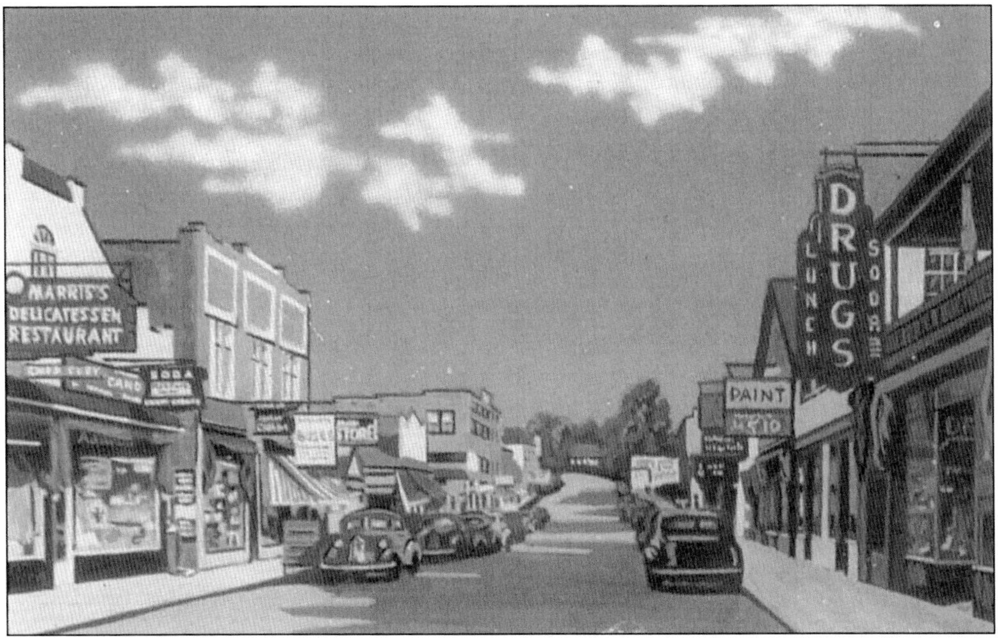

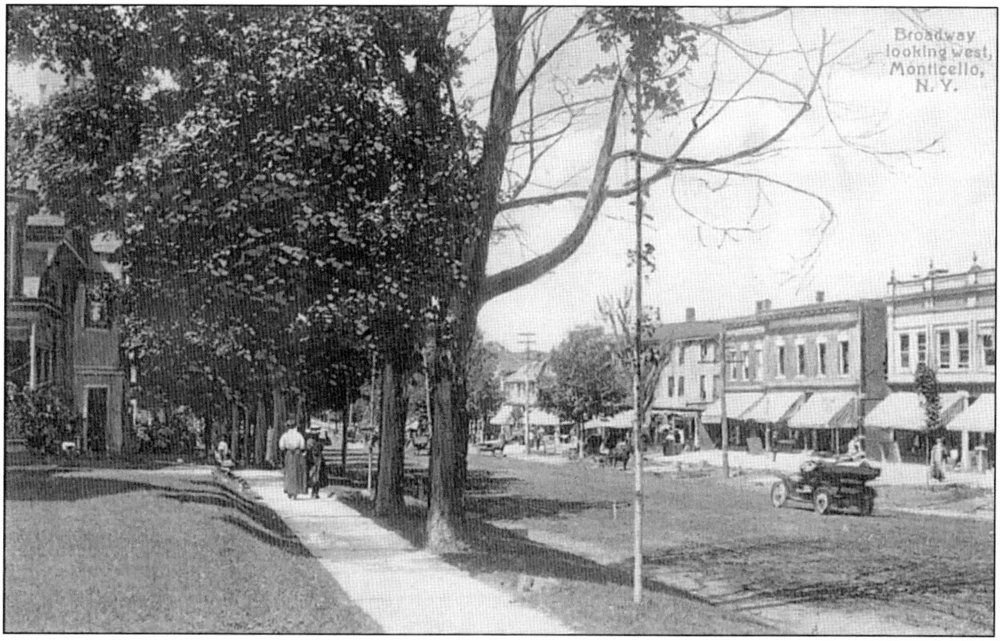

Monticello was founded when Thomas Jefferson was president and was named for his Virginia estate. In 1912, Monticello was the prosperous county seat of Sullivan County, with a substantial downtown that had recovered from a disastrous fire three years before. Some 40-plus years later, the town reached its economic zenith. As shown here, every store is filled, and most have new post–World War II facades. *Carpetbaggers* is showing at the Rialto Theatre. The legend on the back of the card proclaims, "View shows part of the Broadway business district. Monticello is the heart of the famous Sullivan County vacationland—a land of beauty, mountains, lakes, rivers, trout streams, the finest hunting in New York State. Lavish hotels, motels, bungalow colonies, cater to the hundreds of thousands of vacationers every year."

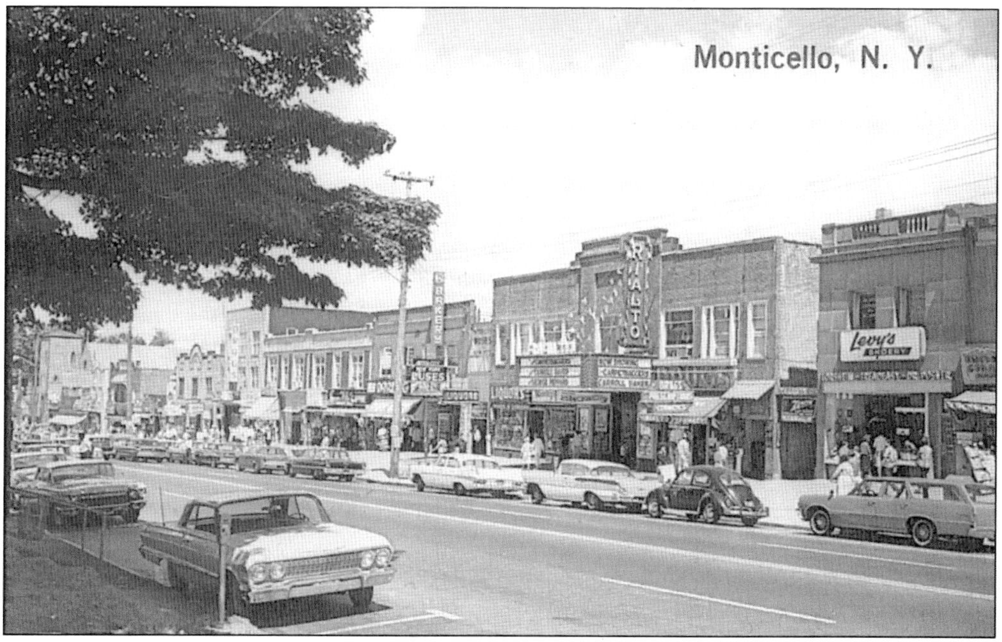

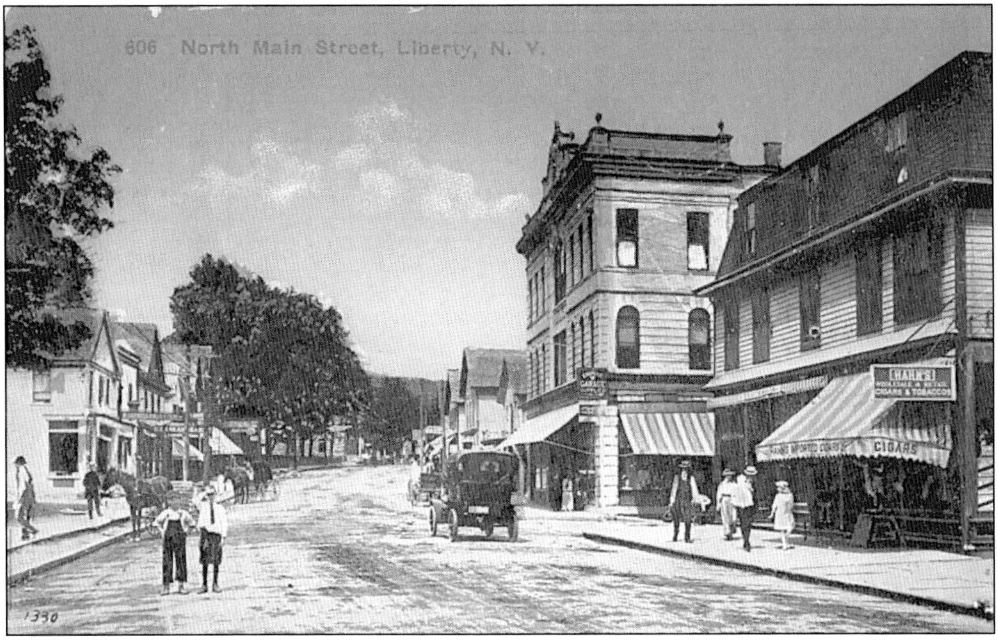

Liberty was Sullivan County's second-largest town. It was not only a center for farmers and a modest summer resort industry, but also the location of several tuberculosis sanatoriums. The view of North Main Street was mailed in 1915 and shows several substantial buildings. The South Main Street view is a few years later. Note that the street has been paved and that gasoline was sold right at the curbside. Liberty was also very proud of Harry Swanson, its first policeman. Despite its name, Liberty tried very hard to remain Christian only. Through the 1920s, many shop windows displayed the sign "No Hebrews or Consumptives Allowed."

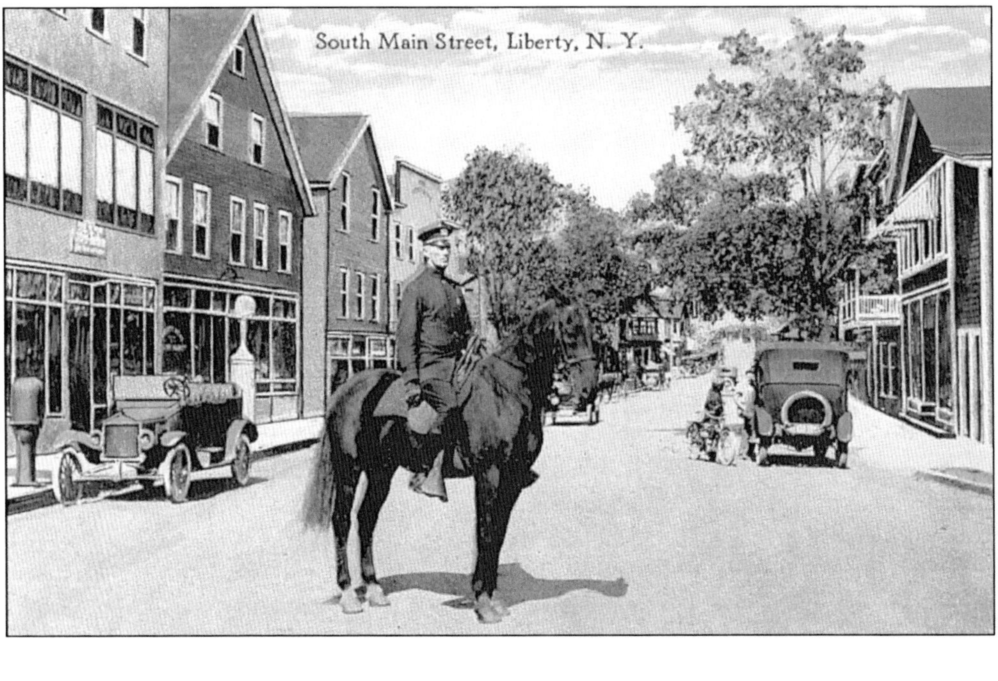

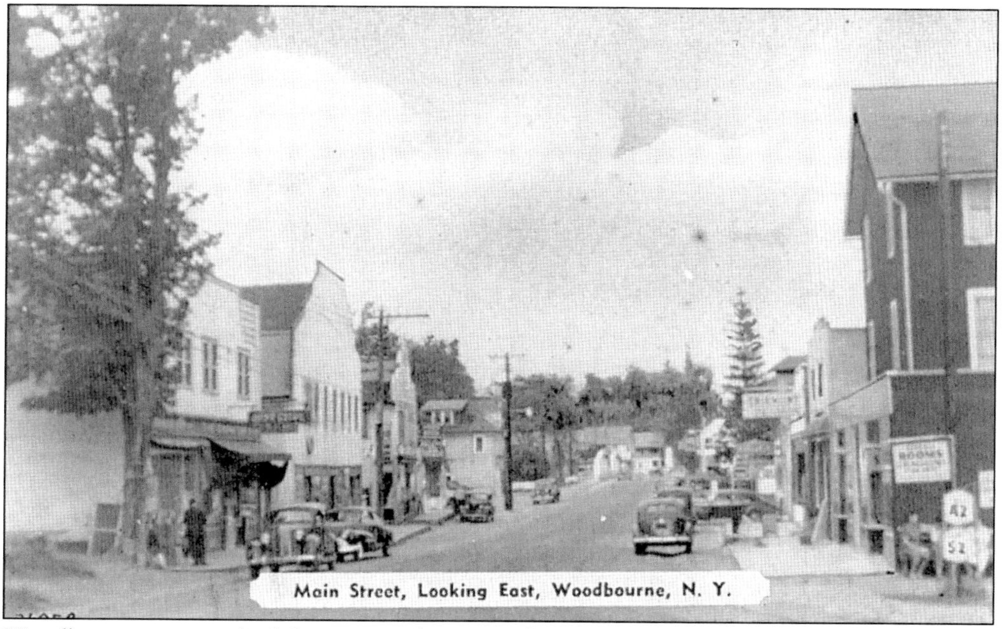

Woodbourne is typical of the many vibrant small towns that had year-round businesses and also catered to vacationers. A disastrous fire in 1964 destroyed many of the buildings shown in this *c.* 1950 view. On the left are Kanowitz's Dairy, Bernstein's Five-and-Ten, Smiley's Bar, Lebed's Drug Store, and Herben's Grocery. The building with the shed-roof dormer housed Dominion's Barber Shop, which survived the fire only to be destroyed by a runaway garbage truck in 1998.

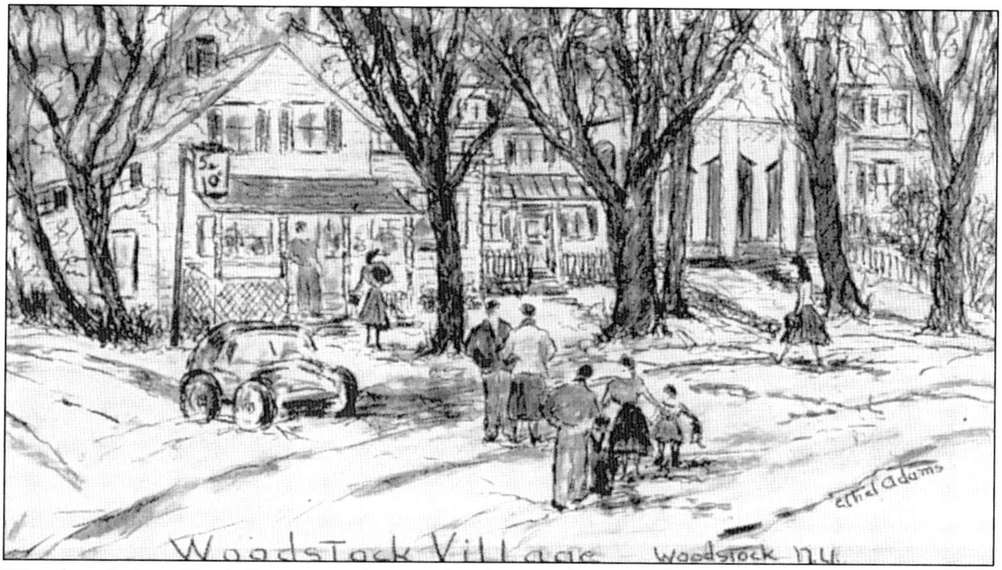

Woodstock is a Catskill center of art and culture. The Woodstock Festival of 1969 was not allowed here by the town authorities and was actually held near Bethel in Sullivan County. Woodstock has, for many years, prided itself on being different. This artist-drawn card mailed in 1951 bears a message that reports, "This is the 5 & 10, but it does not have a big red front like the ones at home. All the stores are like this—sort of little white cottage houses, so that the village is very pretty and doesn't look so much like a town."

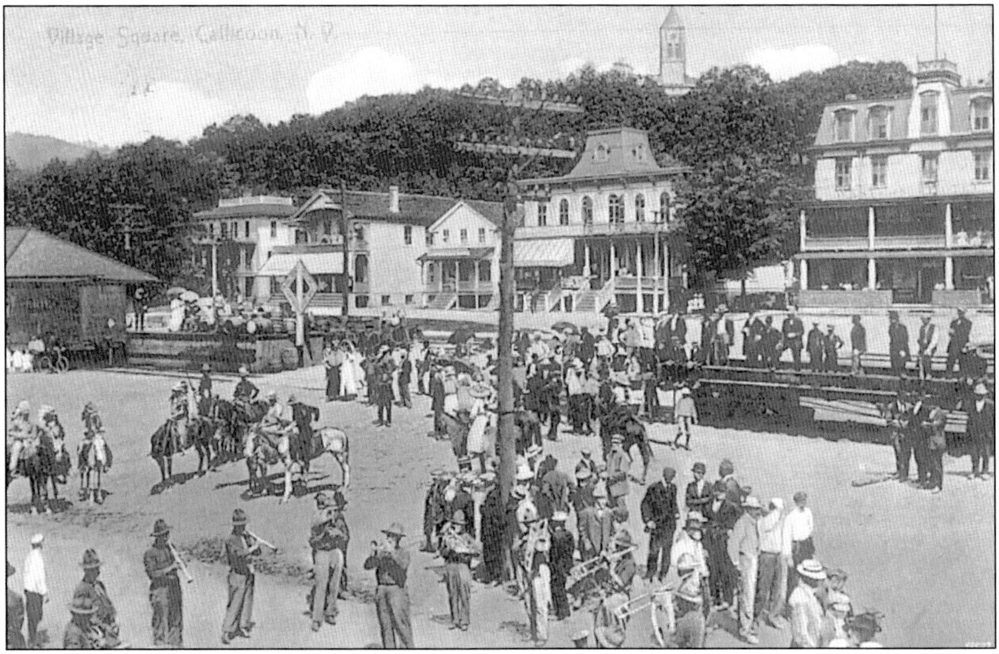

St. Joseph's Seraphic Seminary looms over the railroad station at the center of Callicoon in western Sullivan County. In this card mailed in 1914, perhaps as a teaser for a traveling wild west show, a brass band plays while cowboys and Native Americans in warbonnets sit astride horses.

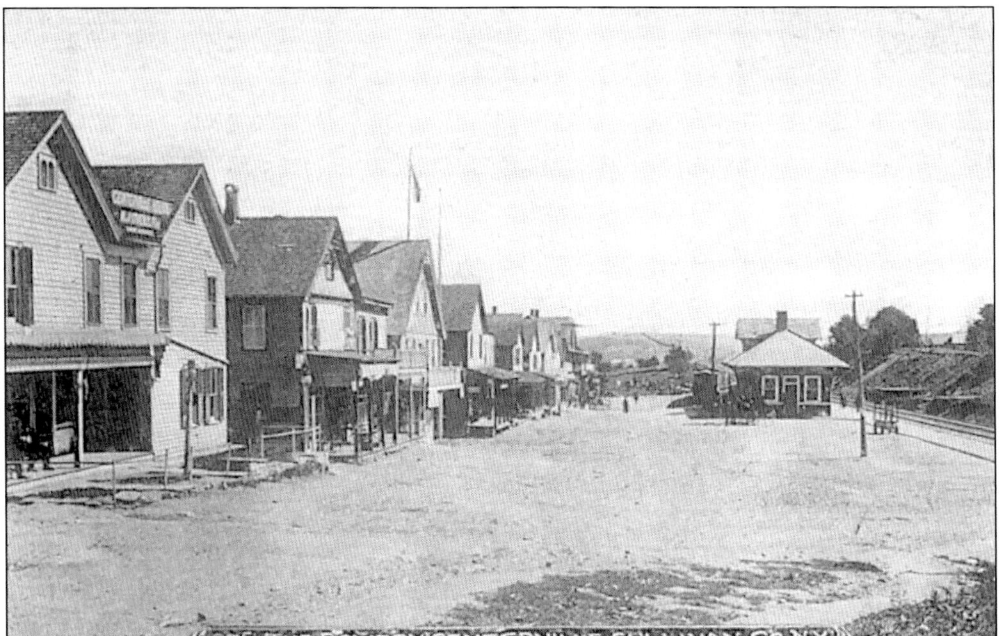

Centerville of 1906 soon became the more sylvan-sounding Woodridge, as tourism increased in importance. The Bowery, probably named for the wide, somewhat notorious New York City street, became The Railroad Plaza. The first Jewish resort in Sullivan County, Jana Gerson's farm-boardinghouse was a few miles from here.

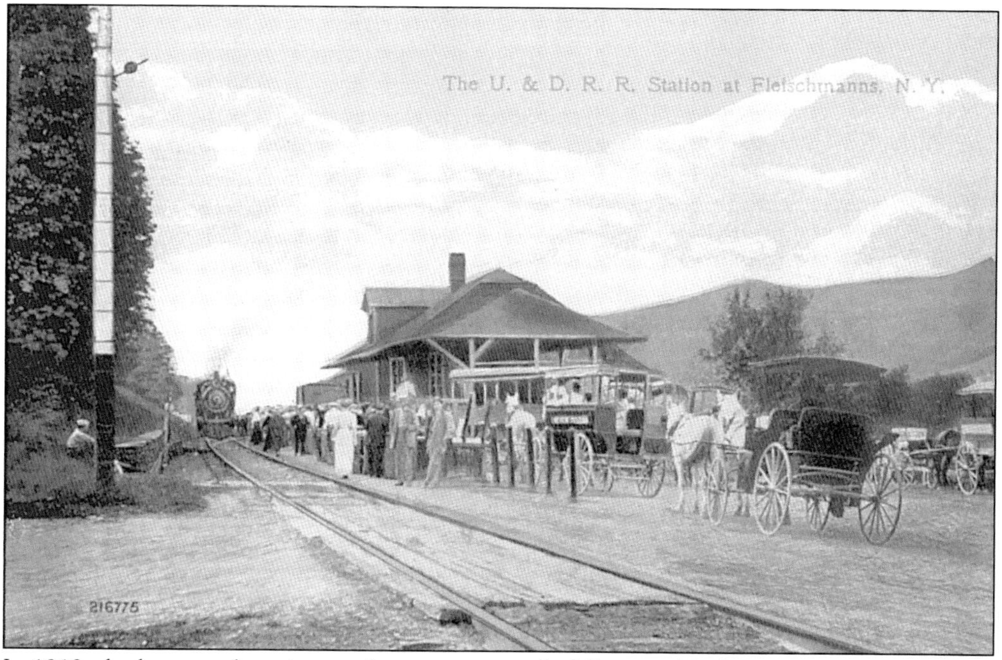

In 1912, the horse and carriage took passengers to the Ulster and Delaware Railroad Station in Fleishmanns. The Friday afternoon train that brought fathers and husbands to the mountains was called the "Bull Train." A brass band often played when the men arrived. In the 1920s, the Ontario and Western Railroad Station at Liberty was crowded with automobiles in a card photographed by Otto Hillig, perhaps the most significant photographer and card publisher in the Catskills.

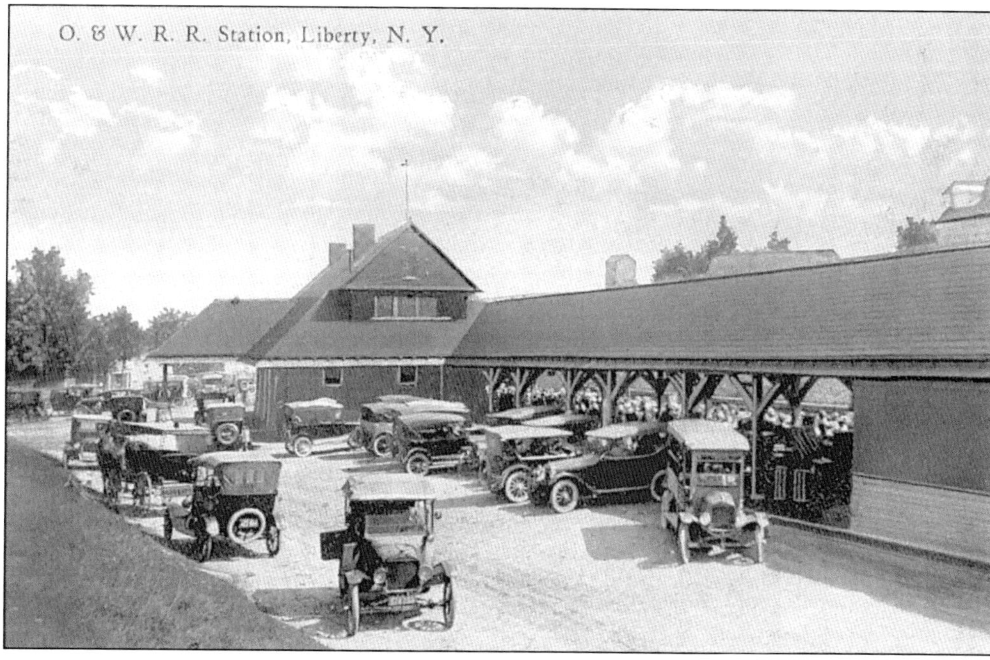

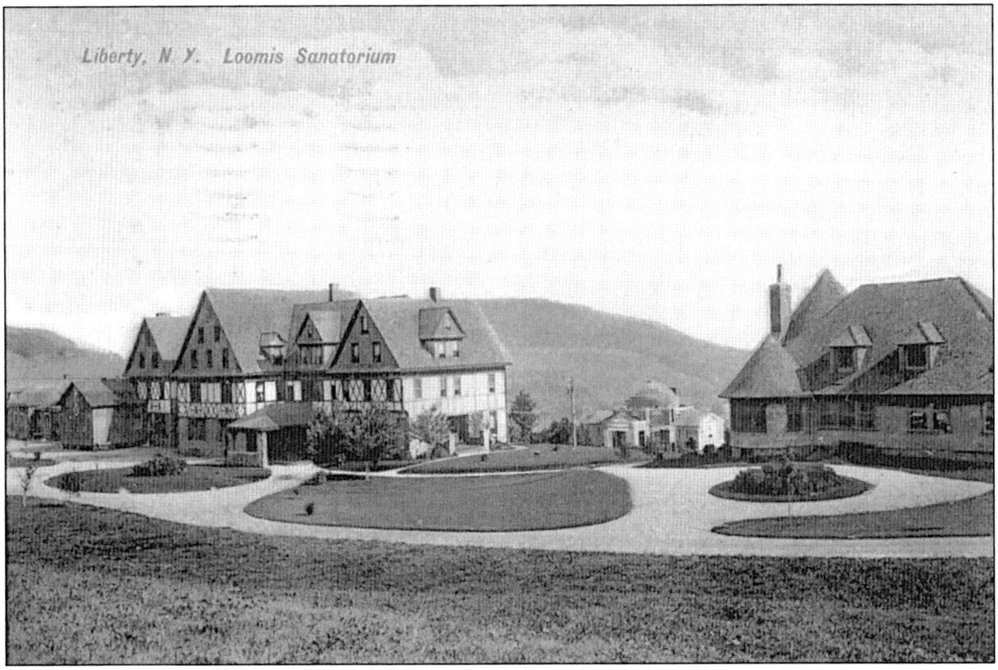

Community hospitals were a source of self-esteem in many communities. More distinctive and perhaps more bizarre, but typical of the age of civic pride, are these images of tuberculosis hospitals in Liberty. Set against a Hudson River–derived landscape similar to a series of paintings by Jasper Francis Cropsey (1823–1900), Loomis Sanatorium presents a picturesque Queen Anne Revival image of gentility and elegance. Gentile and restricted, it was supported by many important New York philanthropists, including J.P. Morgan. The less elaborate Maimonides Hospital, named for British philanthropist Sir Mose Maimonides, served Jewish consumptives.

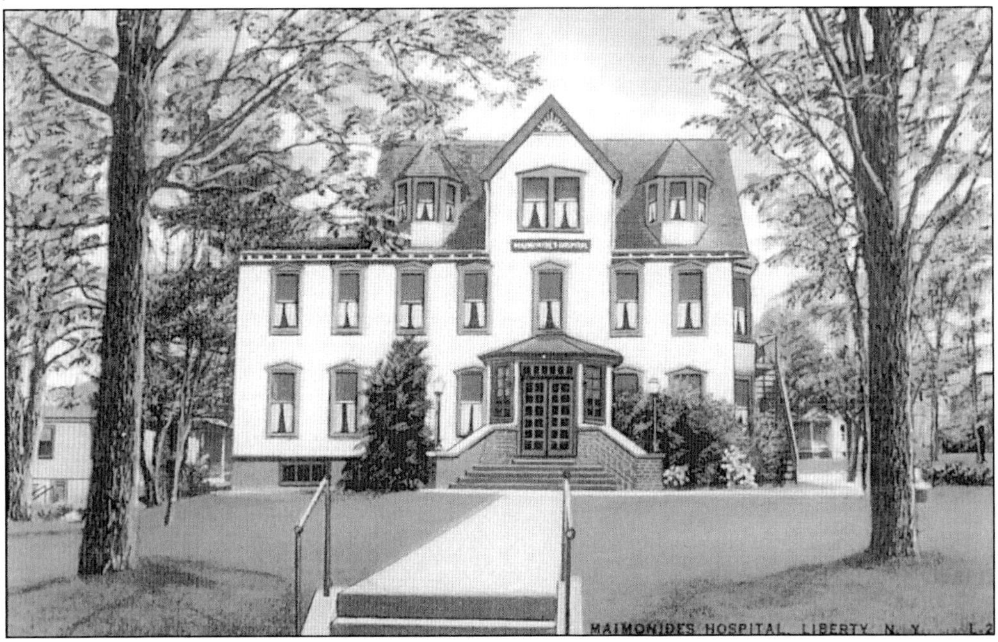

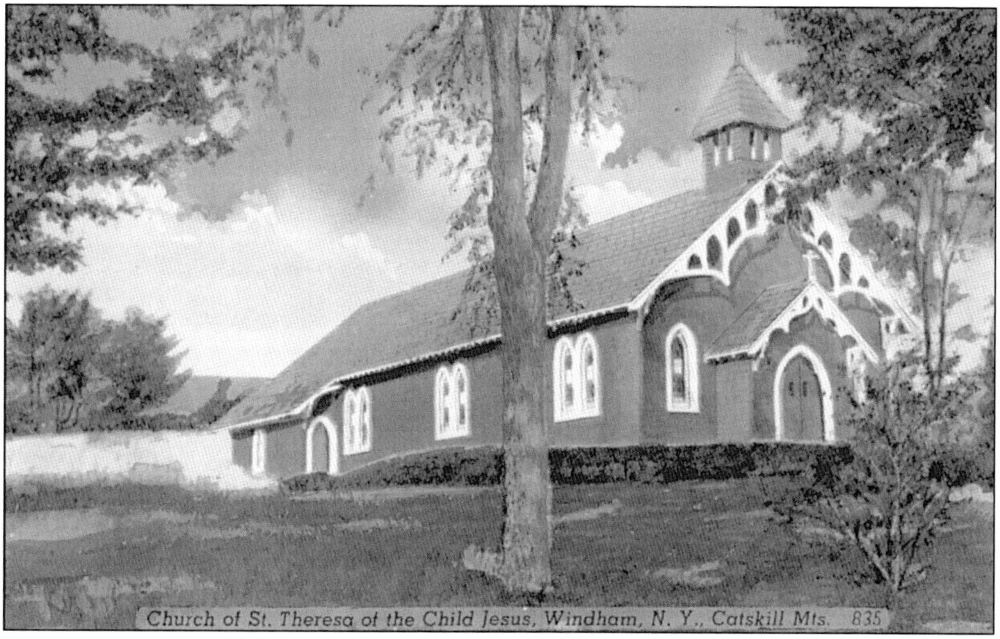

Churches abound in the Catskills, and dozens are depicted on postcards. Church steeples were often seen in paintings by the Hudson River School of artists as a sign of civilization. This card, depicting the picturesque Gothic Revival Church of St. Theresa of the Child Jesus in Windham, was published by George Greenberg and Son in nearby Catskill. Images of synagogues are relatively rare, even though many small towns had Jewish houses of worship. Monticello had several. The Spanish Mission-style facade of the Liberty Street Synagogue was similar to the architecture of many hotels and commercial buildings of the 1920s and 1930s. Reflecting change in the Catskills, this building today houses an African-American Baptist congregation.

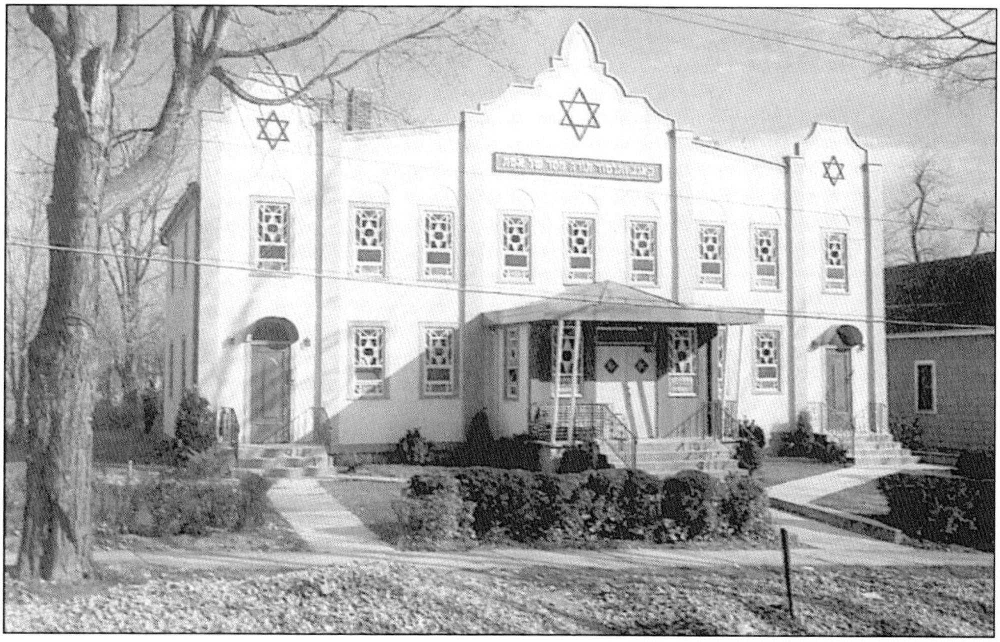

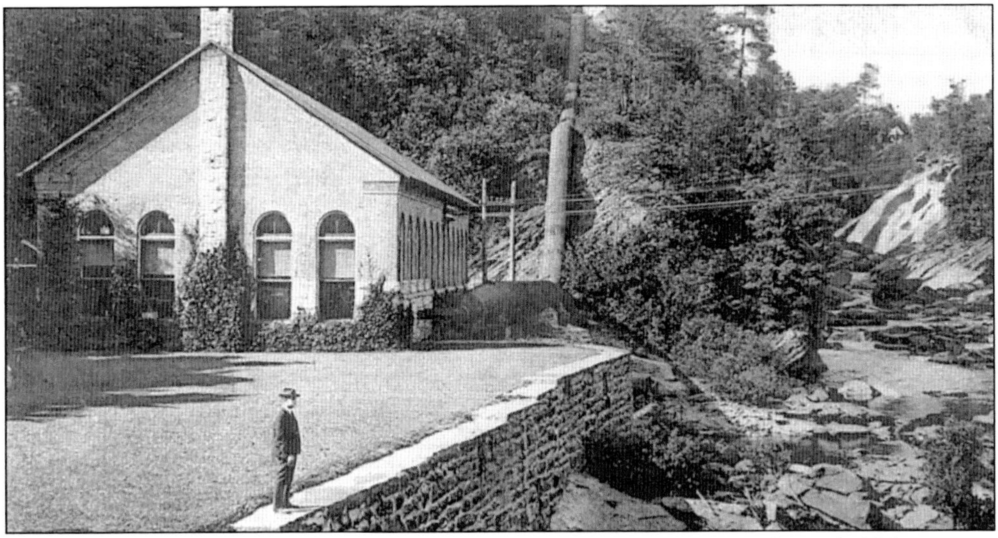

Ellenville, in southern Ulster County, was a very progressive community in the early 20th century. Nestled at the base of the Shawangunk Mountains, Ellenville had been a canal town and was an important railroad stop. There are many cards picturing Ellenville, and various of them feature industrial and commercial enterprises. While no longer in operation, the Honk Falls Power House near Ellenville still exists. Both this hydraulic powerhouse and the Sun Ray Water Works are emblematic of the commercial importance of the area's abundant waterpower.

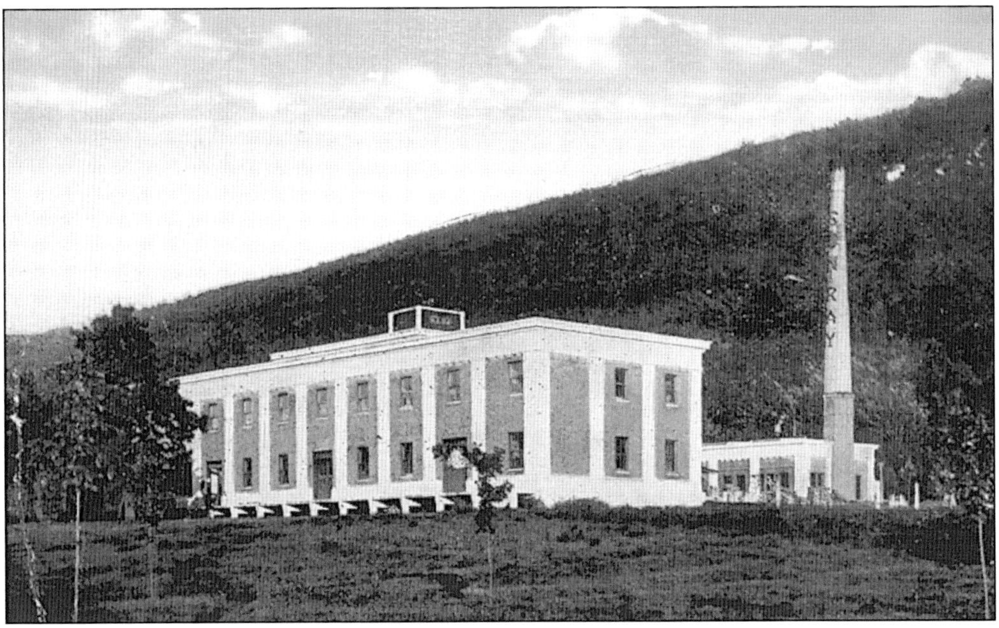

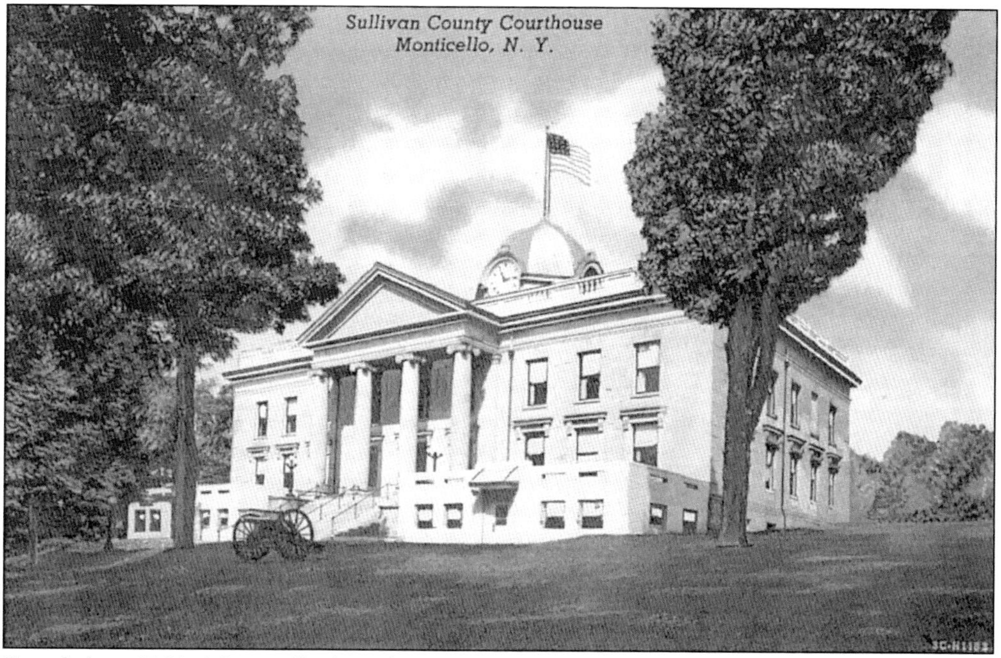

Founded in 1804, Monticello has always been Sullivan County's seat. The Classic Revival courthouse, in its parklike setting in the middle of town, has long been the subject of many cards. It provides an enduring landmark for Monticello's ever-changing Broadway.

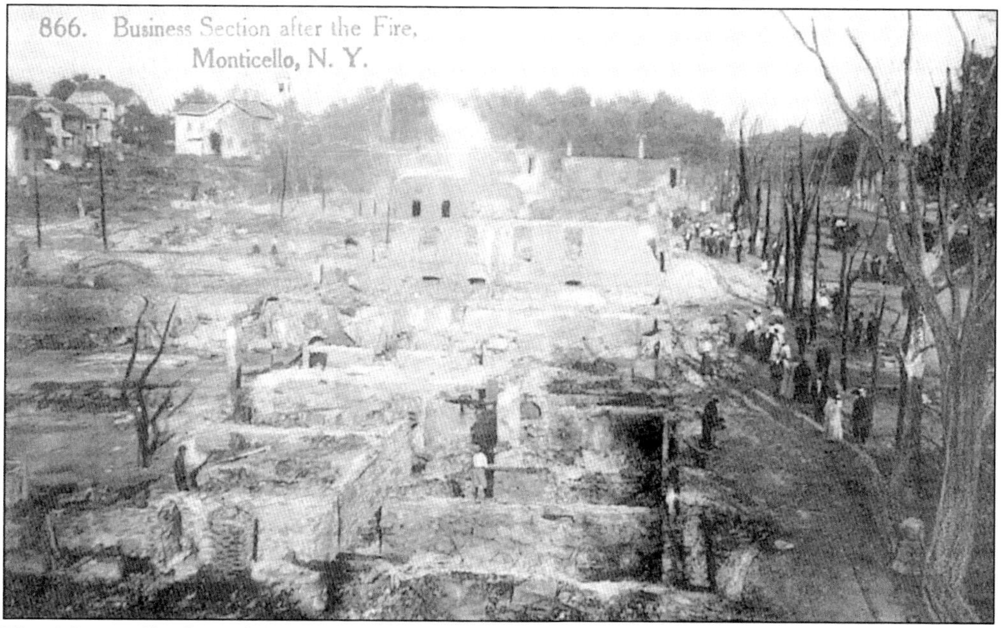

The Monticello fire of August 10, 1909, devastated the county seat and destroyed much of downtown Monticello. Cards of the disaster were not the image makers that many other Catskill postcards were; rather, they follow the conventions set forth in the very well-known earlier series produced after the San Francisco earthquake of 1906, which San Franciscans always euphemistically referred to as "The Fire." The Monticello fire was only one of a number of fires to devastate Catskill communities and resorts.

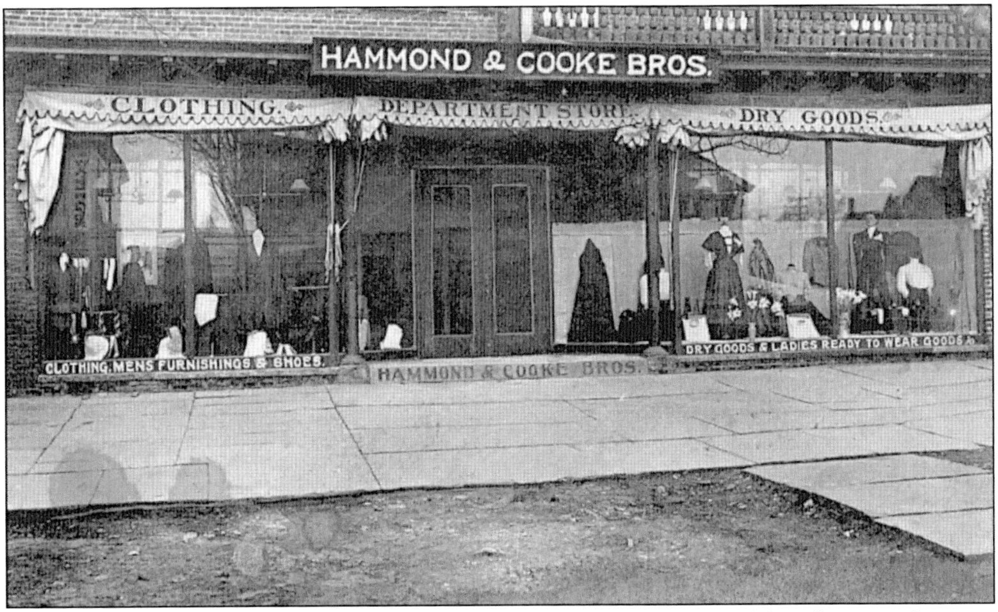

Before the age of the chain store, small towns and villages all had locally owned stores. Monticello, as the county seat, had many. The biggest and longest lasting (over 75 years) was the Hammond & Cooke Department Store on Broadway in Monticello, which on this 1909 card boasted of having 10,650 square feet of floor space.

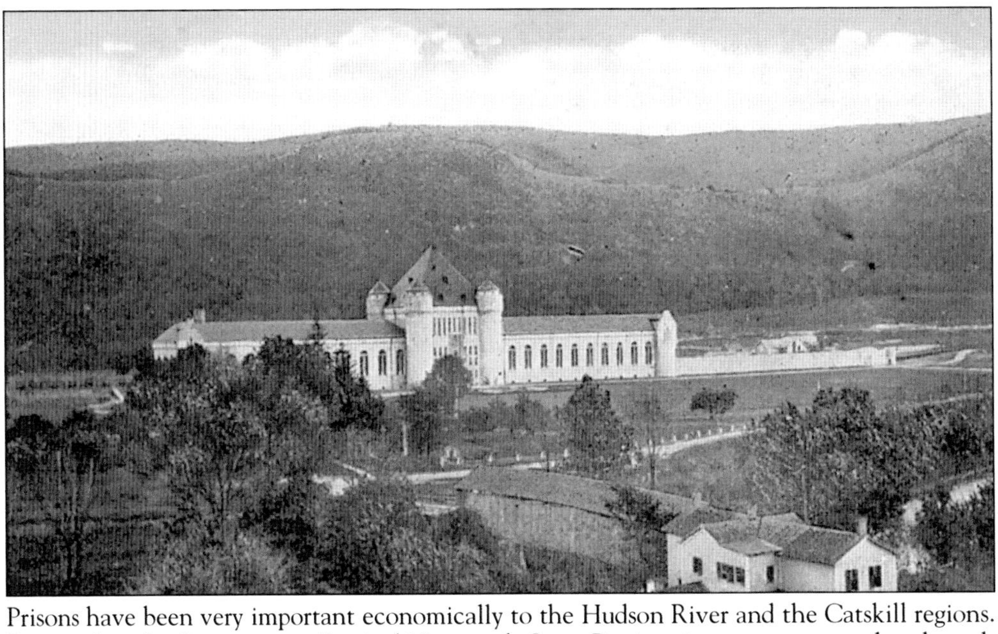

Prisons have been very important economically to the Hudson River and the Catskill regions. Even today, the Romanesque Revival Napanoch State Penitentiary, now renamed and much enlarged, is an economic anchor for southern Ulster County. Woodbourne, in nearby Sullivan County, has another important prison facility where, in recent years, David Berkowitz, the "Son of Sam," was incarcerated.

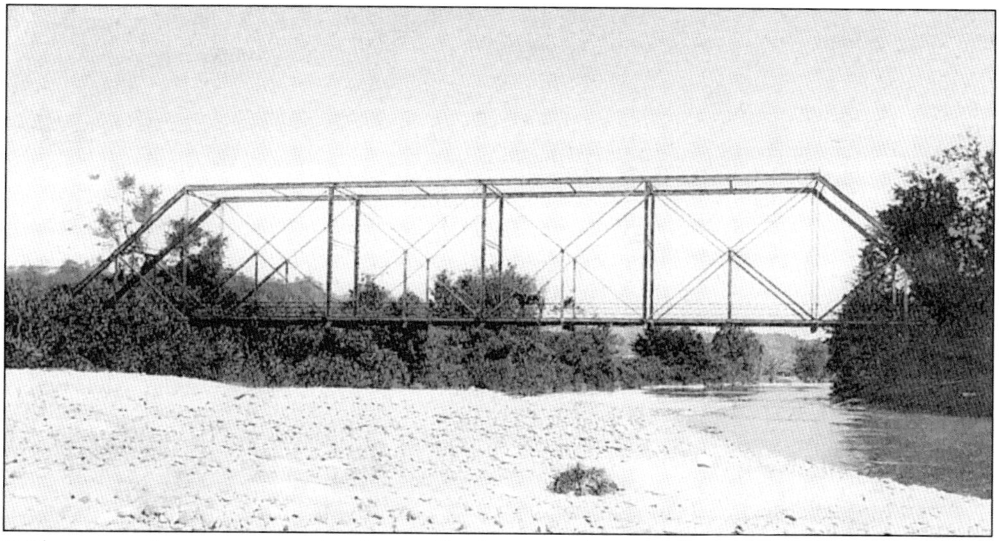

Bridges were often seen on cards. Covered bridges were depicted for their nostalgic value. These two bridges, however, send a different message. The Iron Bridge at Hasbrouck in Sullivan County was new in 1909, when this card was mailed. Crossing the Neversink River, it stood above a favorite riverside beach. It speaks to convenience and modernism. The Swinging Bridge in Palenville was built as a tourist attraction "by the People of Palenville." Apparently, it was truly a "swinging place." The sign on the bridge threatens a $25 fine for "misusing."

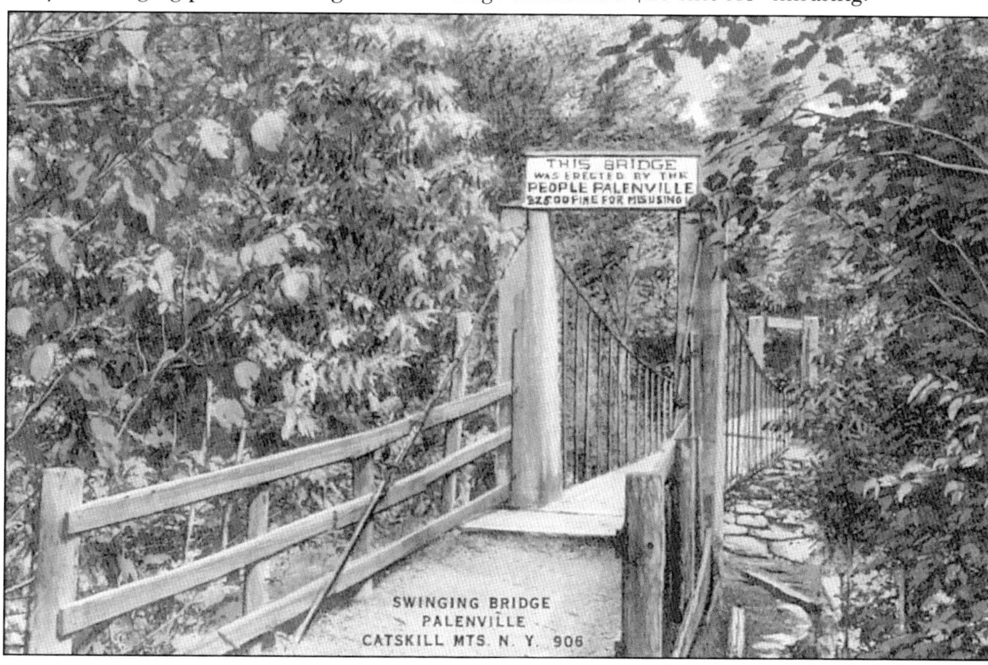

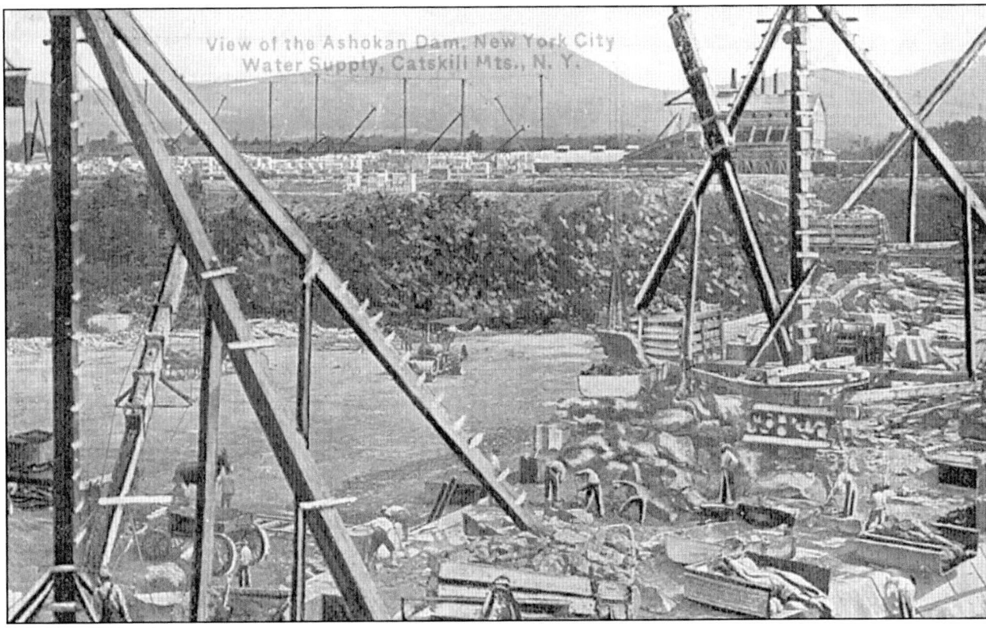

New York City's need for water has changed the face of the Catskills. The Ashokan Reservoir was begun in 1906, and water from the Esopus Creek started to fill it in 1915. In later years, the Rondout Creek, the Neversink River, and the east branch of the Delaware River were also dammed. "When the lakes that filled the valleys aged a little they reflected the surrounding mountains with a charm that made some travelers think of England's Lake District." But the lack of signs of longtime human activity along the lakesides give them all a very antiseptic aspect. Few realize that these reservoirs flooded out pioneer villages, picturesque falls, and, indeed, a whole way of life.

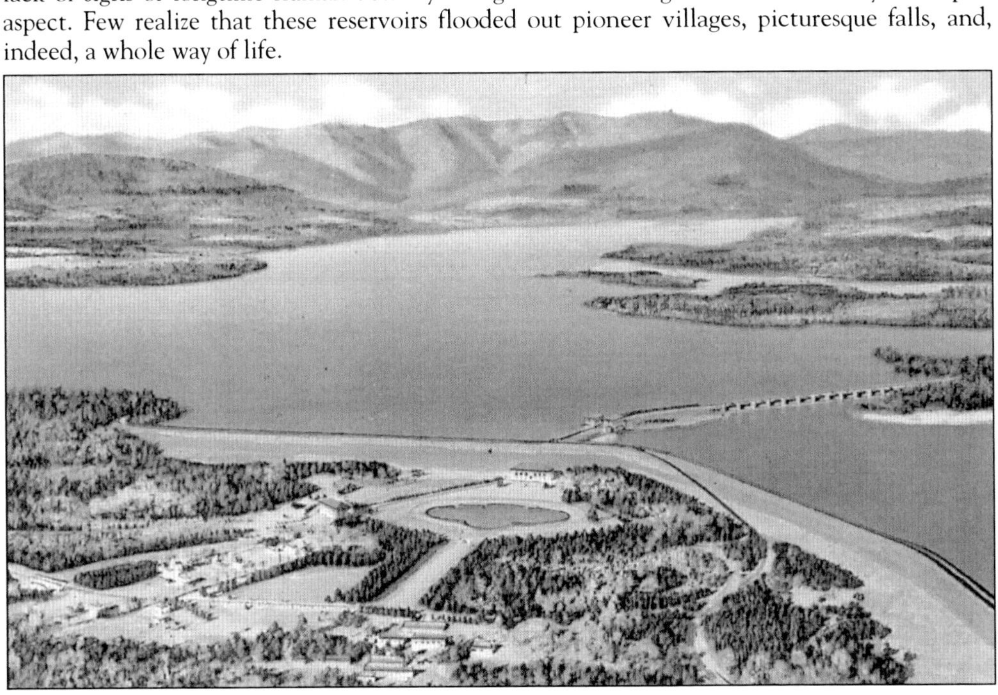

Five

The Vacation Revolution:

Pluralism and the Borscht Belt

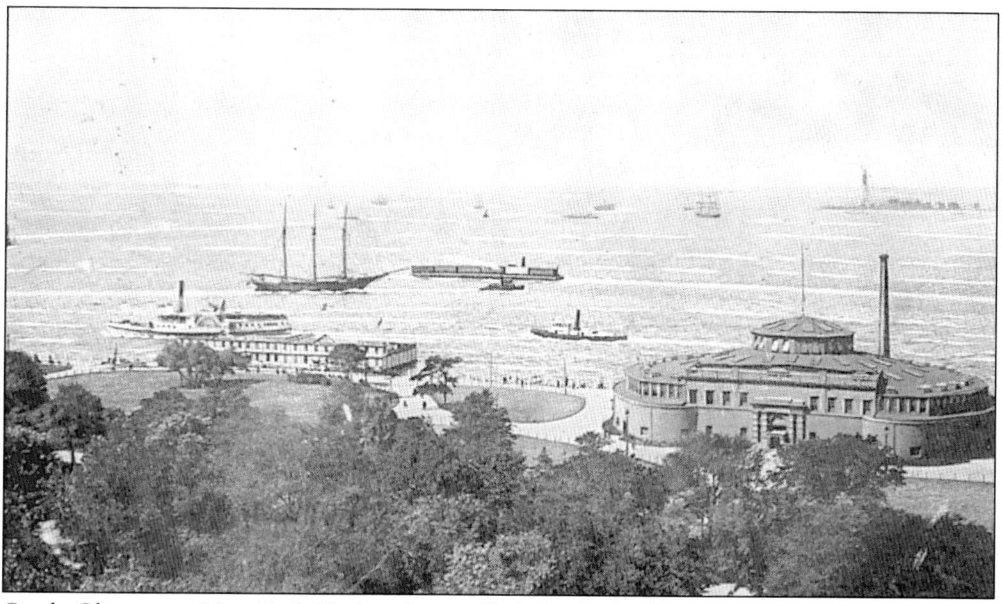

Castle Clinton on New York Harbor, later called Castle Garden, was the gateway for the new immigration before being supplemented by, and then being replaced by, Ellis Island. Later generations knew the distinctive round building as New York's aquarium, the first such facility in America. Note the Statue of Liberty in the background.

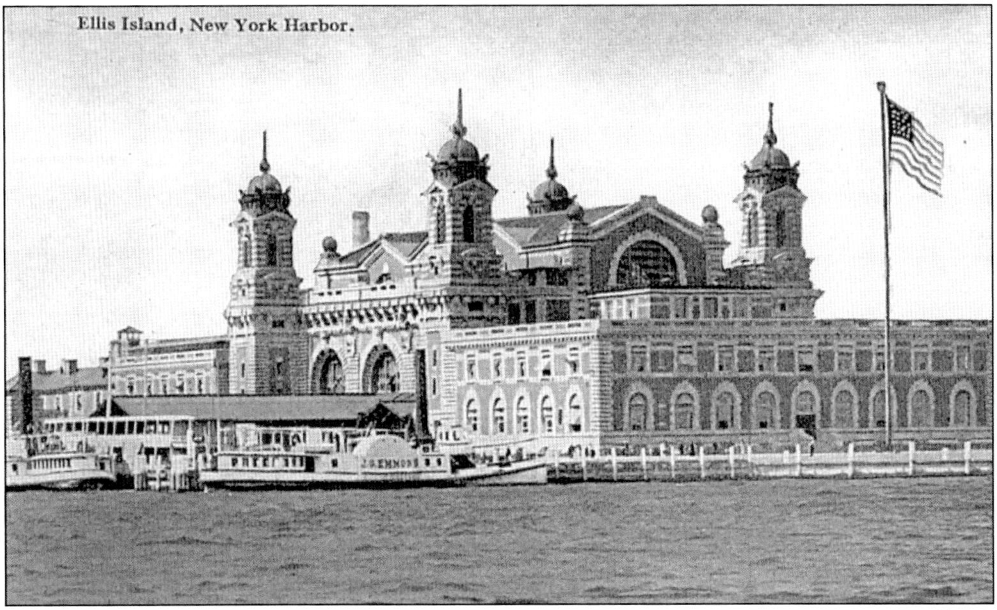

For millions, Ellis Island was the entrance to what Jewish immigrants called *der Goldeneh Medina*, "the golden land." Immigrants from southern and eastern Europe were accommodated but not really welcomed. The terse message on the back of the upper card says a great deal about an earlier time: "Ellis Island. Immigration Depot since 1892, where all immigrants are landed and examined before being admitted to this country. Undesirables are deported at the expense of the steamship company that brings them. Visitors are admitted to the balcony free. Ferry connections from the Battery."

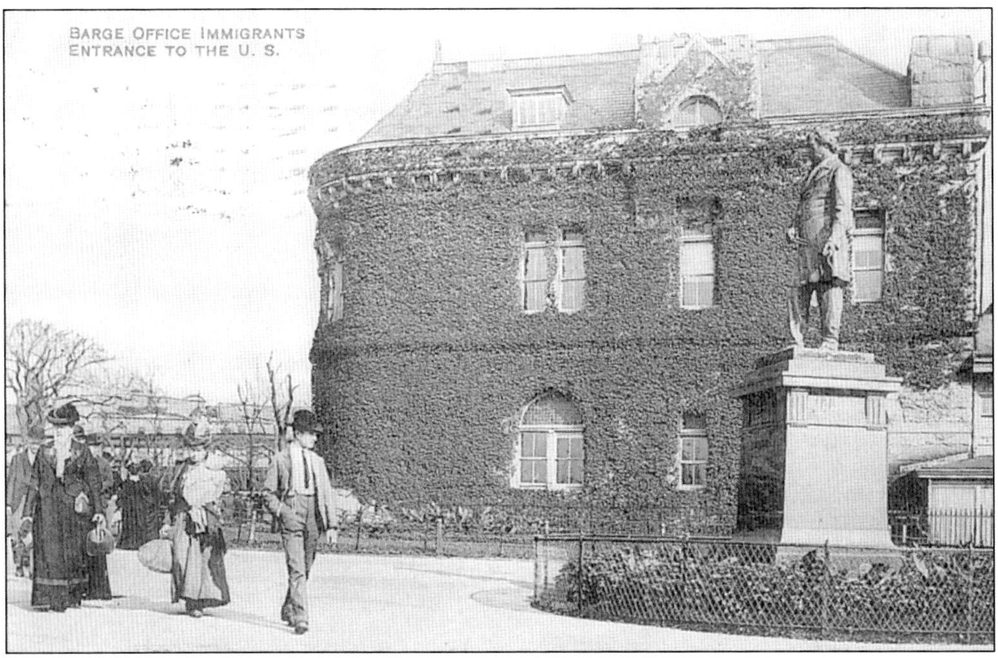

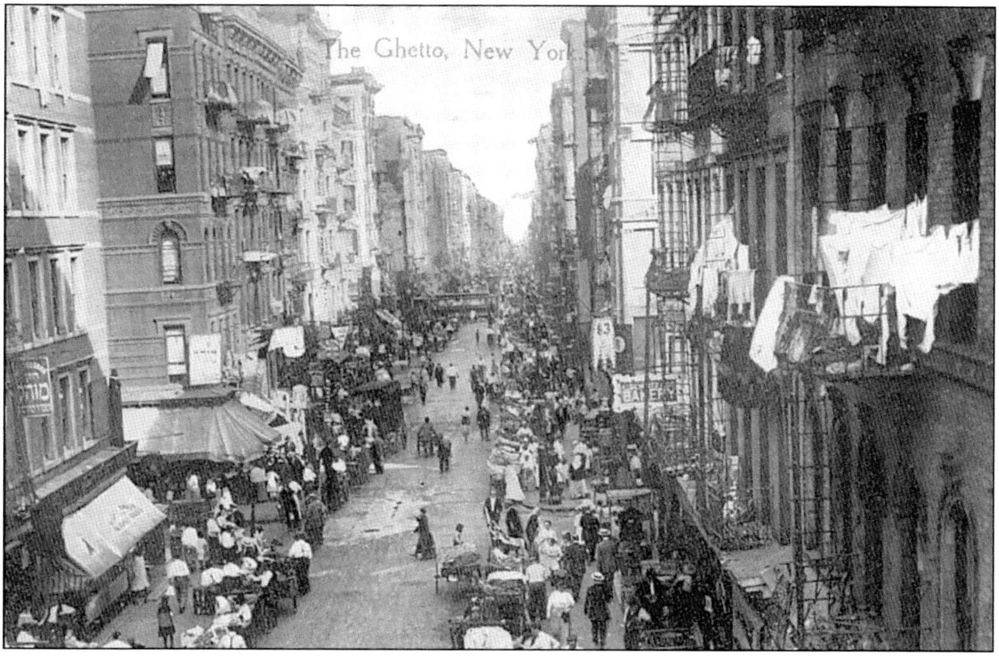

The world of the new immigrants fascinated and horrified old-line American stock. "The Ghetto" is one of several similar early cards the author owns that were mailed to Wasp recipients in Pennsylvania. The legend on the back reads, "The Ghetto. The East Side as it is commonly known stands from Chatham Square east of the Bowery. It is an agglomeration of over 1,000,000 people that fill the old apartment houses to their full capacity. The narrow streets are always crowded with pedestrians as well as street venders. Most anything is sold in the pushcarts." Schools offered promise for betterment, but like the living conditions, they were often dismal and very far removed from nature. The need to escape the summer heat and the concrete streets of New York led millions to the nearby Catskills.

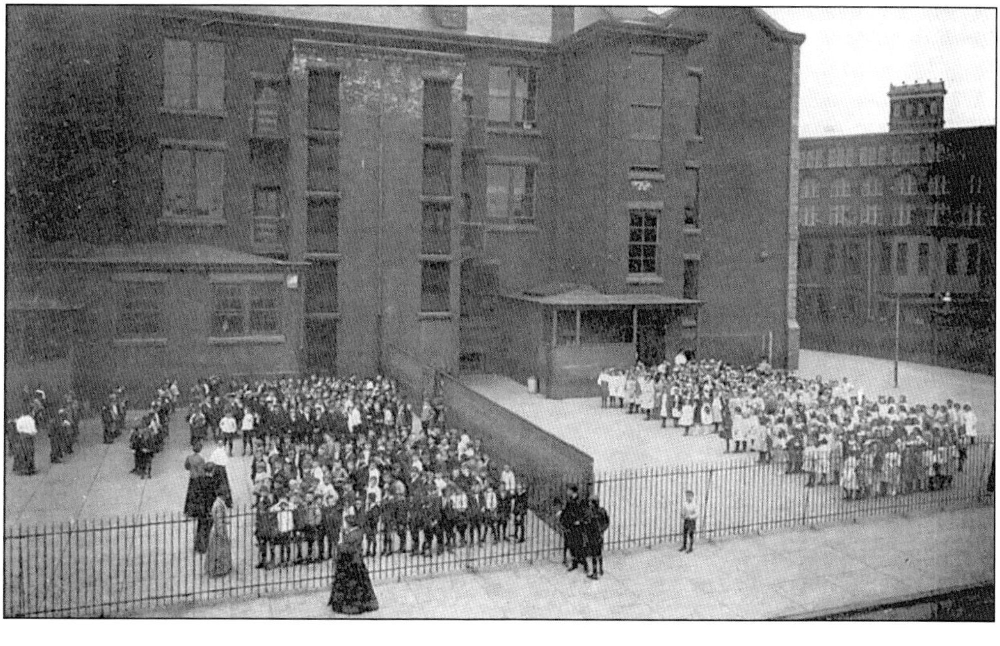

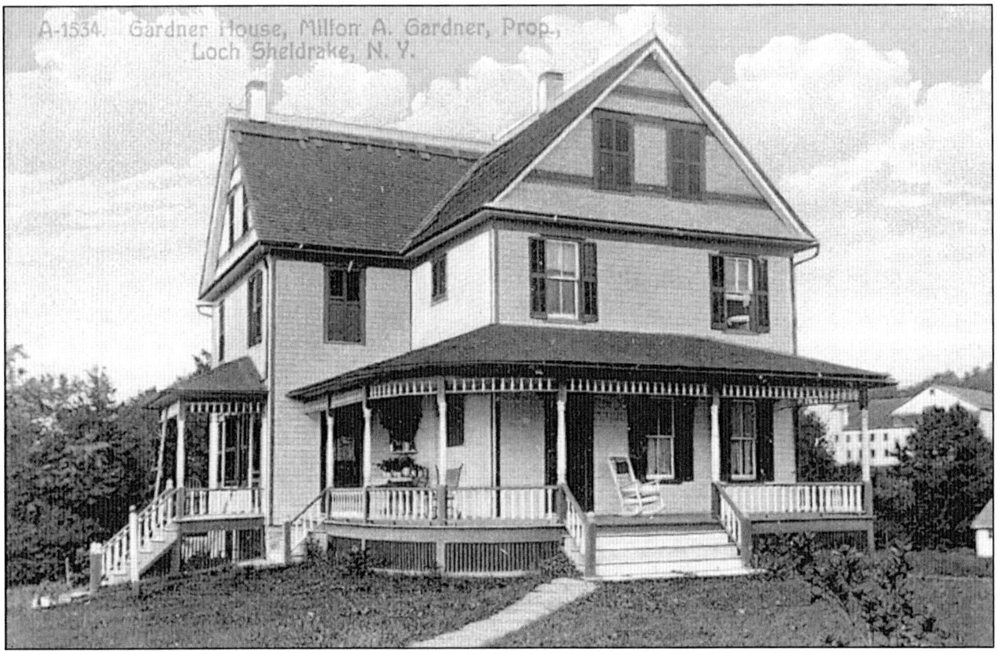

The Gardner House in Loch Sheldrake was typical of the many boardinghouses that sprang up in Sullivan and Ulster Counties beginning in the 19th century. Many originally served a native-born clientele, but most soon catered to the newer immigrant groups, especially the Irish and the Germans.

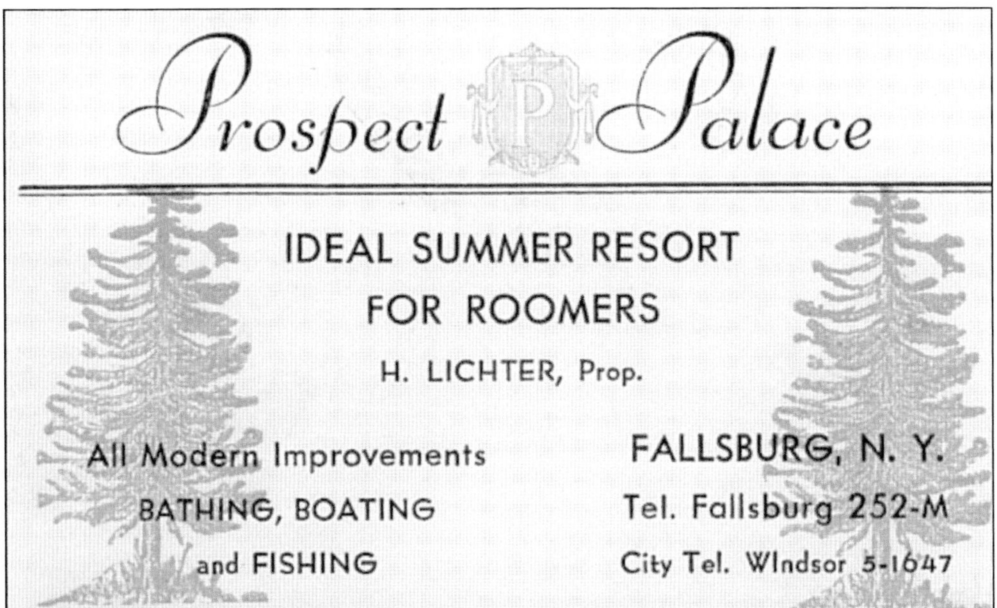

Rooming houses, or *kuchaleins*, were especially popular with poorer Jewish vacationers in the period from 1900 to 1940. At the *kuchaleins* ("cook for yourself"), customers rented a sleeping room and shared community kitchens and bathrooms. The author knows of no *kuchalein* postcard, but this business card is a good stand-in.

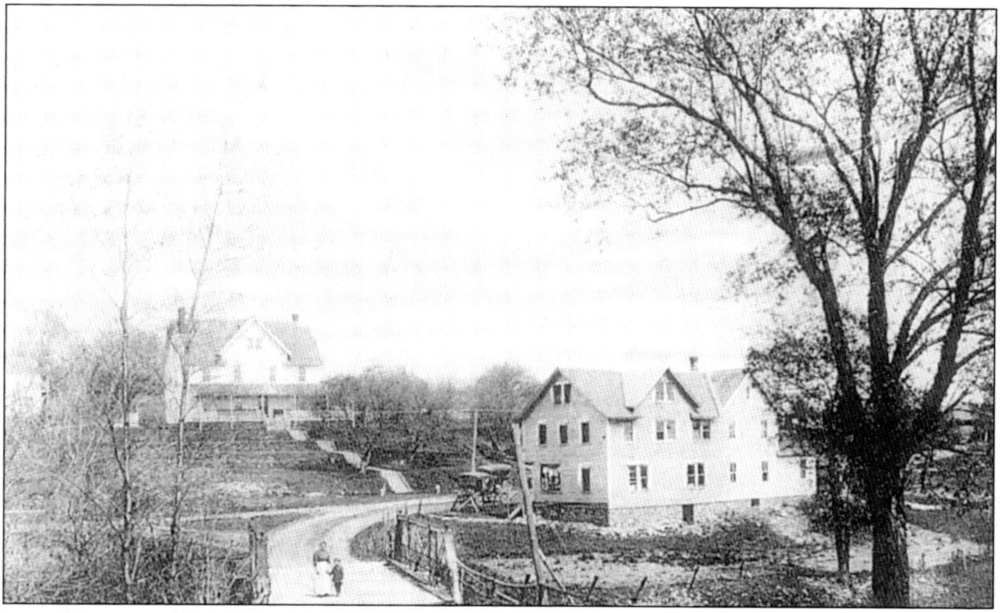

In early views of boardinghouses, scenery is almost never emphasized. Instead, they stress trees, substantial houses, and a general sense of well being. These cards appealed to people who were just happy to be in the country. Common images included those of people walking along the road or posing on the front lawn. The boardinghouses offered few amenities—nor did their clients expect them. The visitors wanted to be in the country, and names helped. Mountaindale, for example, was called Sandburg before the railroad and summer people arrived. The top view is in Ulster Heights. The bottom is in Mountaindale.

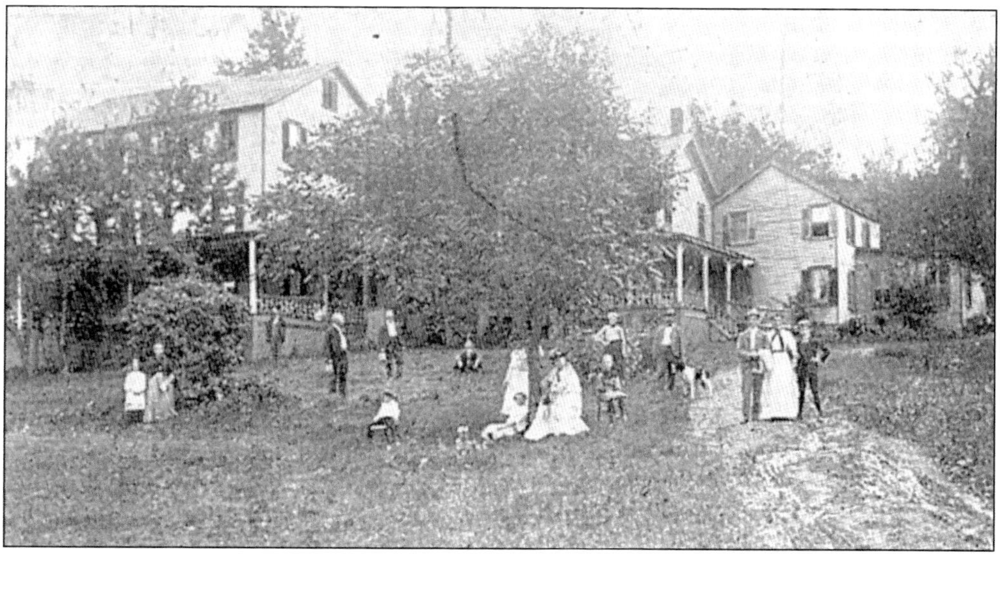

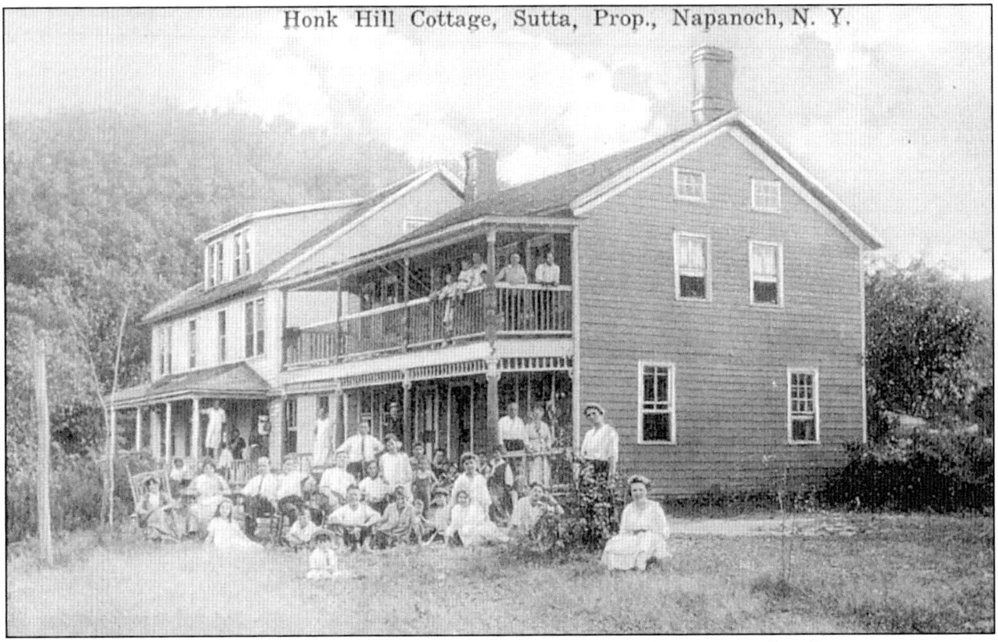

The crowd at Honk Hill was mostly young and probably single. Very early, there are accounts of summer romances at the Catskill boardinghouses and hotels. An especially cheerful lot, the "Honk Hillers" were probably lower-middle-class New Yorkers. Architecturally, the right side of the complex dates from the 19th century and the left side from the early 20th century.

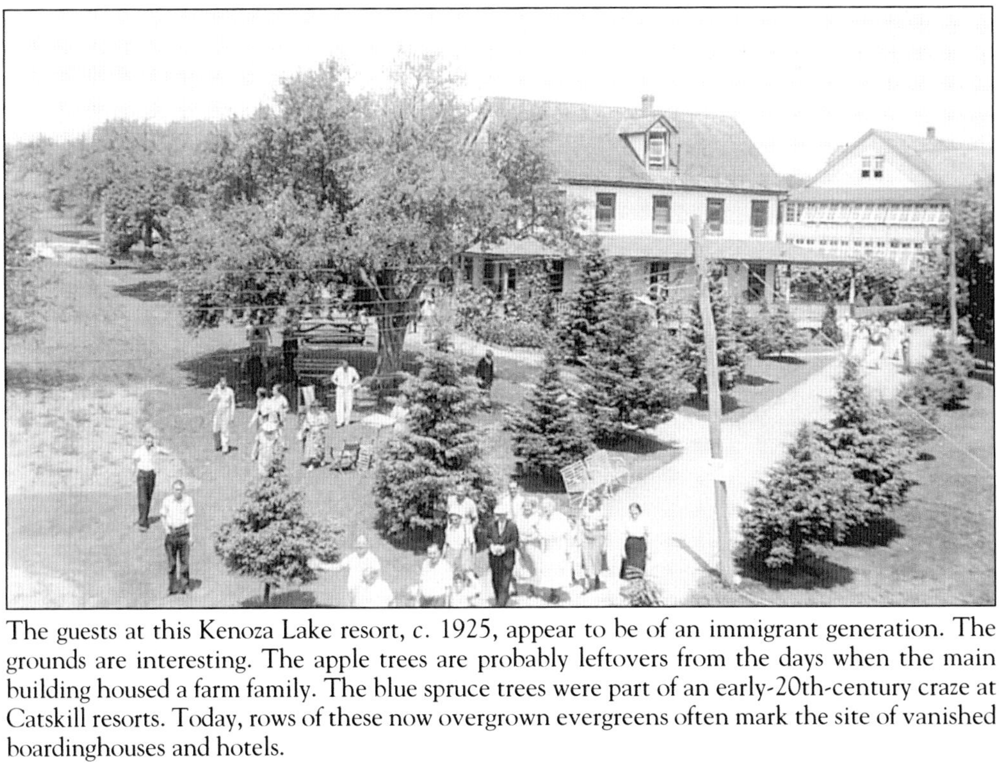

The guests at this Kenoza Lake resort, c. 1925, appear to be of an immigrant generation. The grounds are interesting. The apple trees are probably leftovers from the days when the main building housed a farm family. The blue spruce trees were part of an early-20th-century craze at Catskill resorts. Today, rows of these now overgrown evergreens often mark the site of vanished boardinghouses and hotels.

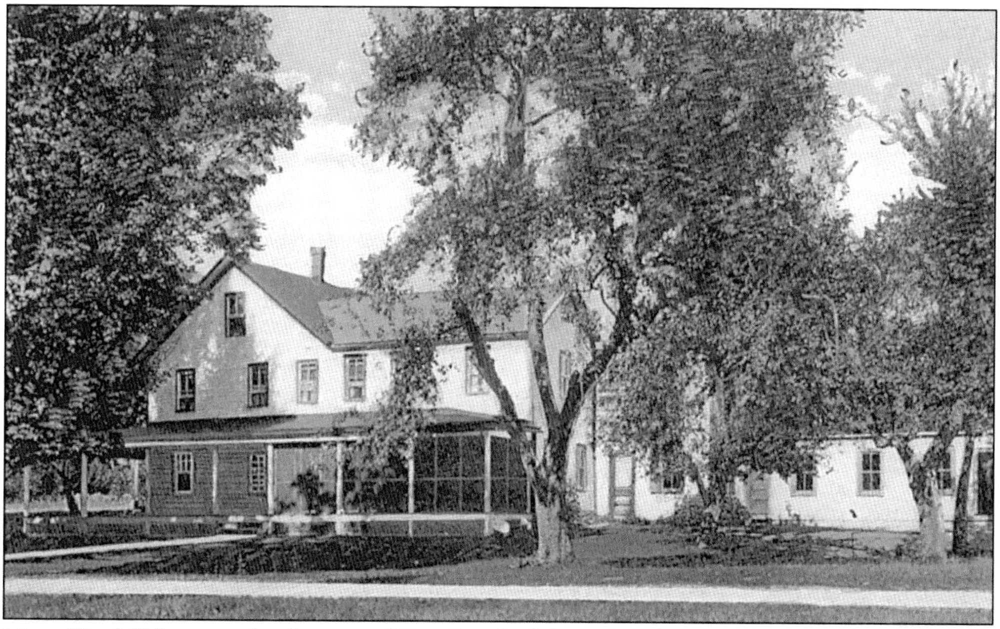

Many Catskill farms evolved into small hotels, which kept the "farm" association and emphasized the simple pleasures of swimming in a natural body of water and going on hayrides. At some farms, the guests helped with the chores, including milking the cows.

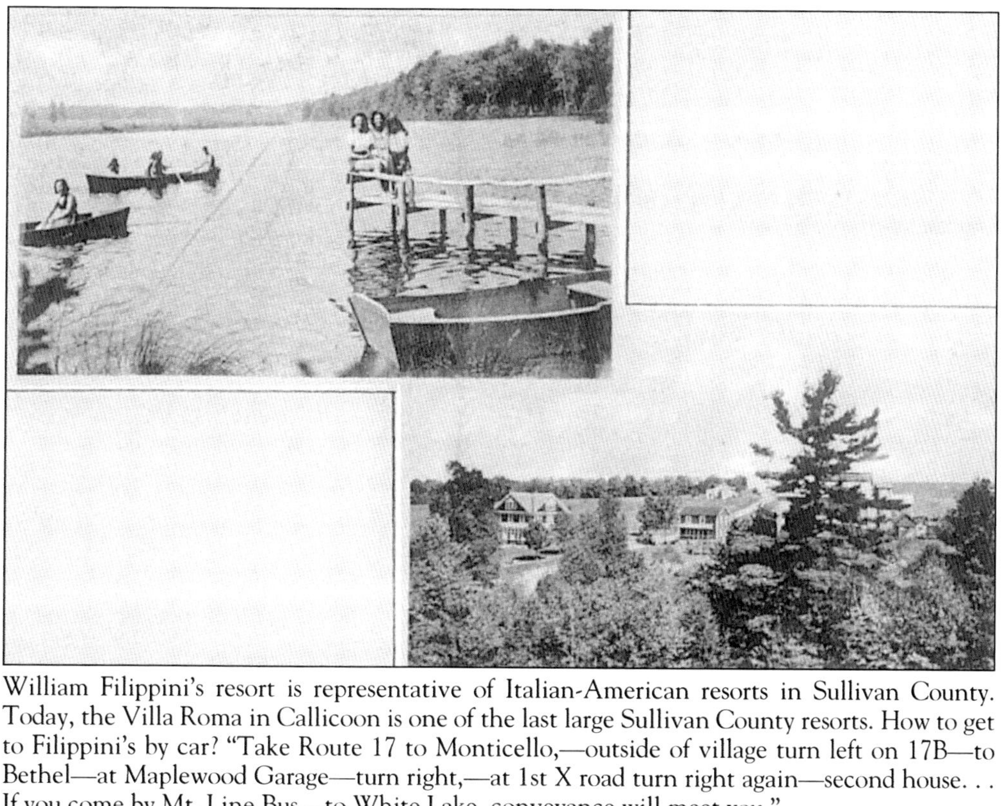

William Filippini's resort is representative of Italian-American resorts in Sullivan County. Today, the Villa Roma in Callicoon is one of the last large Sullivan County resorts. How to get to Filippini's by car? "Take Route 17 to Monticello,—outside of village turn left on 17B—to Bethel—at Maplewood Garage—turn right,—at 1st X road turn right again—second house. . . If you come by Mt. Line Bus—to White Lake, conveyance will meet you."

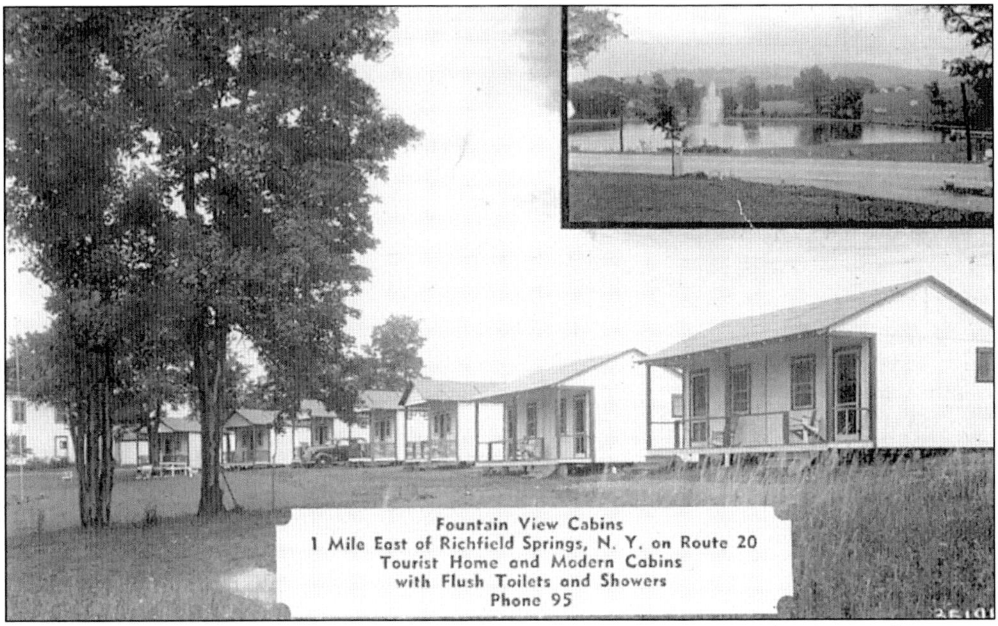

The automobile brought the tourist cabin, the forerunner of the motel. These cabins were often groups of cheaply built frame structures containing one or two rental units each. Albright Cabins on Route 9W, which runs along the west bank of the Hudson River, proudly offered electric lights and running water. The 1920s Fountain View Cabins boasted of flush toilets and showers and had a telephone, relatively new in the rural Hudson Valley. Note the number: "Richfield Spring 95."

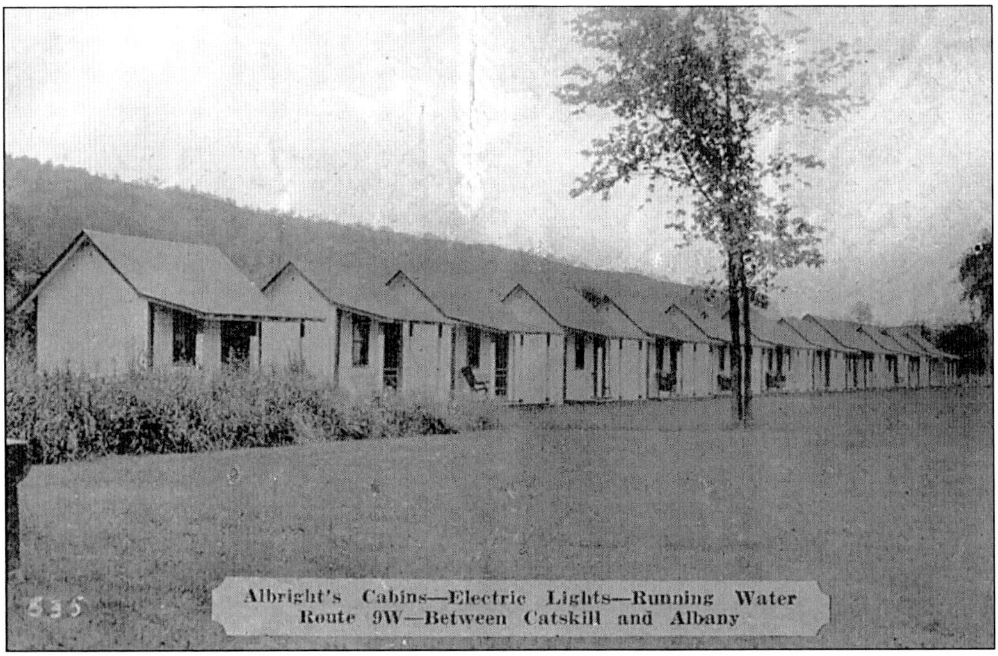

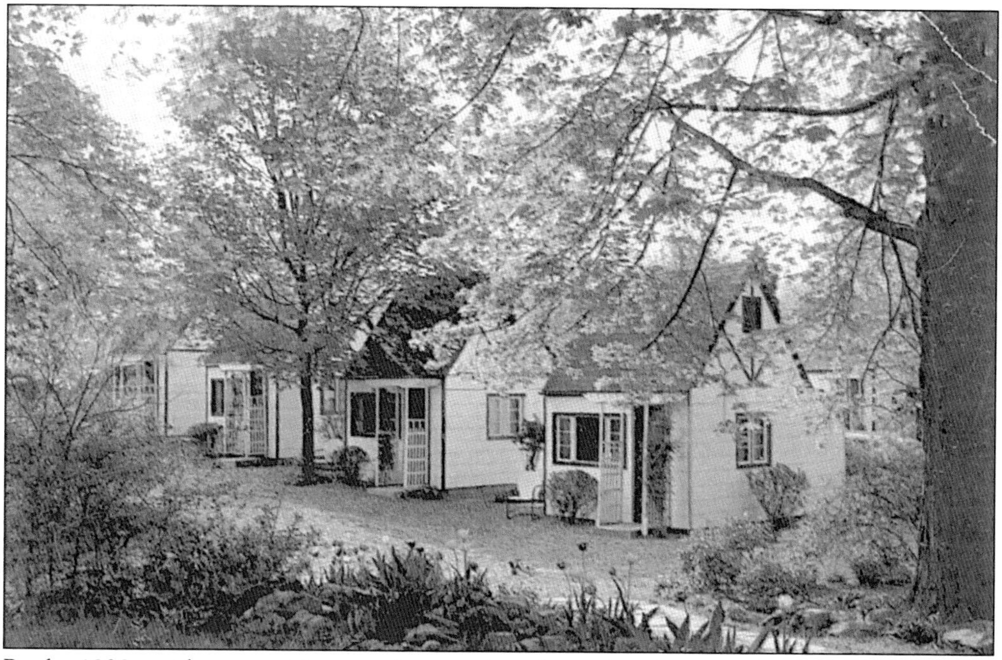

By the 1930s, with competition growing, tourist cabins often became charming, as at Blossom Farm Inn in Milton, which offered "18 Modern Cabins—Private Showers" and a "Beautiful Hudson View." The "picture windows" are probably a 1950s update for these miniature Dutch-style cottages. Progress turned from charm to modernism as cabins and inns gave way to tourist courts and motels. Blossom Farm's new postwar units now offered "Tile Bath Rooms—Radio and Television. . .Air Conditioned Heat."

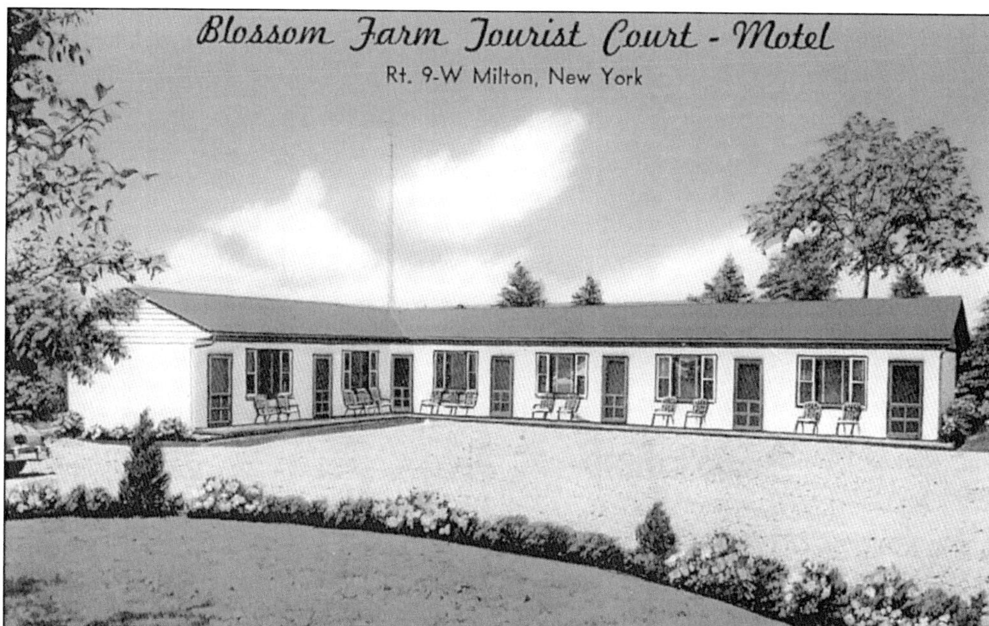

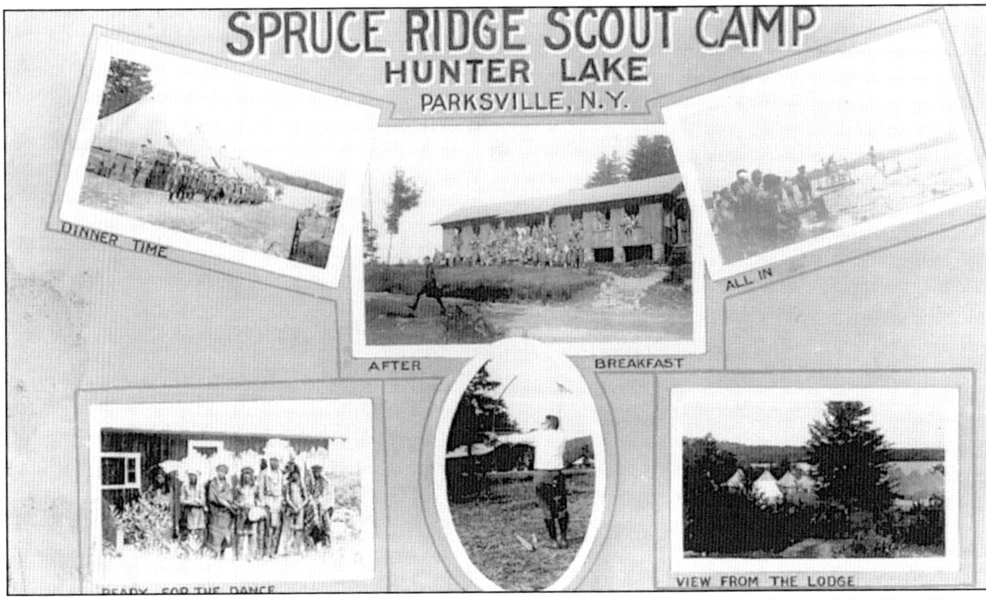

The camp movement matured along with the postcard and with the founding of the Boy Scouts in the early 20th century. Most camps emphasized the rural aspects of the rugged life. At Spruce Ridge Scout Camp, many campers lived in tents and practiced Native American crafts. Judging from the piano, the mess hall at Camp Wallkill was probably also the entertainment center. The flags and the Japanese lanterns suggest that the room was decorated for the Fourth of July when this photograph was taken.

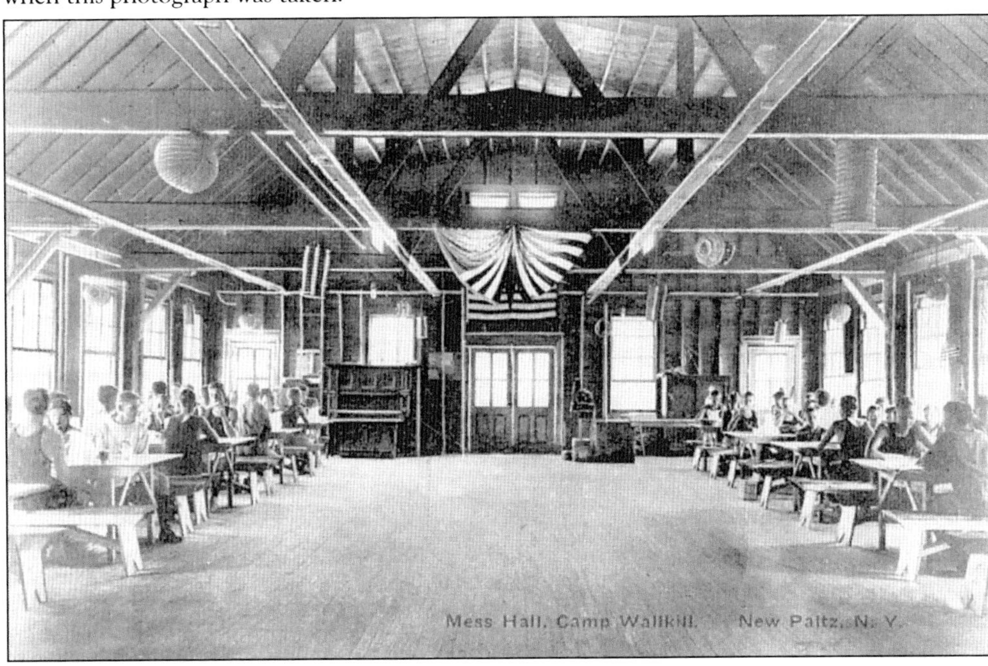

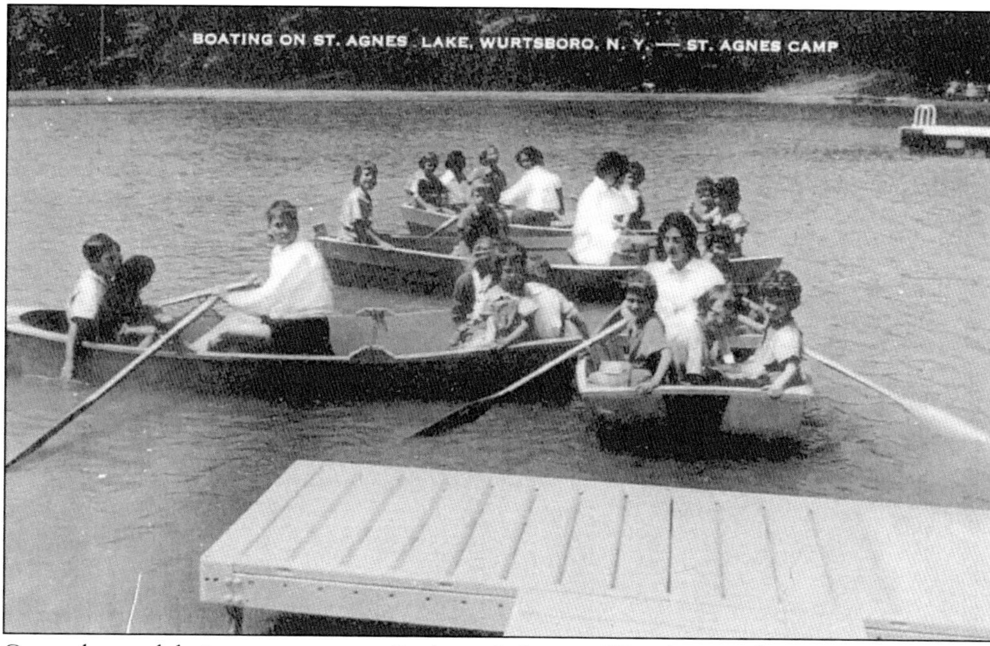

Counselors and their campers row on St. Agnes Lake near Wurtsboro in the 1920s. Many camps, like Catholic St. Agnes, had a religious affiliation. In line with today's new secular religion, physical fitness, there are several Catskill camps devoted to helping, or forcing, overweight youngsters to become slim.

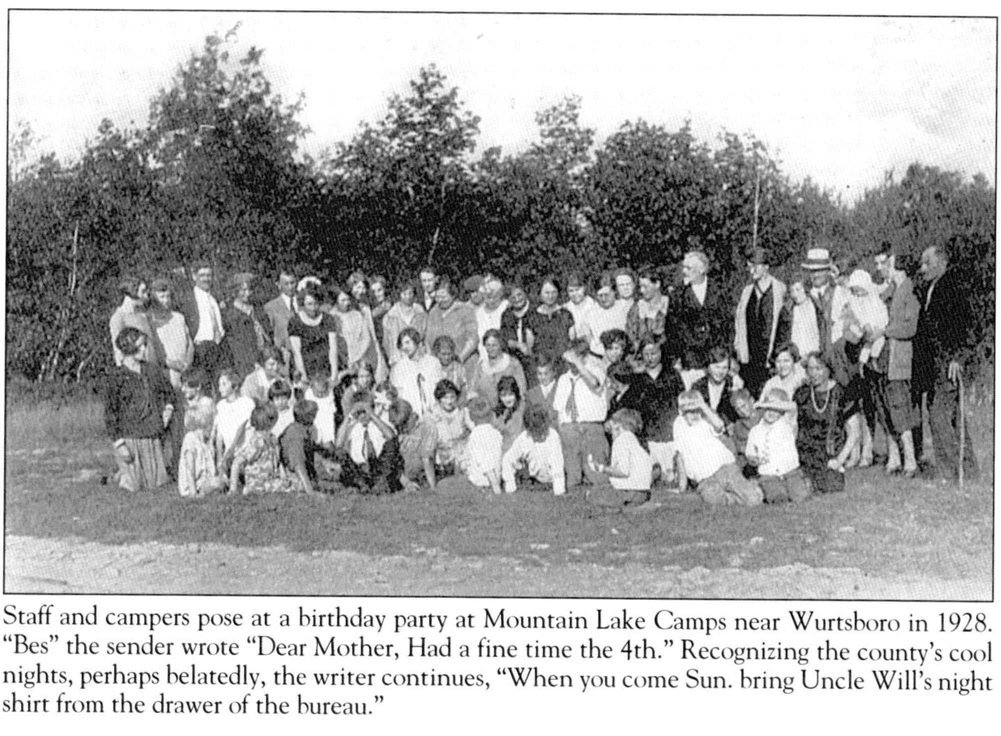

Staff and campers pose at a birthday party at Mountain Lake Camps near Wurtsboro in 1928. "Bes" the sender wrote "Dear Mother, Had a fine time the 4th." Recognizing the county's cool nights, perhaps belatedly, the writer continues, "When you come Sun. bring Uncle Will's night shirt from the drawer of the bureau."

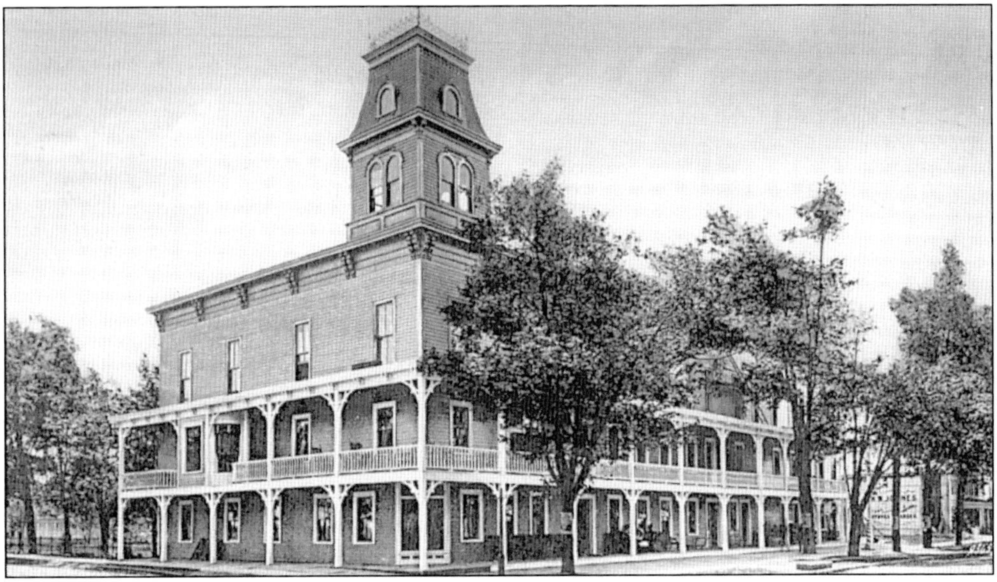

The Hotel Rockwell stood on Broadway near the courthouse. In 1890, a New York City paper claimed it was "second to none of the houses of the same class. . . visited in the larger cities of this and neighboring states." While tourists were its mainstay, the Rockwell was also "popular with traveling boys." It burned during the Monticello fire of 1909, along with 75 other buildings.

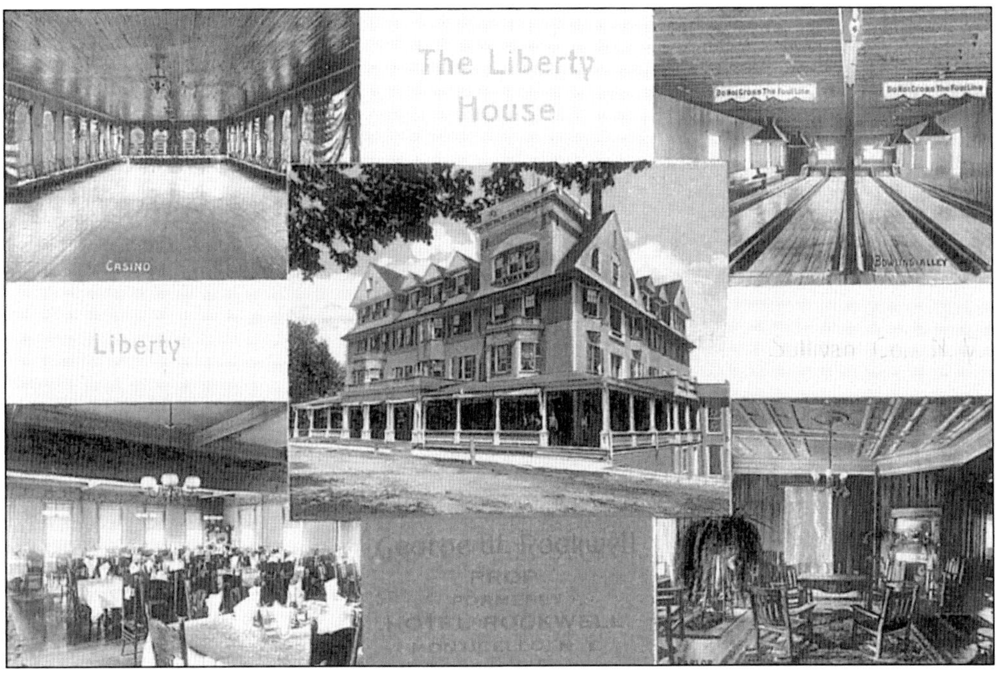

Incorporating an earlier Liberty House, built in the 1860s, the new Liberty House opened to the public on January 20, 1896. When state Route 4 between New York City and Binghamton was developed, it became a popular halfway stopover for early motorists. It offered a large casino, bowling alleys, and elegant interiors. It burned April 3, 1926.

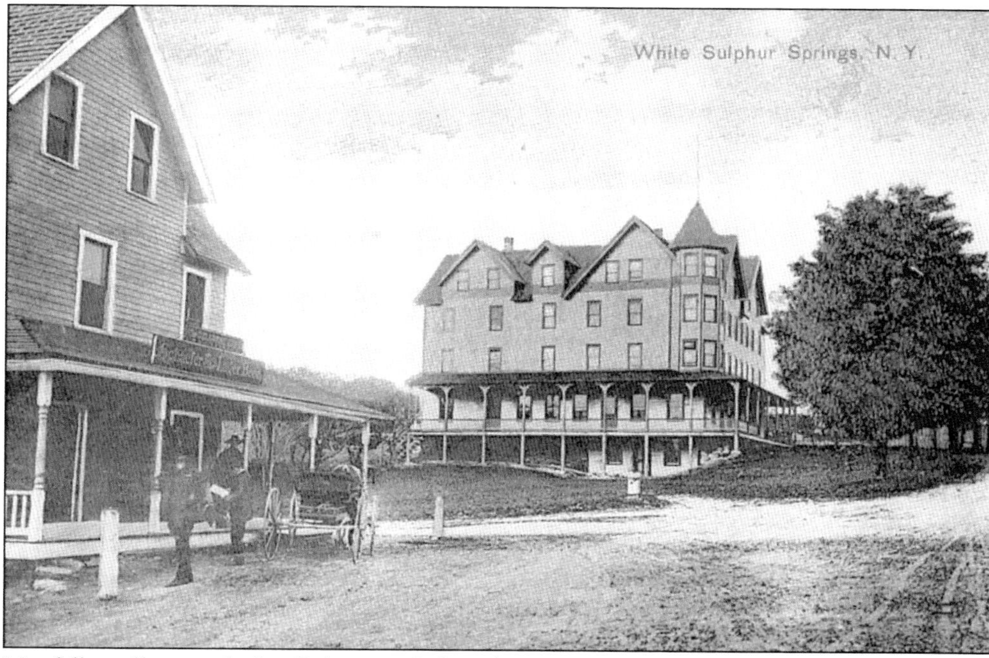

Menfolk mill around the Delaware Cafe, whose sign proclaims "Schaefer Lager." In the background of this scene in White Sulphur Springs, Sullivan County's premier spa, is the Lawrence House. A late-19th-century success, the hotel limped into the mid-20th century. Finally abandoned, it was torn down in 1964.

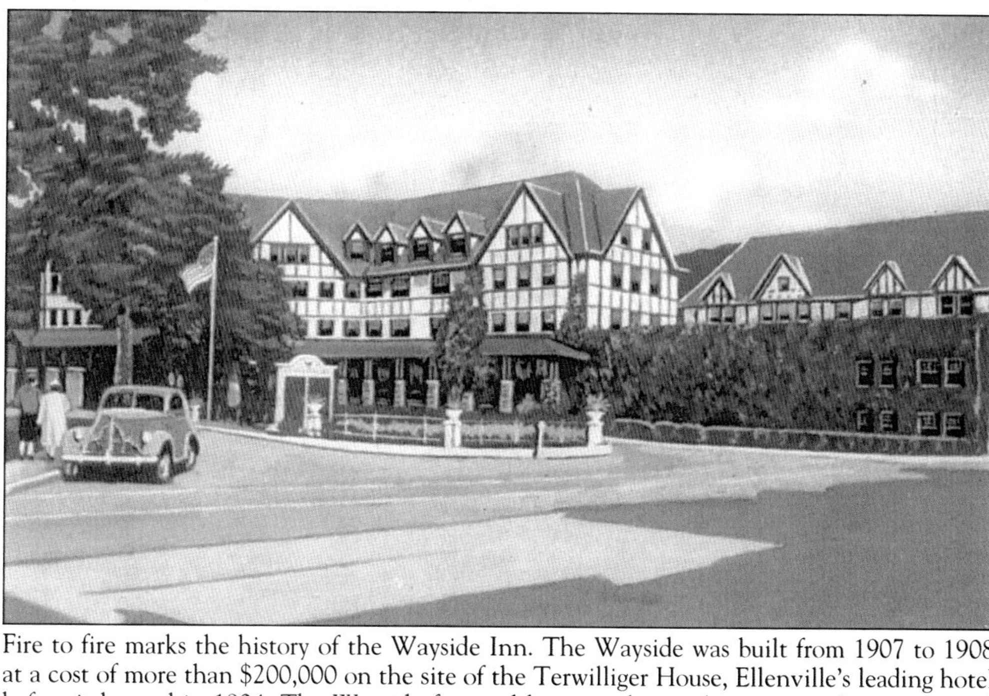

Fire to fire marks the history of the Wayside Inn. The Wayside was built from 1907 to 1908 at a cost of more than $200,000 on the site of the Terwilliger House, Ellenville's leading hotel before it burned in 1904. The Wayside featured long porches and a porte cochere supported by pillars built of a local stone called Shawangunk grit. After passing through many hands, the Wayside burned on October 25, 1967.

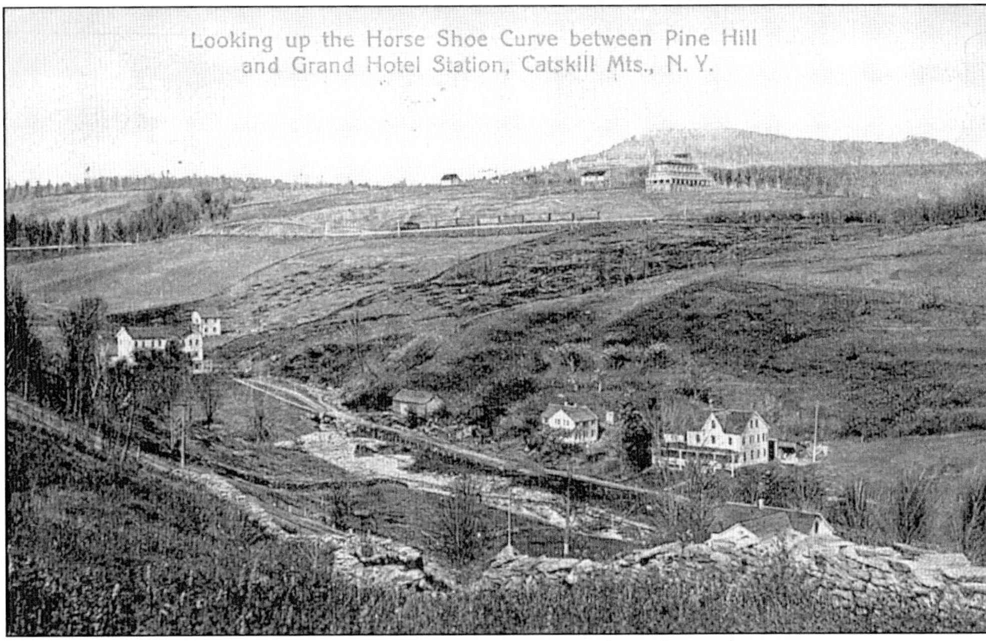

Emulating the grand hotels of the region, many more modest places chose picturesque settings. However, they seldom were sited in the splendid isolation of the earlier hostelries, once the railroad became increasingly important to the development of the resort areas. Note the train rising from the Ulster County resort town of Pine Hill to the Grand Hotel Station.

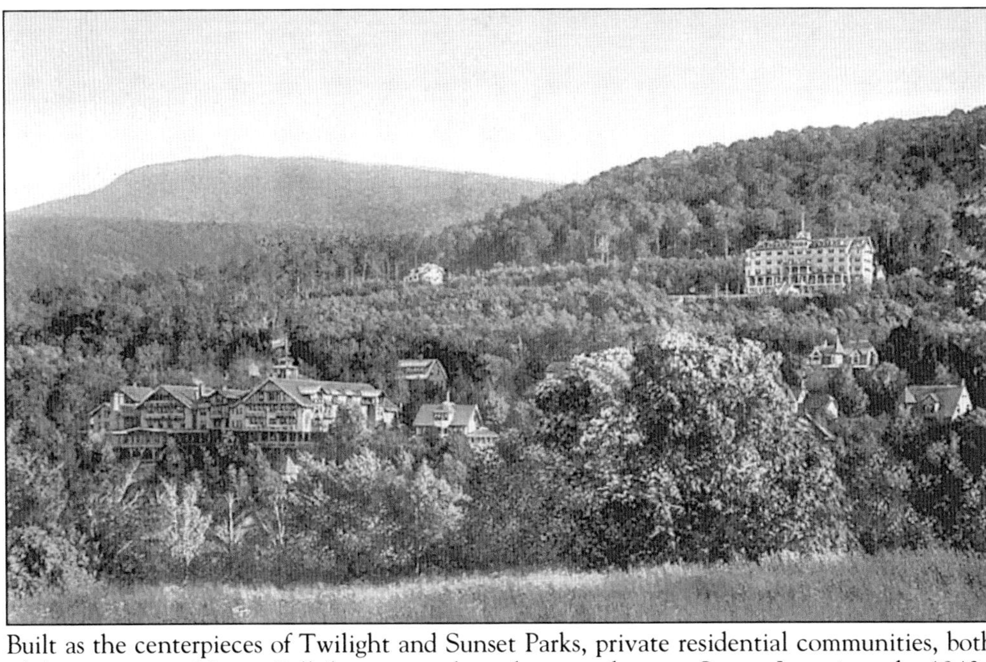

Built as the centerpieces of Twilight and Sunset Parks, private residential communities, both of these inns near Haines Falls have gone through many changes. Sunset Inn, since the 1940s, has catered to a Greek clientele. "Its Queen Anne style has not been altered at all; instead a Greek band plays ethnic songs in the nightclub. The rule of architecture as a non-clue to ethnic identity is consistent throughout the Catskill Resorts."

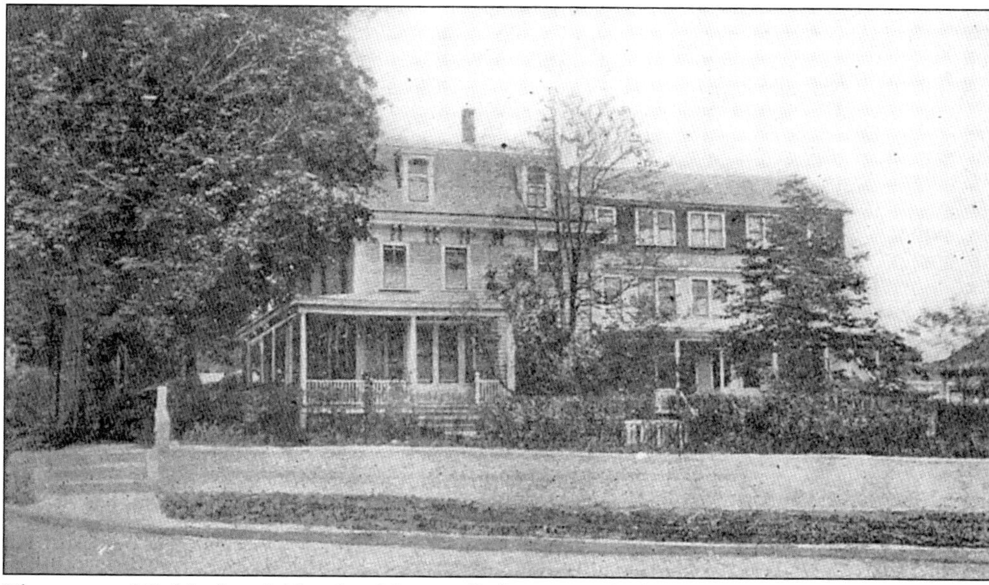

The name of Goldenberg's Hotel in Monticello leaves no doubt about the religion of its owners. Typical of the in-town hotels built by Christian entrepreneurs, Goldenberg's changed ethnic complexion in the early 20th century.

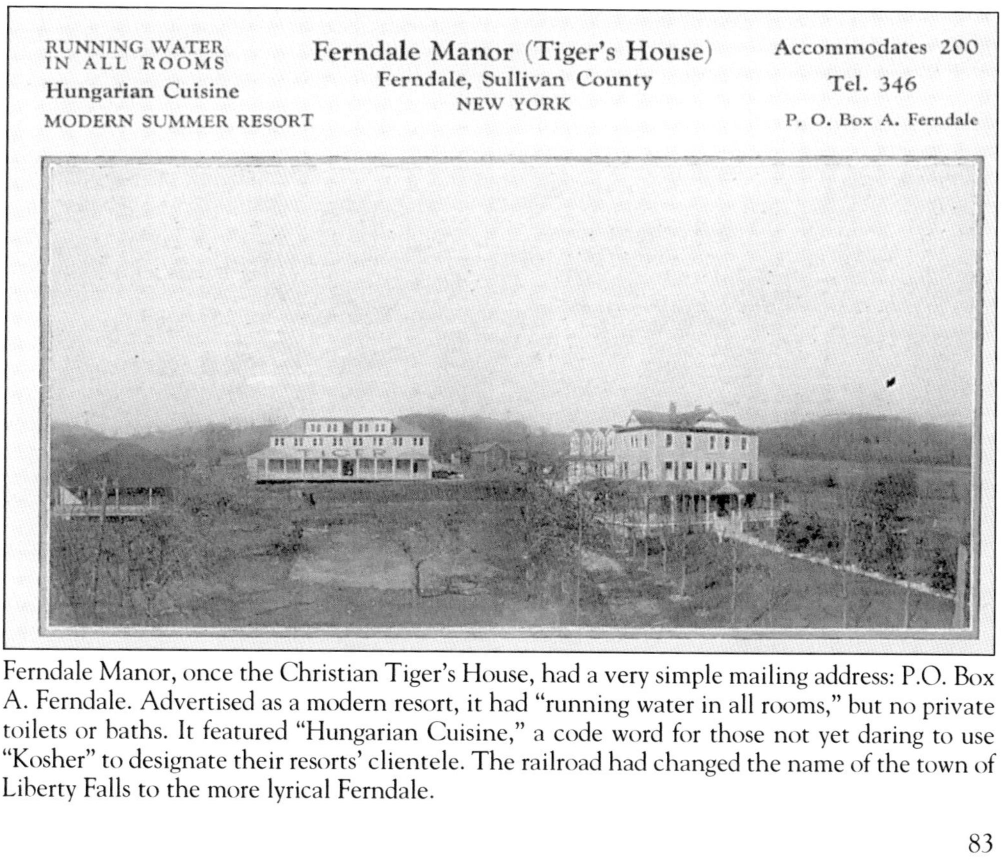

Ferndale Manor, once the Christian Tiger's House, had a very simple mailing address: P.O. Box A. Ferndale. Advertised as a modern resort, it had "running water in all rooms," but no private toilets or baths. It featured "Hungarian Cuisine," a code word for those not yet daring to use "Kosher" to designate their resorts' clientele. The railroad had changed the name of the town of Liberty Falls to the more lyrical Ferndale.

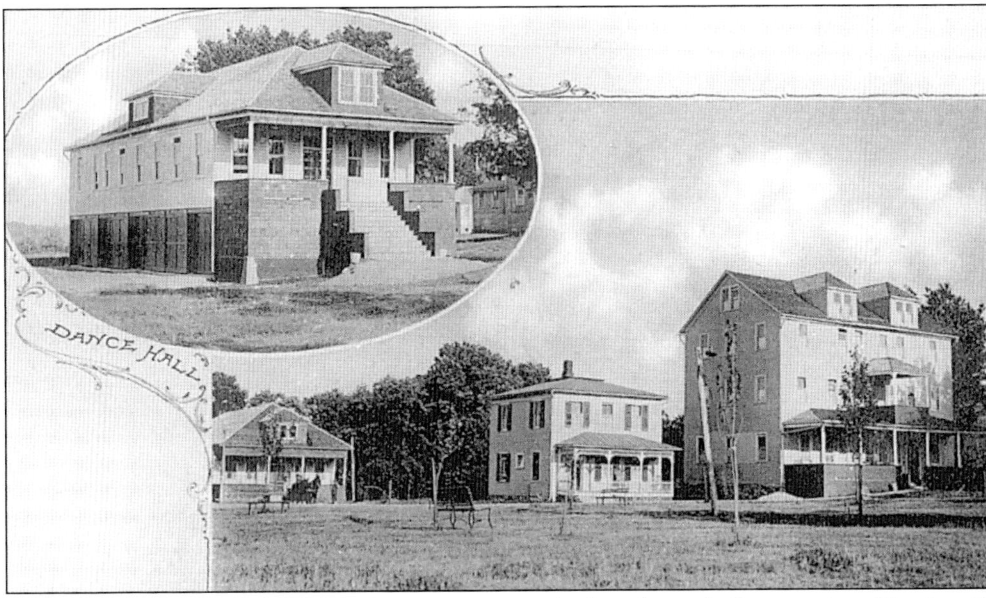

The Evans Hotel at Loch Sheldrake was very proud of its dance hall, or casino. The hotel's original farmhouse is seen in the center of this 1920s view. A very popular hotel into the 1960s, Evans today is the site of Vacation Village, a very costly bungalow colony and summer home complex, patronized by modern Orthodox Jews.

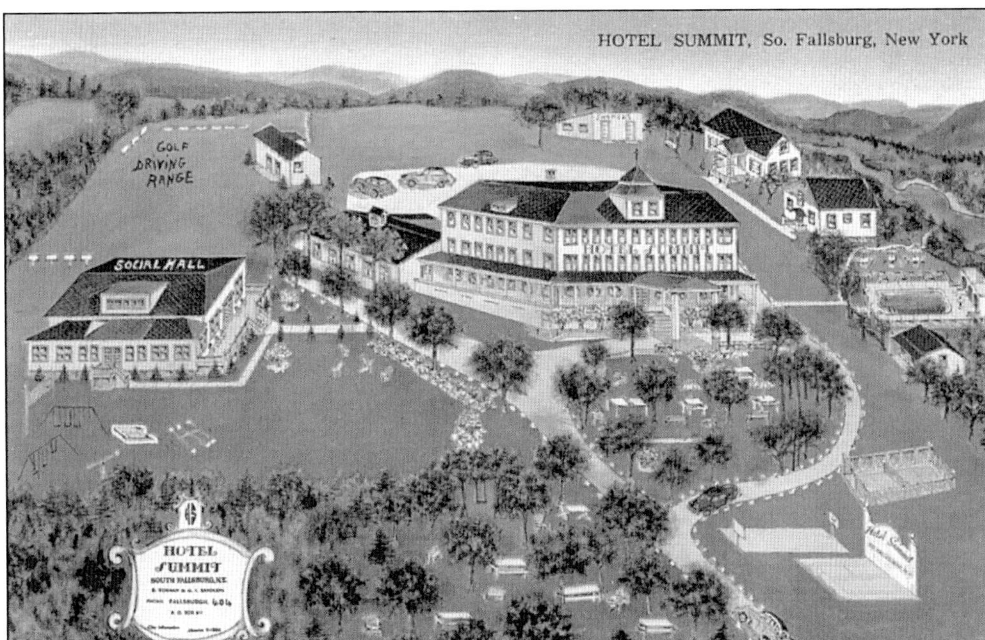

The Hotel Summit is shown in a card by Sullivan County artist-postcard publisher A.S. Landis, who specialized in aerial views, never employing an airplane. The Summit shows a range of facilities, but Landis often enhanced his views to fit client demands. Note the apparent proximity to the Neversink River, at the right, which was actually much more distant.

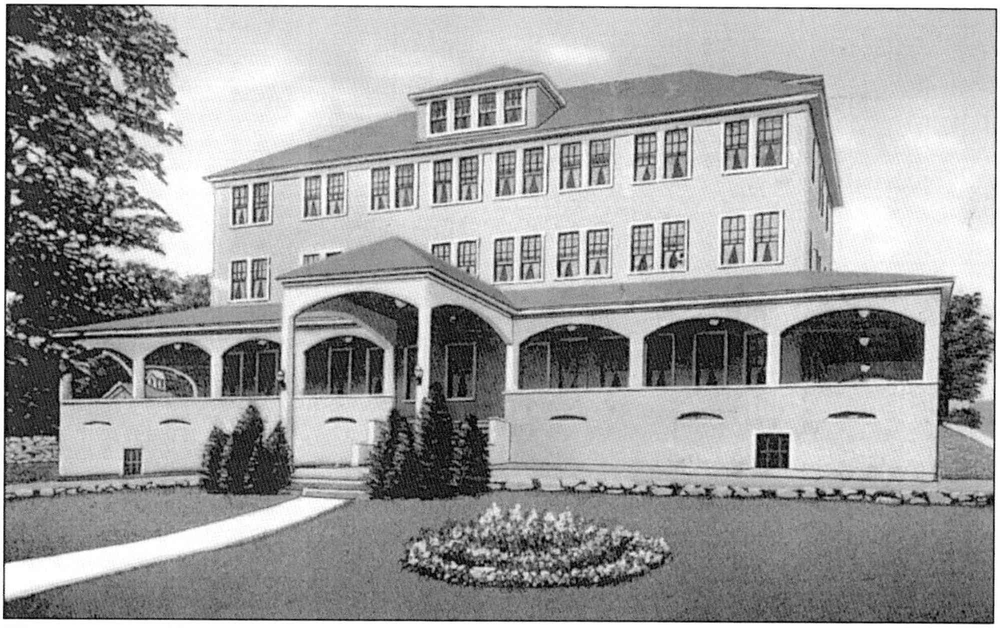

The Murray Hill Hotel promoted itself as "A modern hostelry open throughout the year. A haven for rest and recreation." Large porches were common in the bungalow style, popular with many small and medium-sized hotels. Note the flowerbed on the lawn. Circular beds of colorful annuals were a Catskill hotel feature. Today, remodeled and renamed, the former Murray Hill houses the Dynamite Youth Center, a drug rehabilitation facility—a fate that has befallen a number of former resorts.

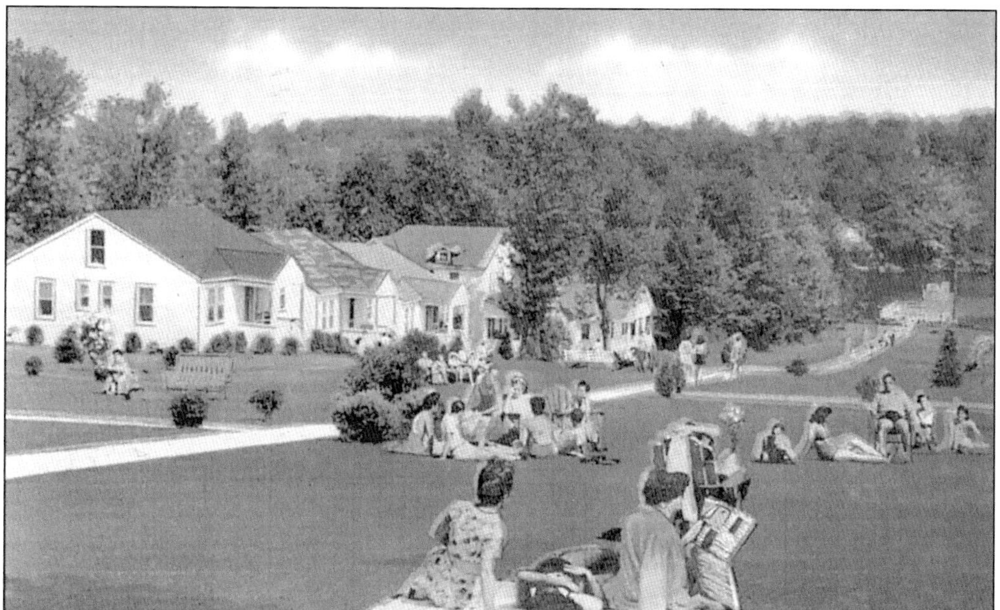

The Waldemere on Shandlee Lake, "the preferred resort of smart young men and women," had many "deluxe" bungalows to house its guests, who apparently enjoyed lounging on the lawn. "Dear Folks" reads this 1948 card, "Having a wonderful second honeymoon. Place is nice and we are taking everything in. Love, Gladys & Leo."

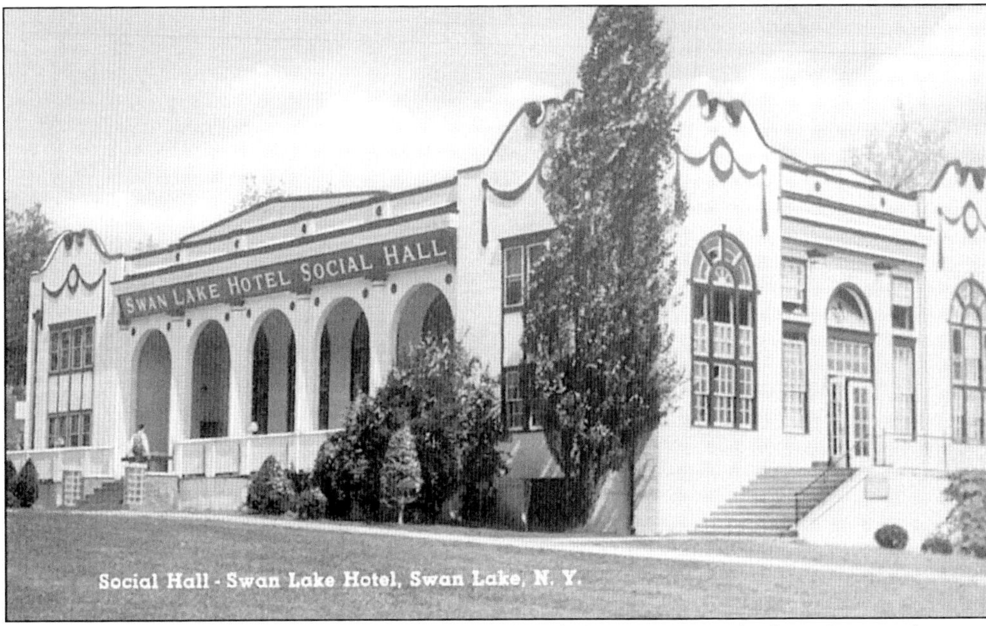

The Swan Lake Hotel was built on the estate of local physician Dr. Abraham Swan, who gave his name to the community. The 1920s social hall, or casino, was in the very fashionable mission style. The hotel, which had also acquired a mission facade, burned in 1954 while an elevator was being installed.

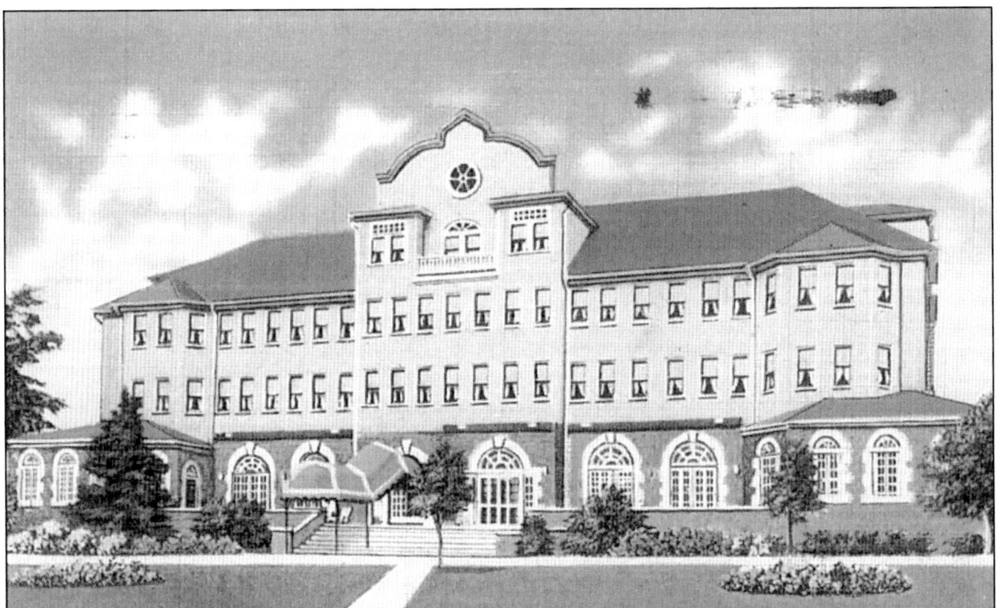

The Brickman Hotel started as a simple farm. Under the Posner family, it developed into a major hotel. Its mission-style facade of the 1930s later gave way to the International style of its grandest period. To attract a young crowd, the hotel developed "a college campus" suggestive of Ivy League housing. It is now part of an ashram, a Buddhist center of worship, which has many Jewish-born followers.

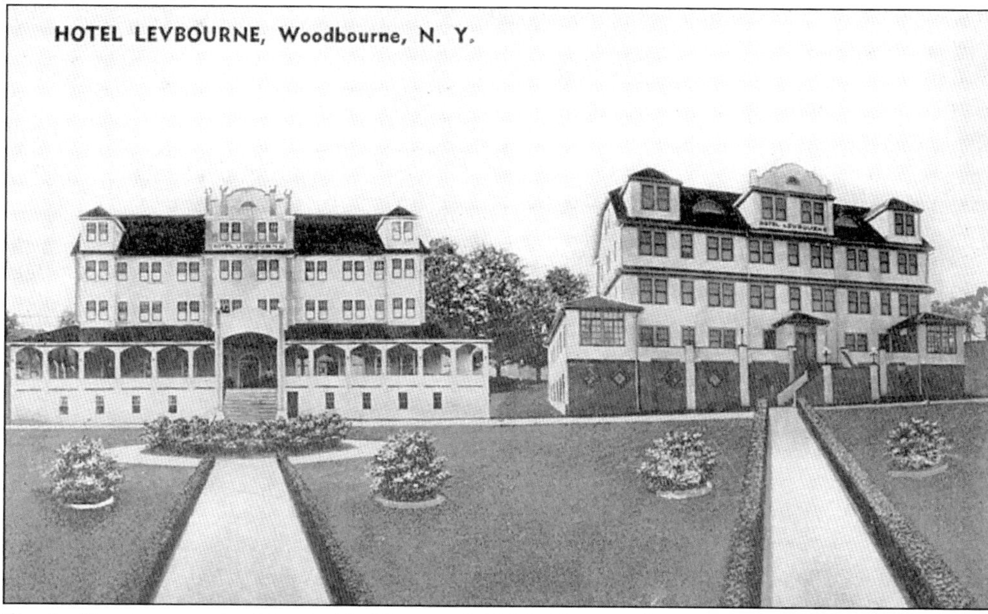

Carrie Komito ran the Hotel Aladdin until 1998. Now in her nineties, she recalls that her parents, after ten years as guests at the Hotel Levbourne, bought the resort. In the 1950s, to make the hotel seem fresher, the family changed the hotel's name to the Aladdin. When they built a nightclub, they named it the Ali Baba Room, naturally. The International-style facade transformed the appearance of the first floor of the building on the left. It is shown in a night view for a very good reason. The upper floors were not changed at all. As the hotel business soured, Carrie Komito moved many bungalows onto her property and rented them to "snowbirds," or Floridians. The hotel is now being transformed into an Orthodox Jewish resort cooperative.

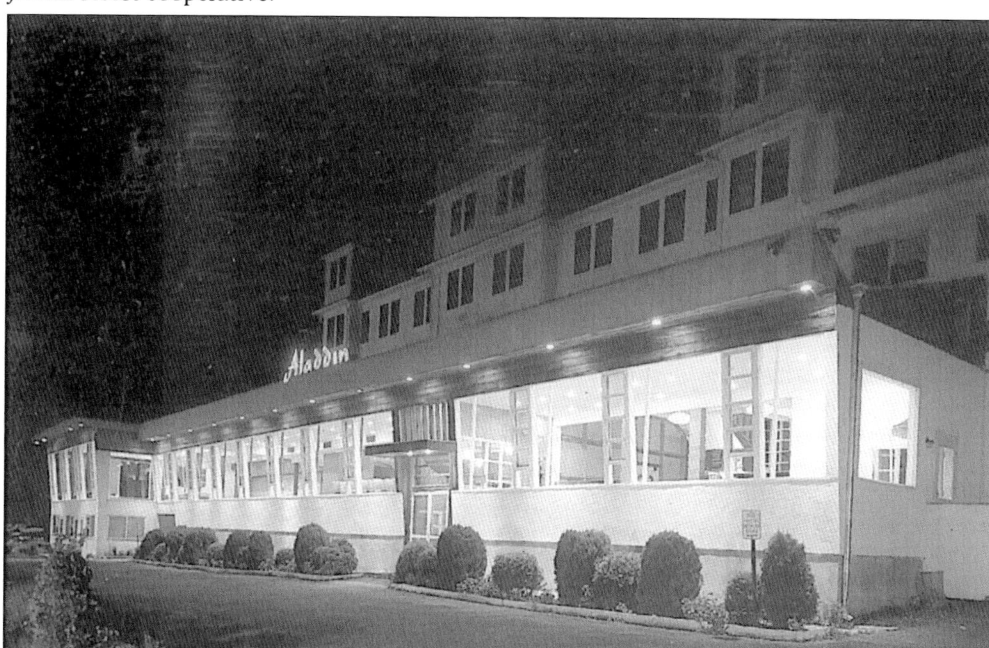

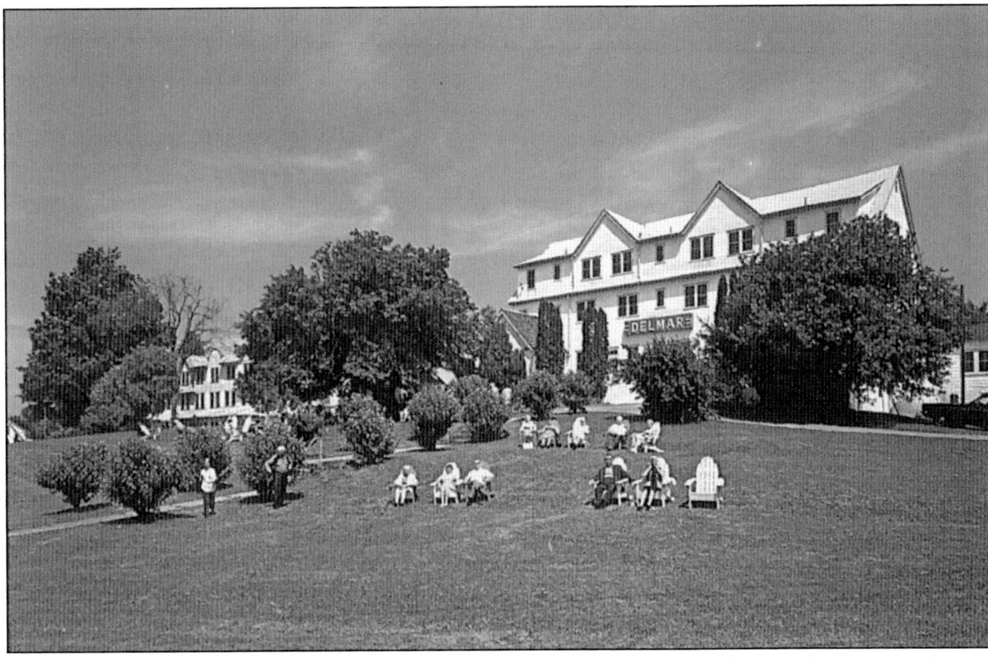

October 15, 1929, less than two weeks before the great stock market crash, Hyman Jacobs bought the Cozy Nook, a farm with a 20-room guest house and a barn, for $1,000. He renamed it Jacobs Inn. His son and daughter-in-law, who operated the hotel until 1986, renamed it the Delmar Hotel. It always remained a small family hotel. In 1971, it featured a "big filtered swimming pool" and boasted having "All Public Rooms Air Conditioned, Dietary Laws, Music and Entertainment Nightly."

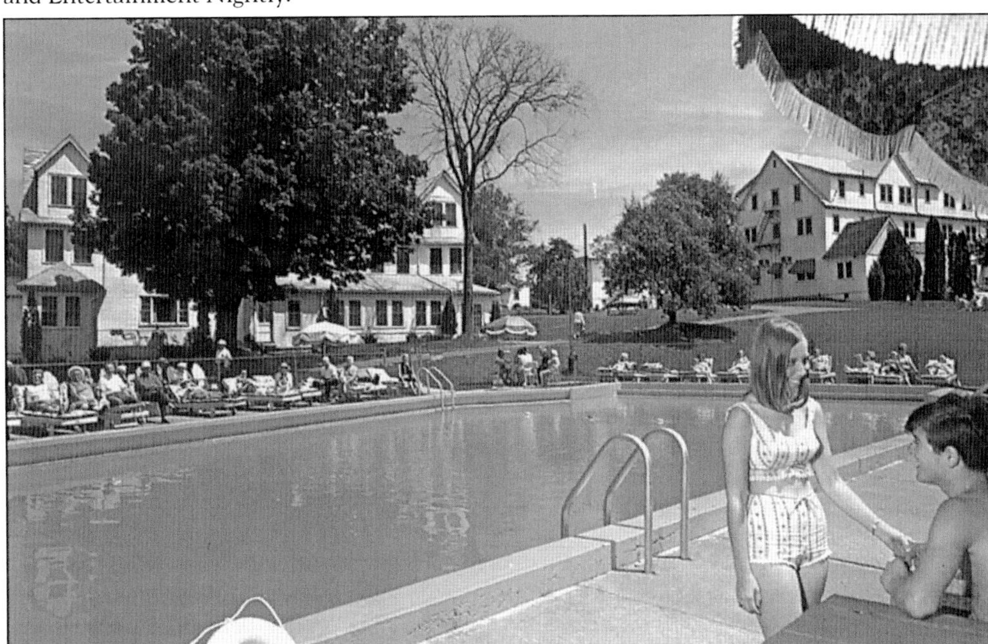

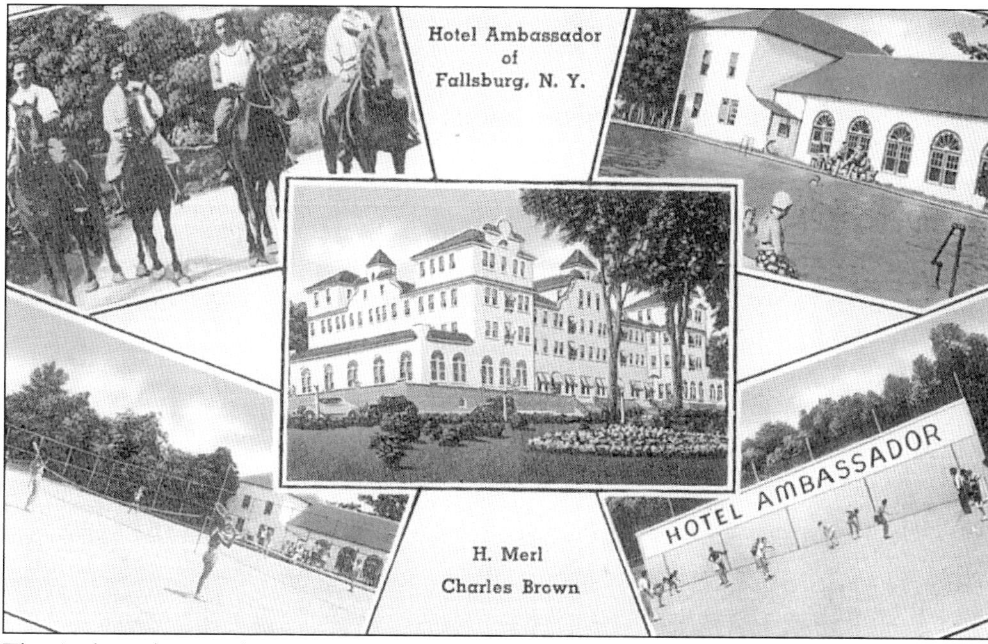

The Ambassador Hotel emphasized its Spanish-style ambiance. Along with many large hotels, it hired college basketball players as dining room and bell help. Hotel teams played one another for the amusement of guests and for the guests' desire to gamble. The Ambassador had the first real nightclub in a Borscht Belt hotel. Today, it is the site of Catskill Playland, a small summer amusement park catering to ultra-Orthodox Jews.

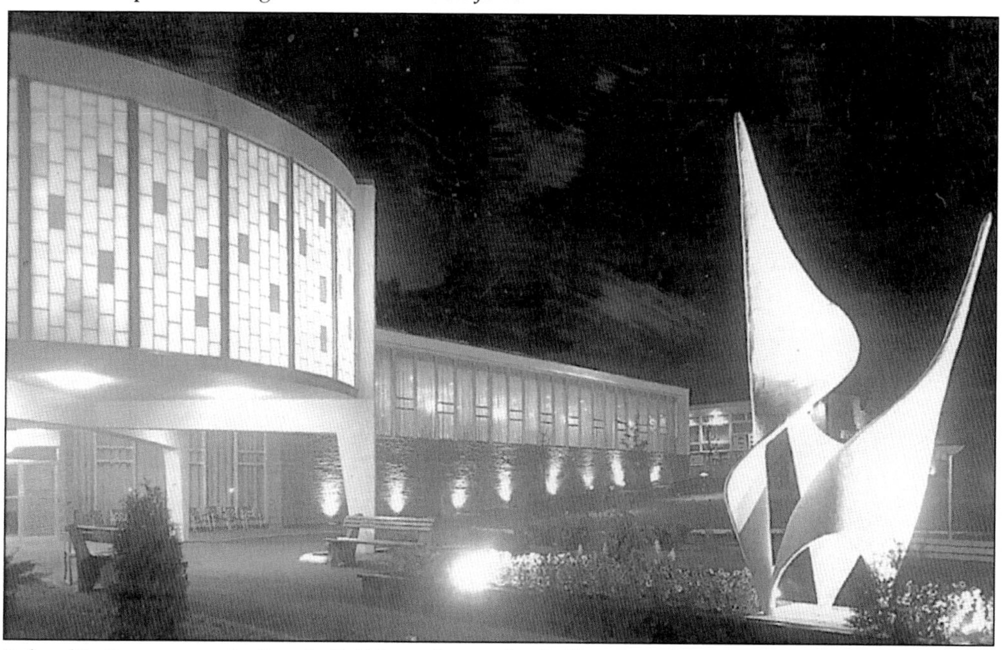

Schenk's Paramount in South Fallsburg bragged of offering "The Ultimate in Resort Living." Its grand International-style facade and abstract sculpture brought a touch of Miami Beach glamour to the Catskills. Today, it is a Hasidic camp, where the dynamic sculpture looks especially forlorn.

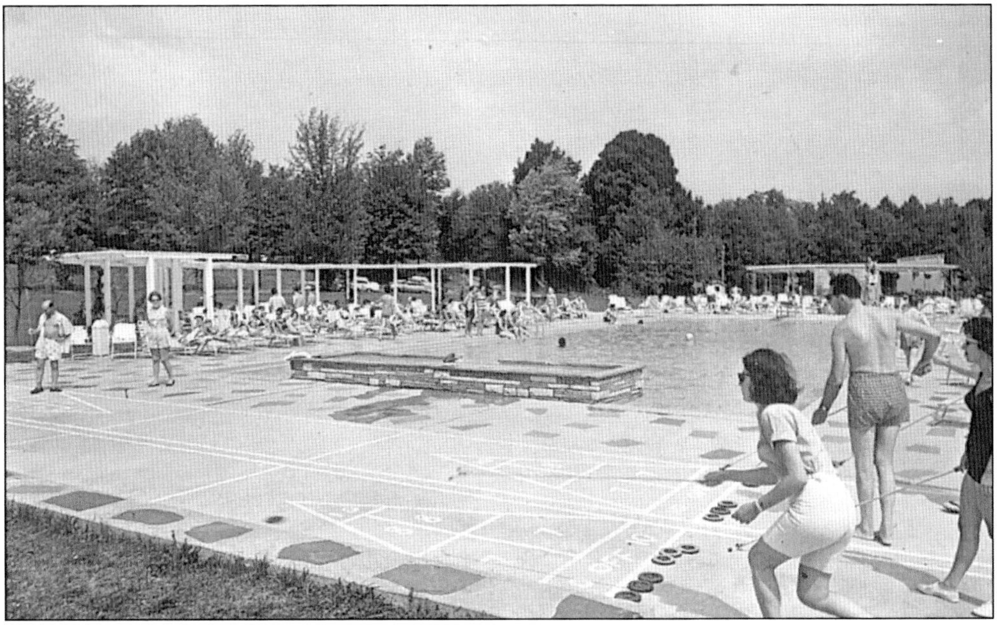

Chester's Zunbarg, "sun hill" in Yiddish, was founded during the Depression by Ann Chester and her family, most of whom were left-wing activists. The hotel, which later dropped "Zunbarg" from its name, was a destination for liberal-thinking young people. It was essentially a singles resort, before the term was invented. Over the years, the resort became known for its intellectually oriented entertainment and its very good athletic facilities. During the 1950s, Ann Chester employed many black-listed artists, such as tap dancer Paul Draper. By the 1950s, every resort had to have tennis courts, even though they were seldom used, and, of course, a pool.

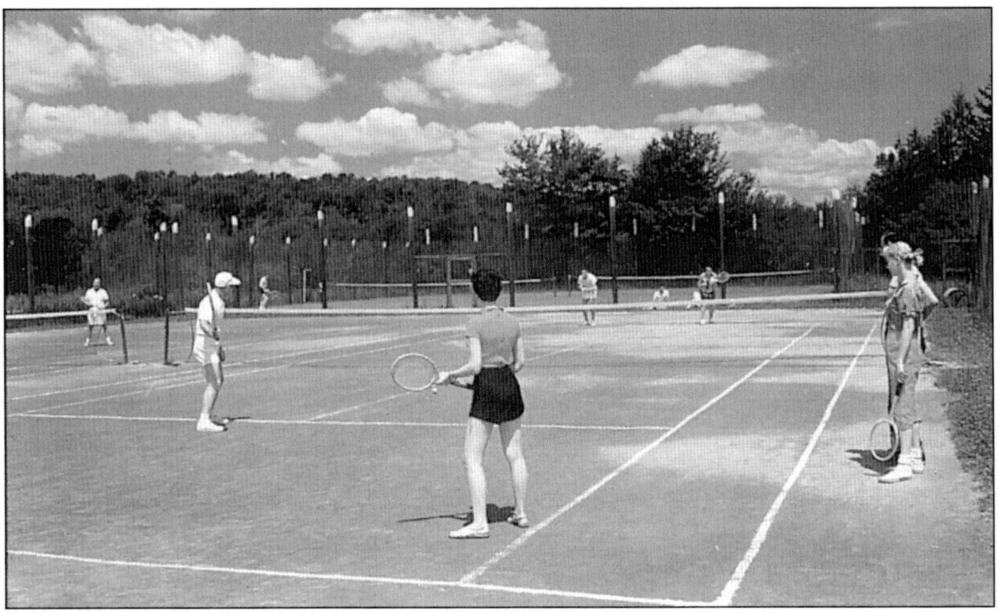

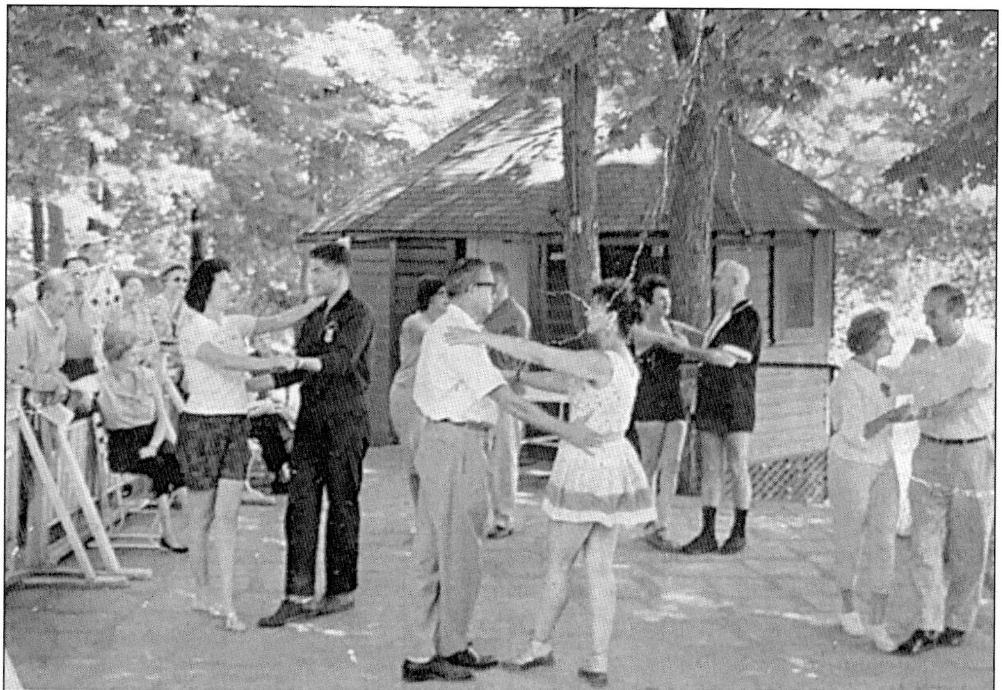

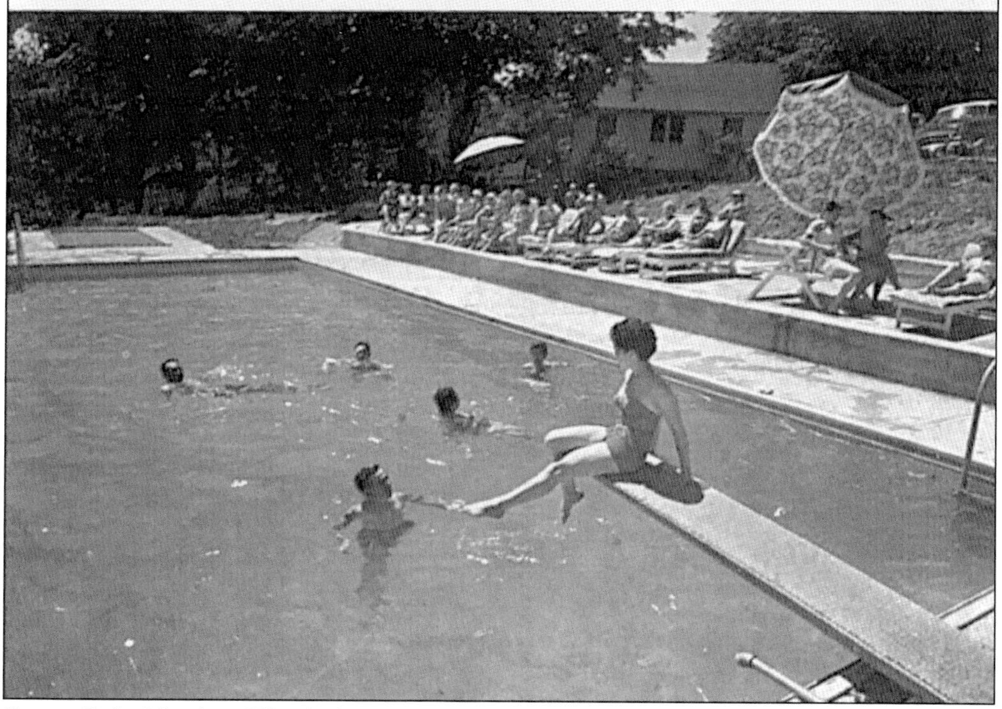

Sunny Oaks Hotel in Woodridge is now in its fourth generation of matrilineal ownership. Always small, the hotel provided accommodations for "80 nice people," when this card was printed in the 1960s. For five years, the resort has been the site of the annual Catskill Institute Conferences, which are dedicated to studying, recording, and preserving the area's unique heritage.

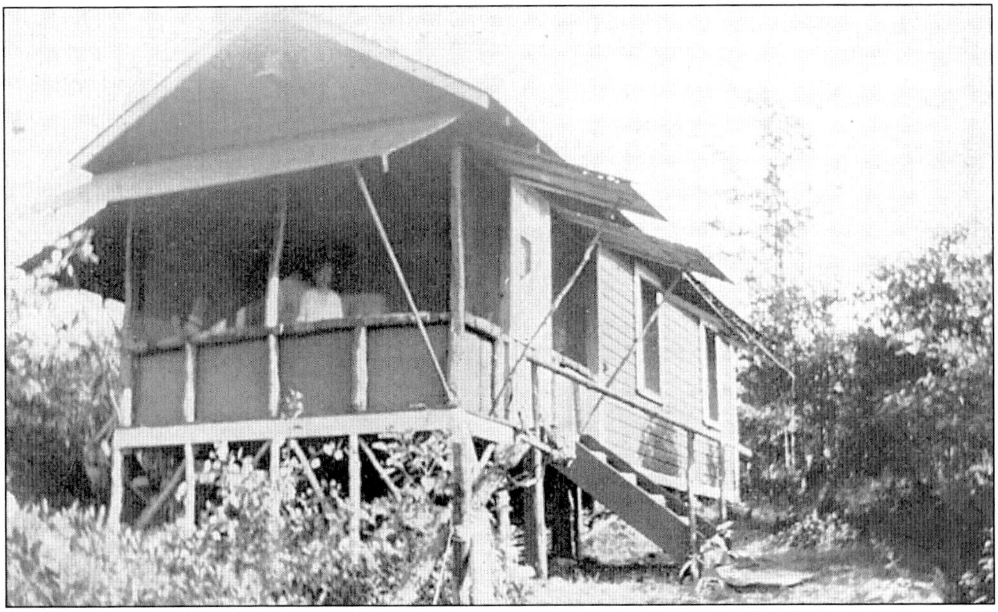

Bungalow colonies were a characteristic Borscht Belt resort, where families rented a small cottage or bungalow for the season. Mom and the children stayed for the summer. Dad came up on the weekends and for his vacation, if he was lucky enough to have one. "Summer Comfort" (above) was probably an individually owned vacation shack. The structure shown in this card, published in Wurtsboro *c.* 1920, is similar to the earliest bungalow colony structures. Later resorts, such as Six Lake Bungalow Colony, offered a variety of accommodations: a casino, a handball court, and a "Spring Fed Private Lake."

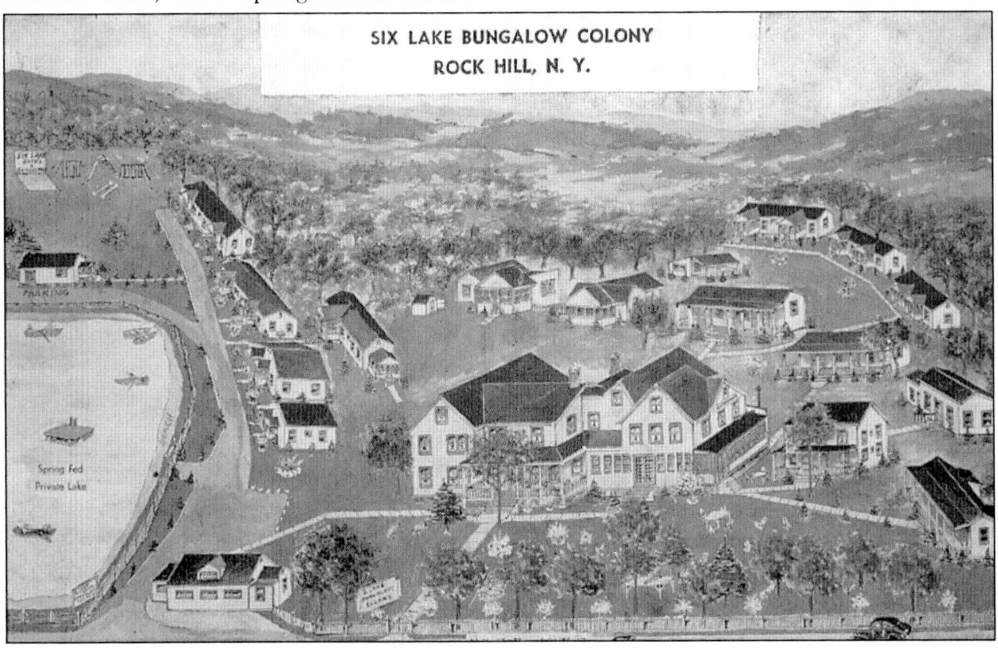

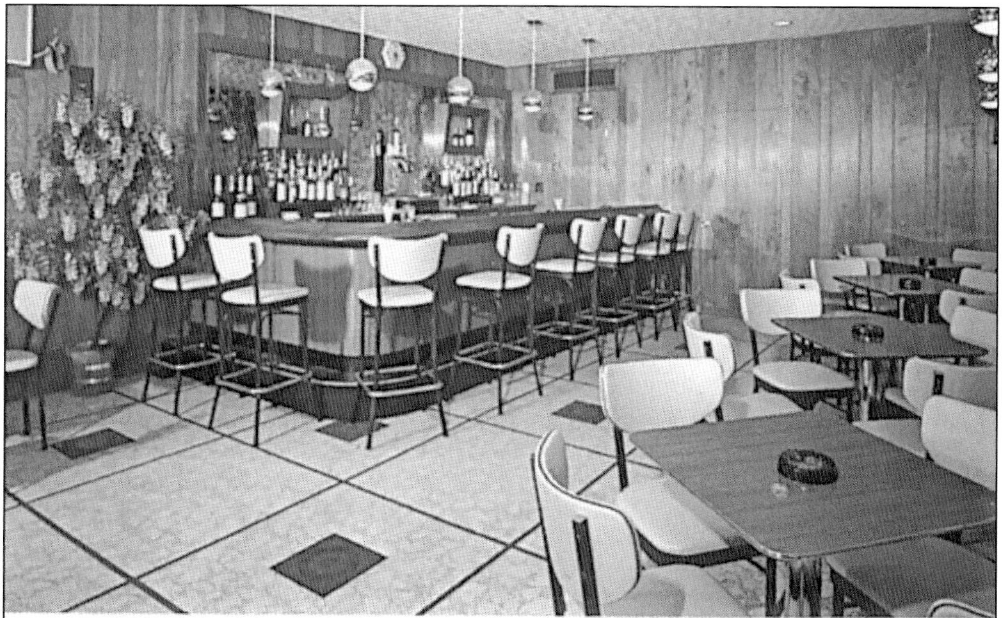

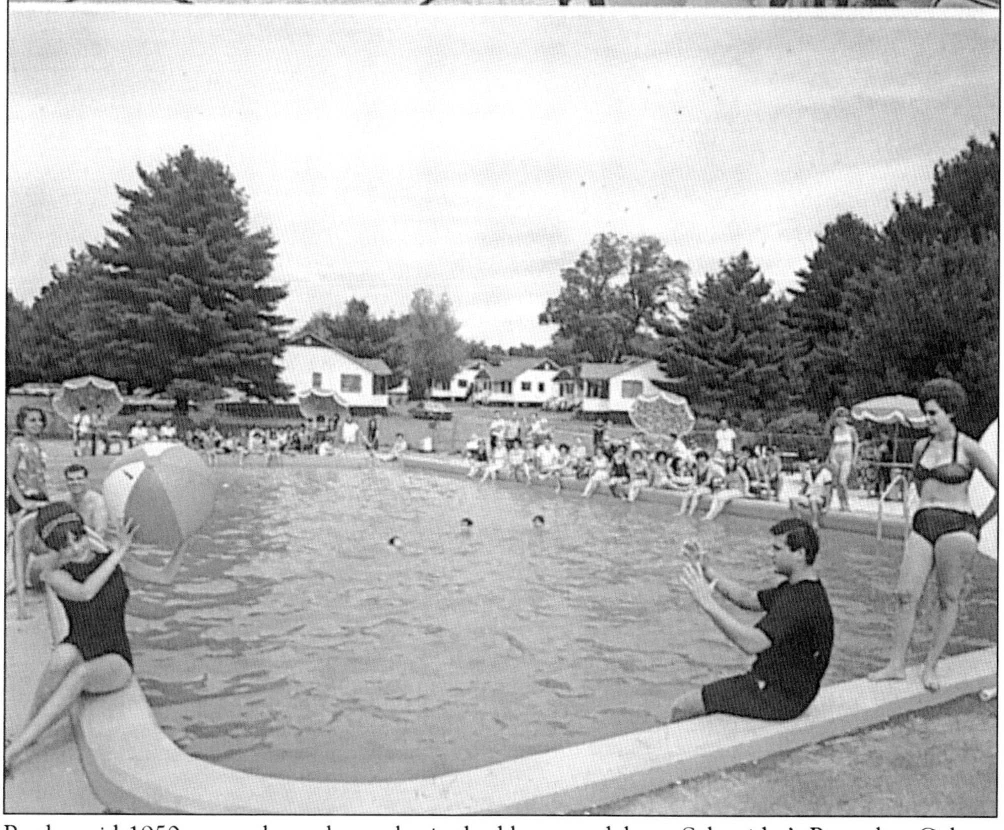

By the mid-1950s, some bungalow colonies had become deluxe. Schneider's Bungalow Colony in Monticello offered "A Modern Bungalow Colony—new air conditioners, cocktail lounge, two coffee shops, all-star Broadway entertainment, two bands, supervised day camp, two filtered pools, and private lake."

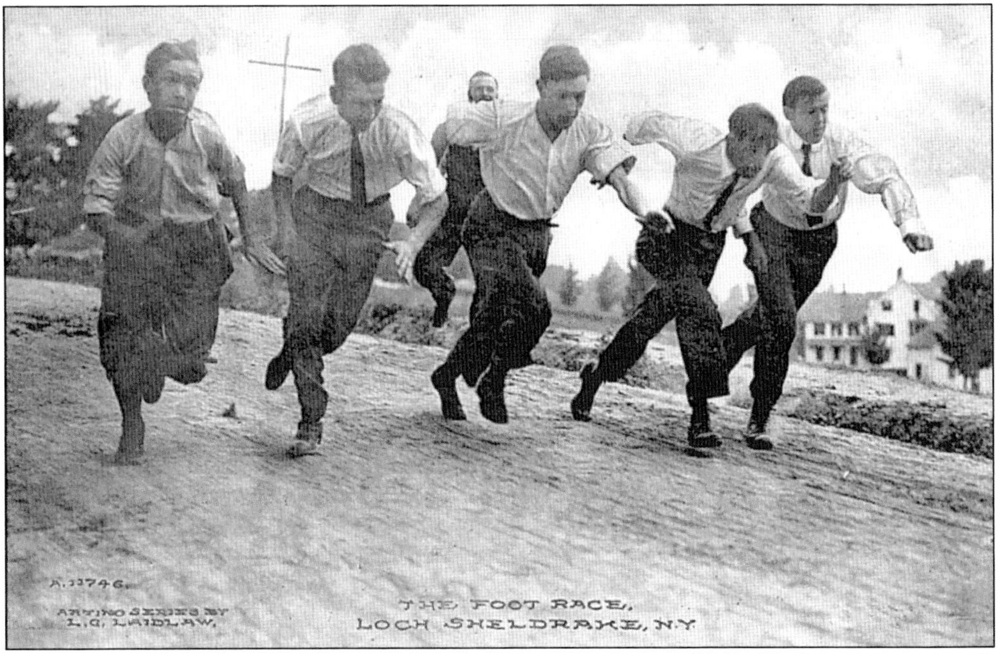

The cross in the background suggests that the "Foot Race" at Loch Sheldrake was at a church outing and is similar to an informal event beautifully depicted in the film *Chariots of Fire*. Note the absence of special athletic attire.

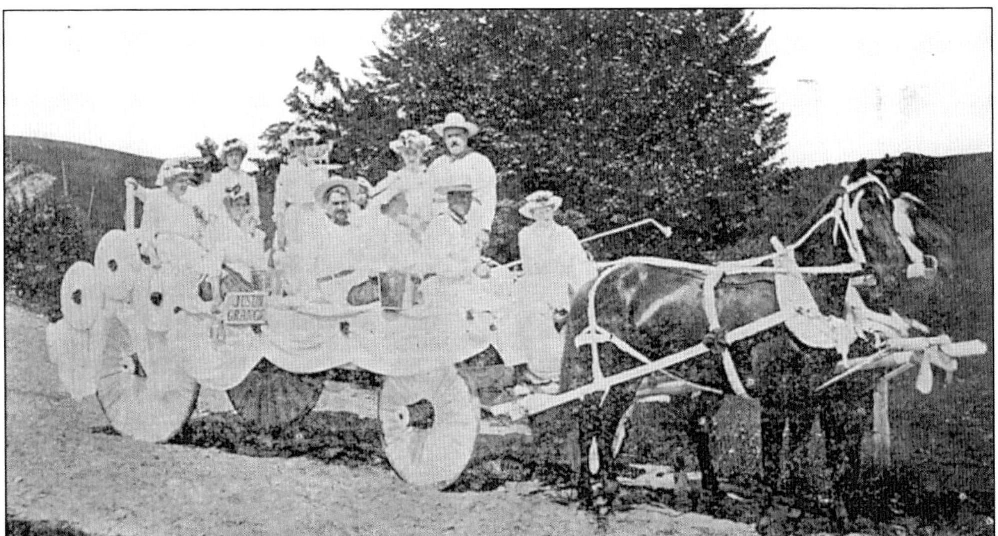

Local hotels and boardinghouses decorated their farm wagons and carriages, and passengers dressed up to be consistent with a theme, as in this 1905 card, for the resort festival called Coaching Day. Usually a parade was held along the village street.

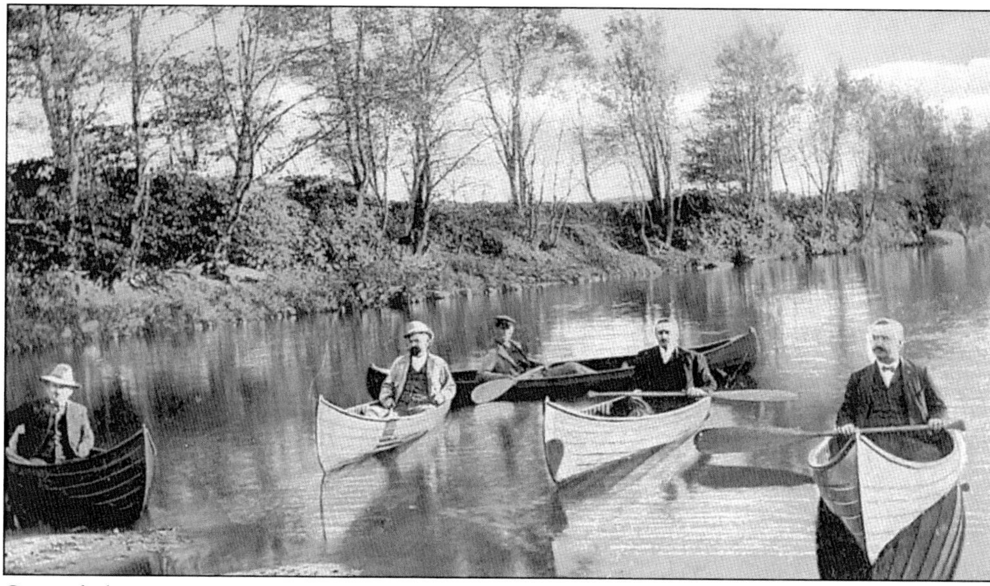

One of the most amusing canoeing cards shows these formally attired men, presumably Christian, paddling on the Neversink River in Woodbourne. Printed in Germany c. 1905, this popular postcard was issued in several editions.

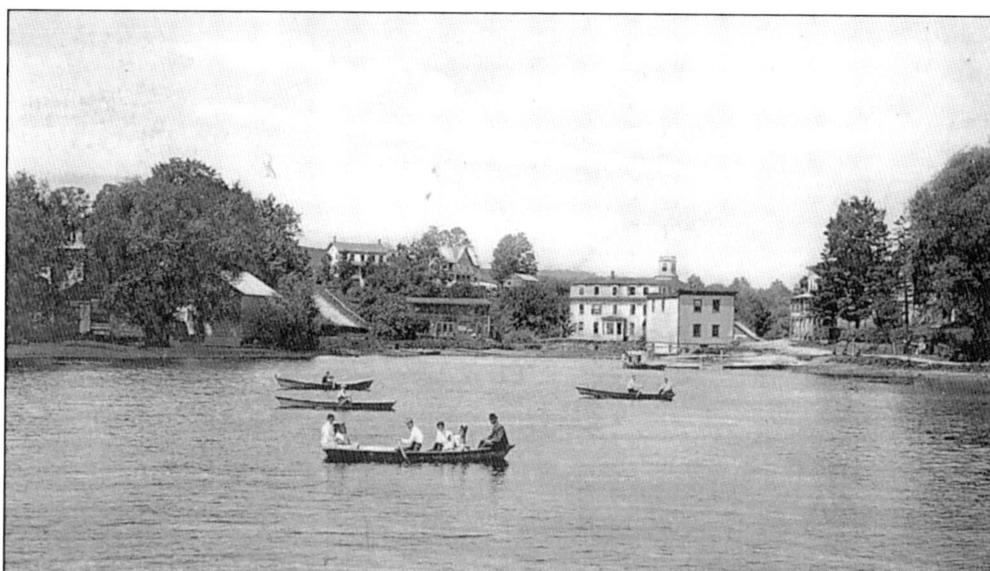

Like many Catskill lakes, Kenoza Lake was bordered by resorts, and vacationers spent a lot of time "On the Rippling Waters." It appears that the people in the front boat may have known that they were going to pose for a picture; the children, especially, are very dressed up.

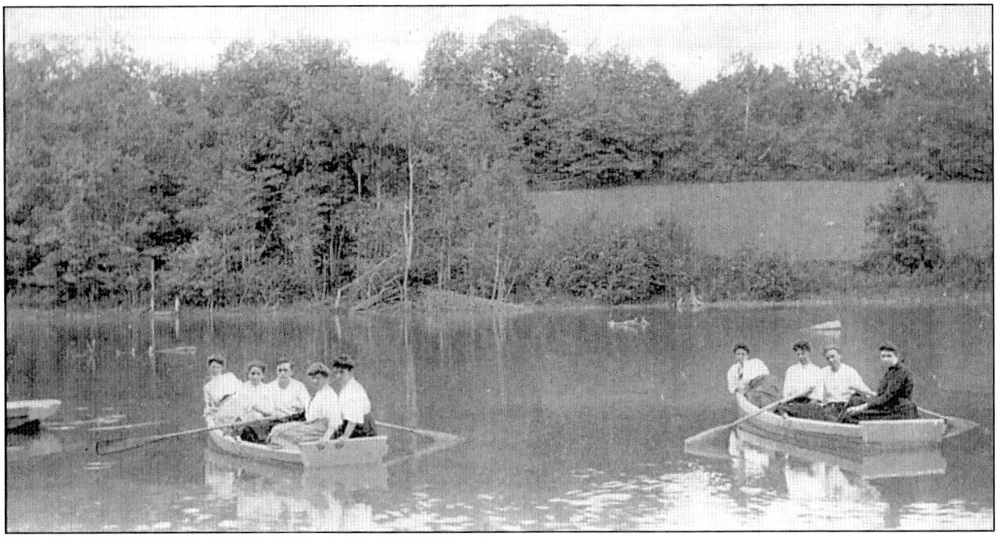

The odds were very much in favor of the women when they boated on Silver Like in 1907. Everyone is informally attired, and the men are wearing open shirts without collars. One woman, in the boat on the right, however, is wearing a tie.

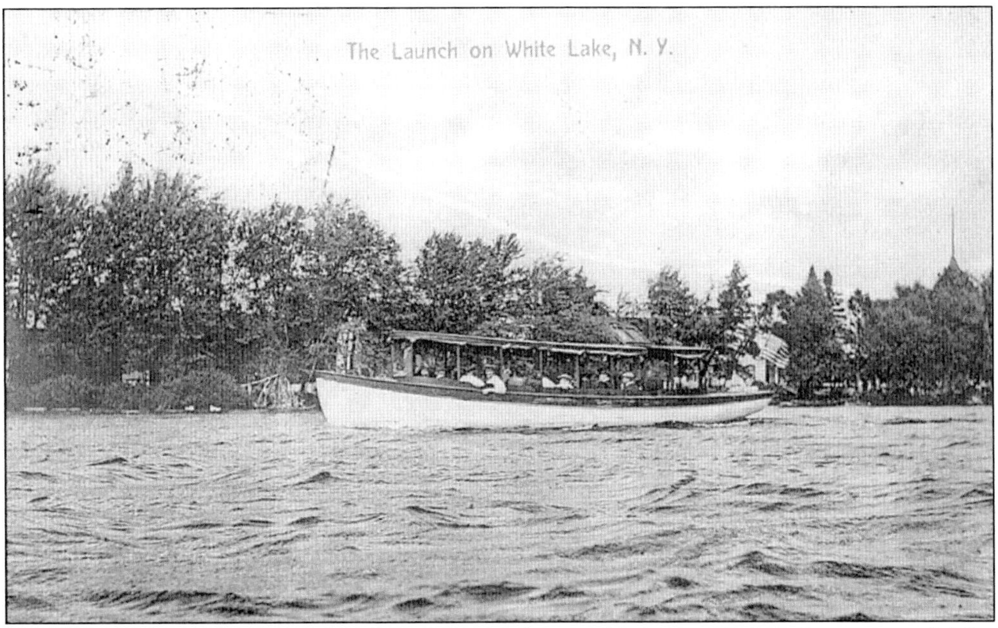

White Lake is named for its very clear water and its visible areas of white bottom sand. The *Queen* was a launch operated by Grey's Casino, a popular entertainment spot. The boat picked up vacationers at the private docks, which most of the lakeside resorts maintained.

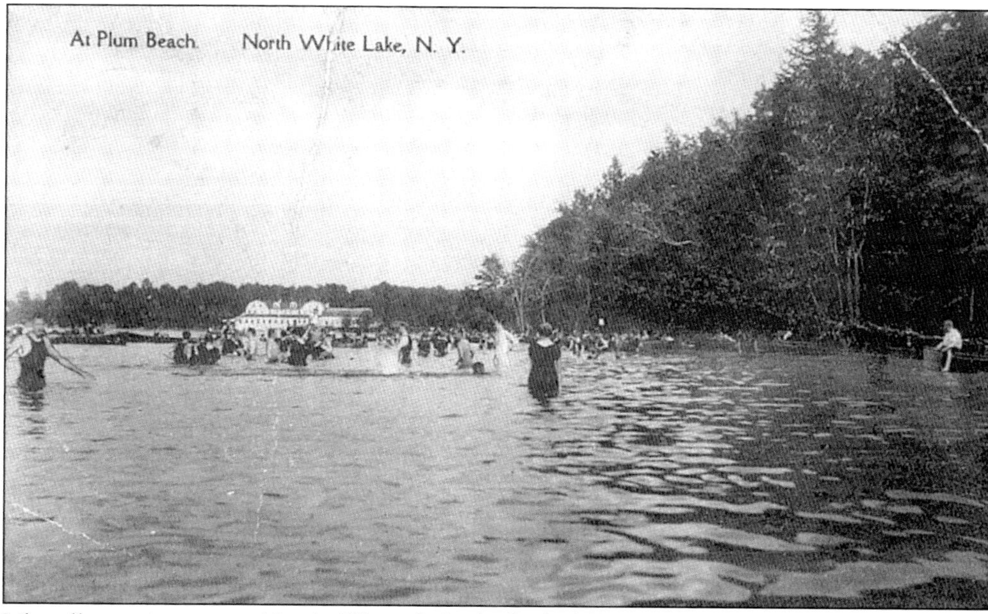

Like all vacation spots, North White Lake looked idyllic on postcards. In 1912, a sad Etta wrote, "Dear Esther, We have been up here two weeks and it has been raining everyday but two days! We expect to come home Monday." More conservative than the livelier White Lake nearby, North White Lake changed its name to Kauneonga Lake so that no one would confuse the two resorts.

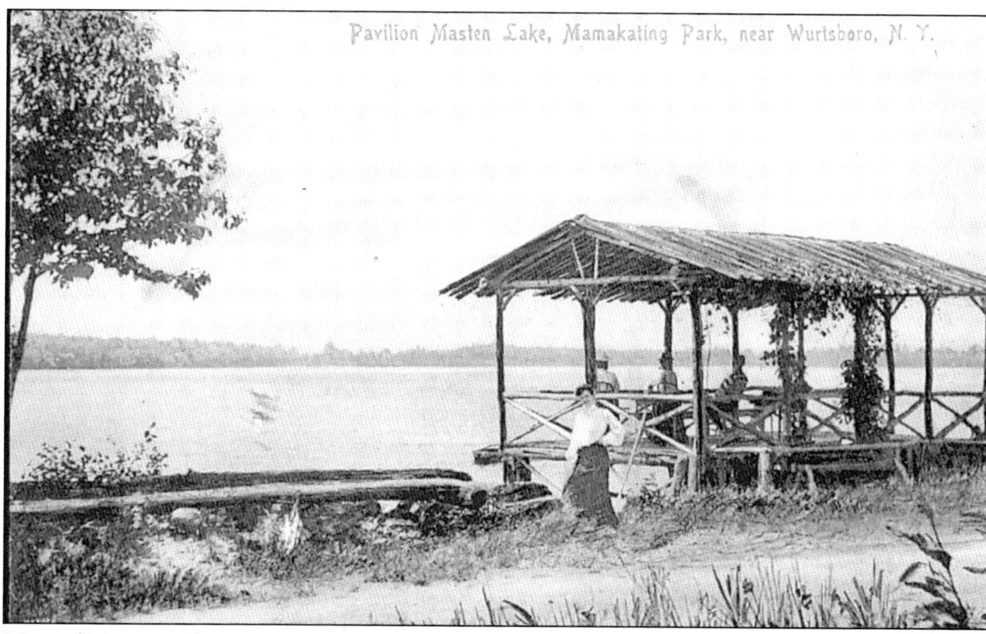

Most of Masten Lake was owned by the restricted and exclusive Sullivan County Club, chartered in July 1893. It was a popular stop for "the right kind" of people. Writing, in 1909, to a friend vacationing at Lake Hopatcong in New Jersey, Rose, who was staying at the nearby Mountain View House in Wurtsboro, noted, "Having a fine time we went here today on a straw ride. We were rowing on the Lake."

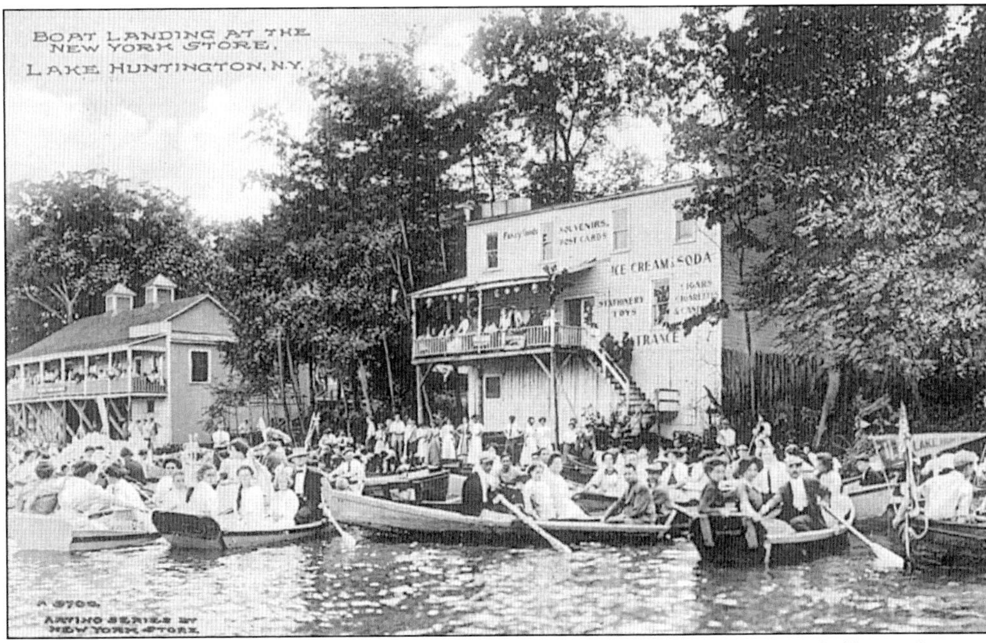

Every lake had its summer meeting place. At Lake Huntington in western Sullivan County, that place was the New York Store, which sold ice cream and sodas, as well as toys, souvenirs, and, of course, postcards. The flag on the porch of the building on the left suggests that the day might have been the Fourth of July.

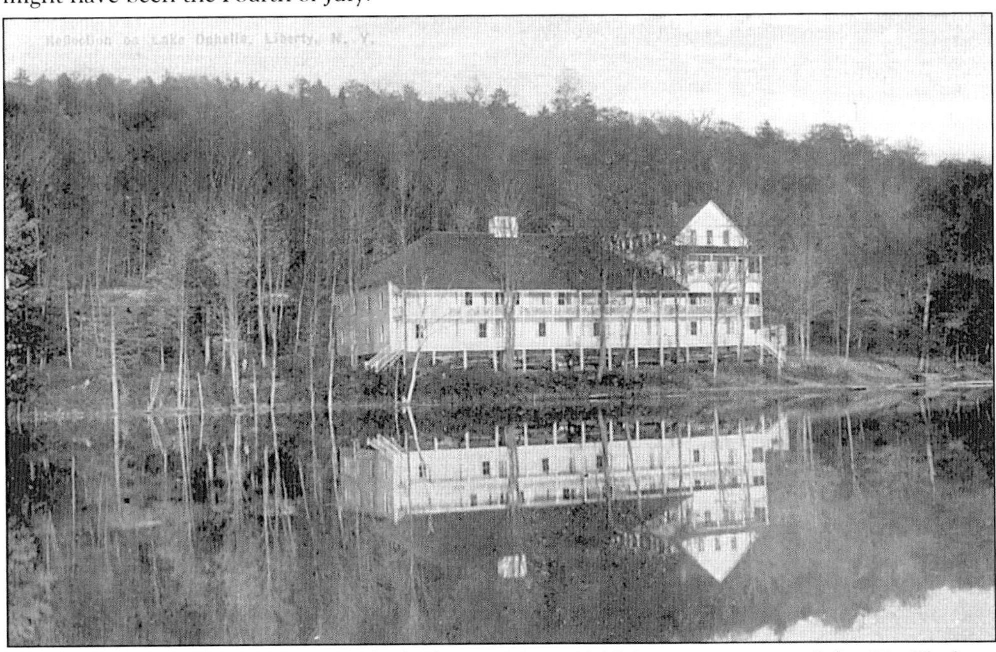

The Casino at Lake Ophelia was built from 1901to 1902 by entrepreneur John T. Clark to serve the guests of the many nearby resorts. It had the largest dance floor in the county, as well as eight bowling alleys and billiard and pool tables. It burned in October 1911. Lake Ophelia itself vanished when the Route 17 Quickway was built through it. This exhibited progress, Sullivan County style!

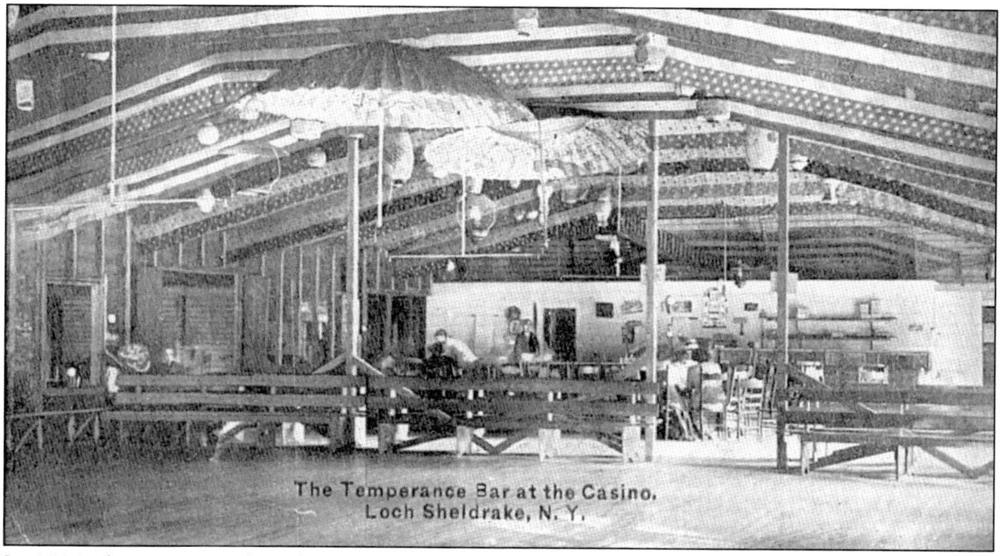

In 1906, there were 23 boardinghouses and farmhouses at Sheldrake (the Loch was added later, after railroad publicists decided it sounded better.). To extract money from summer people, H.M. LeRoy opened his Maple Grove Casino, which boasted the county's first bowling alley. LeRoy offered "free dancing in the casino every afternoon and evening except Sunday." In keeping with the sentiments of the time, the bunting-draped casino featured a temperance bar, which presumably served nonalcoholic beverages only.

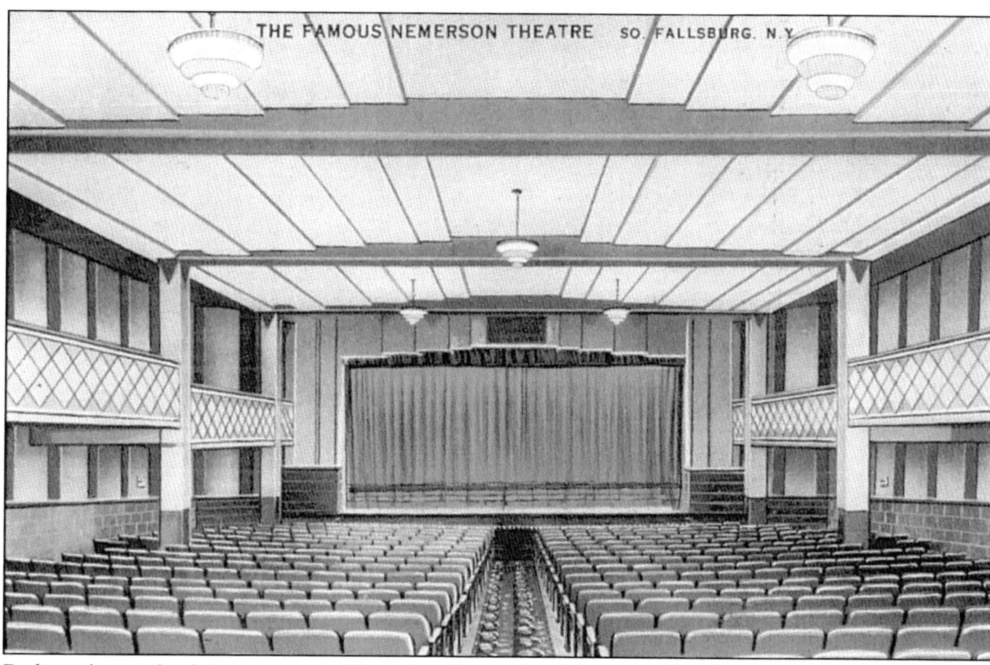

Before the nightclub age, several hotels of note had theatres for their guests' entertainment. The Nemerson's 1,000-seat house was one of the finest in the area. "Here, spectacular Broadway productions with a cast of radio, stage, and screen stars are presented on the large stage."

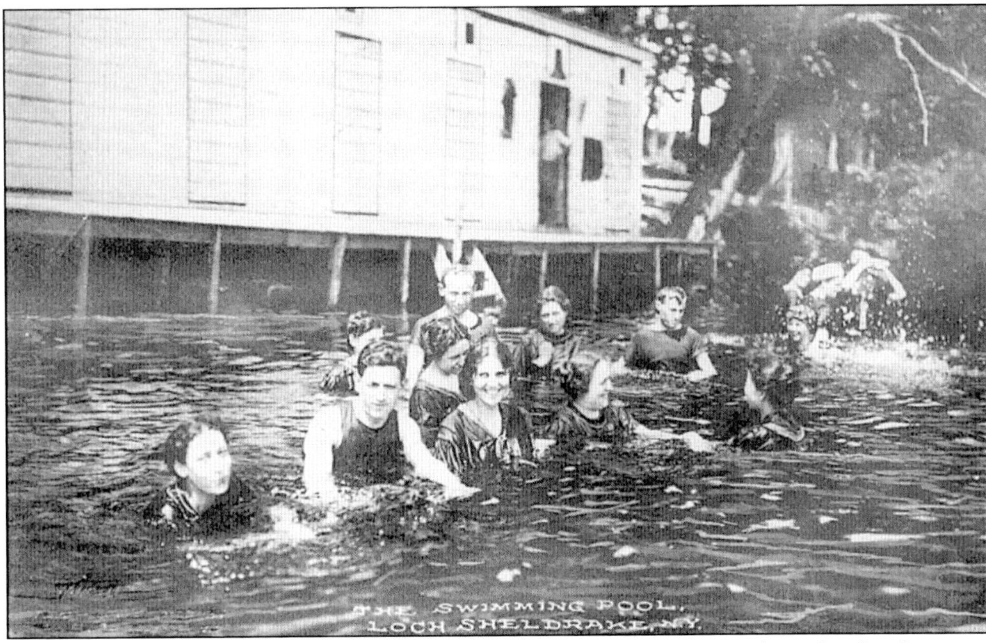

Tourism and swimming go hand in hand. These early-1900s visitors at the redundantly named Loch Sheldrake Lake splash in front of a bathhouse, constructed so that they were able to change into their swimsuits and then plunge right into the water. Mixed bathing and the invention of swimsuits were late-19th-century phenomena. A song of the late 1800s was entitled "I Love to Go Swimmin' with Women (and Women Love Swimmin' with Me)."

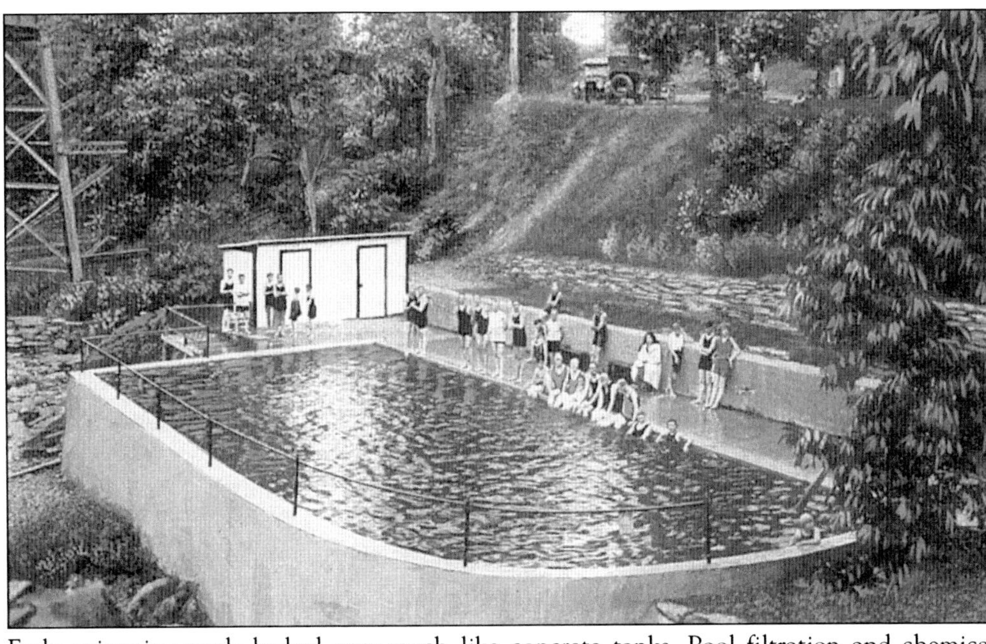

Early swimming pools looked very much like concrete tanks. Pool filtration and chemical treatment had not yet been perfected in the 1920s. Most places advertised their pools as being spring fed or artesian-well fed, and they relied on running water to keep them clean. Seldom clear, the pool water was usually green with algae.

Six

The Age of Glitz: Palaces for the Mostly Jewish People

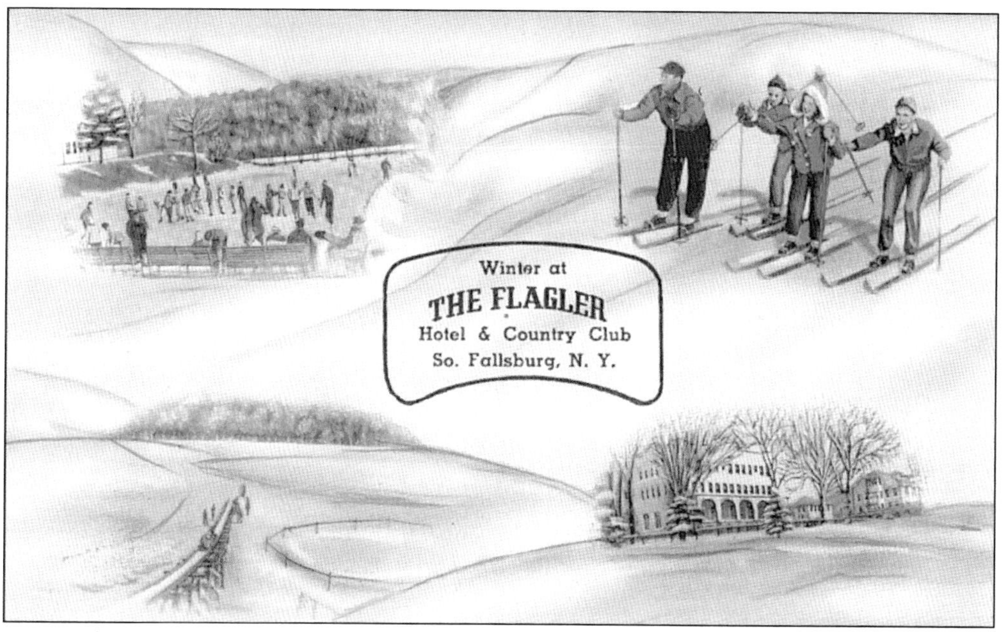

Despite legend, the Flagler had nothing to do with Standard Oil partner Henry Morrison Flagler. Rather it was named for Nicholas Flagler, a partner in the tannery at nearby Old Falls, by his daughter Carrie Flagler Angel, who founded the hotel in 1872. The 35-room Flagler House was purchased by Asias Fleisher and Philip Morgenstern in 1908. They turned it into the a resort that boasted a 1,500-seat theatre and the first in-room telephones in the Catskills. Additionally, the Flagler was one of the first Catskill resorts to open for winter sports.

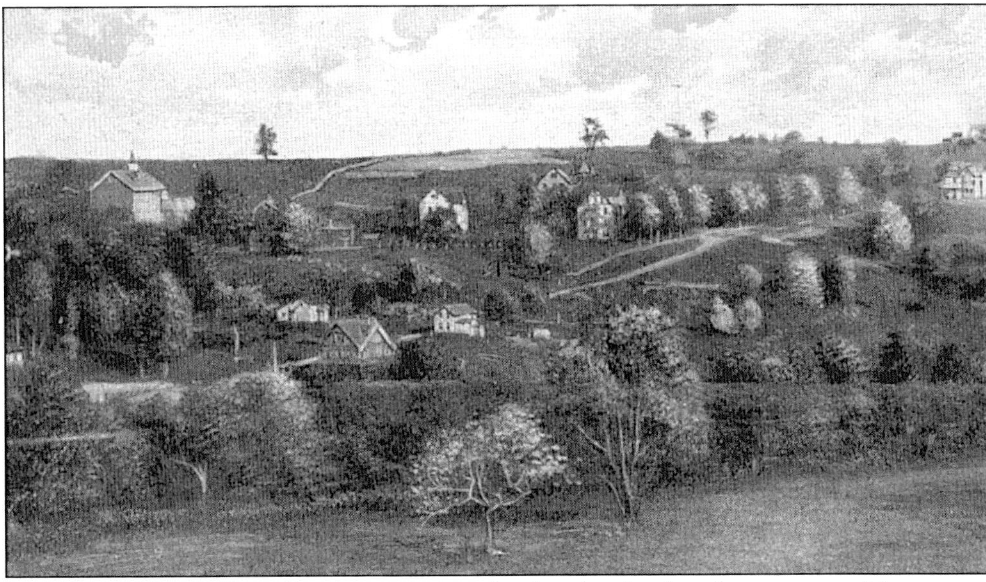

The Nichols was purchased by the Grossinger family, who developed it into one of the premier hotels of the Jewish Alps. This area was generally less scenic than the northern Catskills. Thus, early cards of hotels in the region concentrated on the buildings rather than the setting.

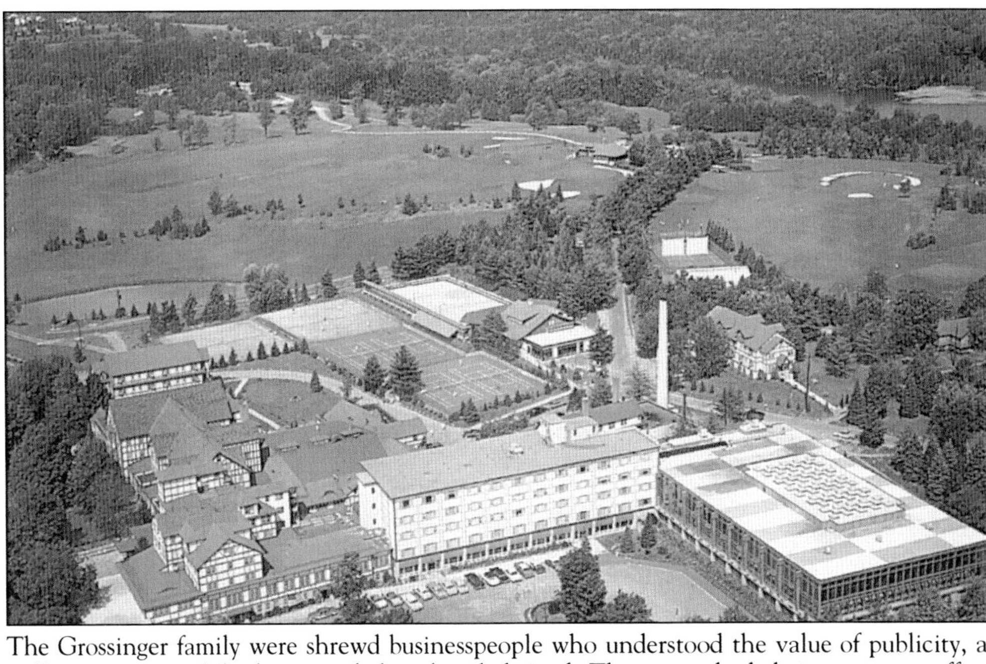

The Grossinger family were shrewd businesspeople who understood the value of publicity, as well as service and facilities, and their hotel thrived. They even had their own post office, "Grossinger, New York." Mailed in 1960, this card bears the classic message "Having a wonderful time here—Wish you were here too—."

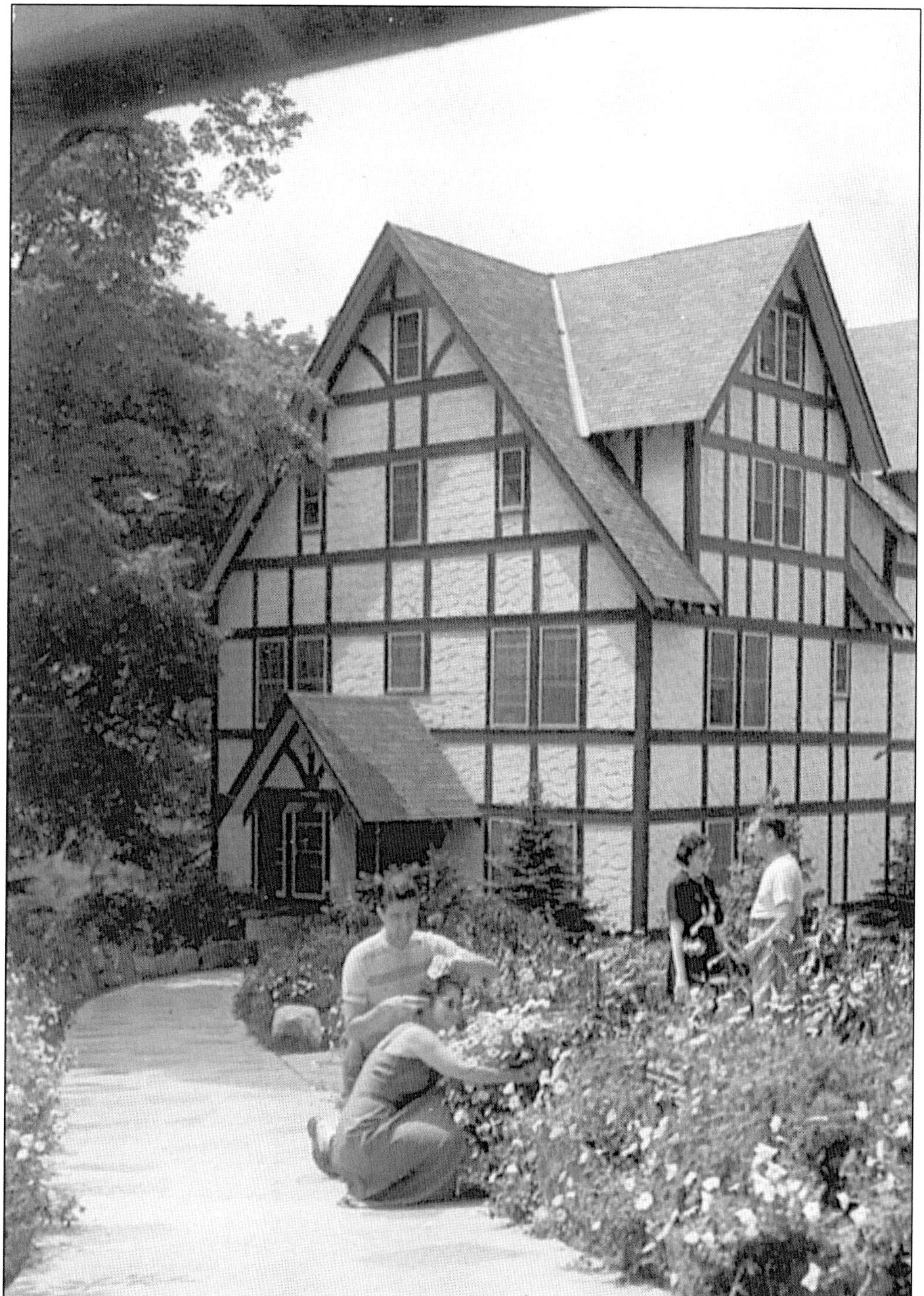

The pre–World War II architecture of Grossinger's was Olde English, a style which meant class to the new middle classes. Roosevelt House, in the background, was named in honor of the president so many American Jews revered. Contrary to this image, guests were not encouraged to pick the flowers.

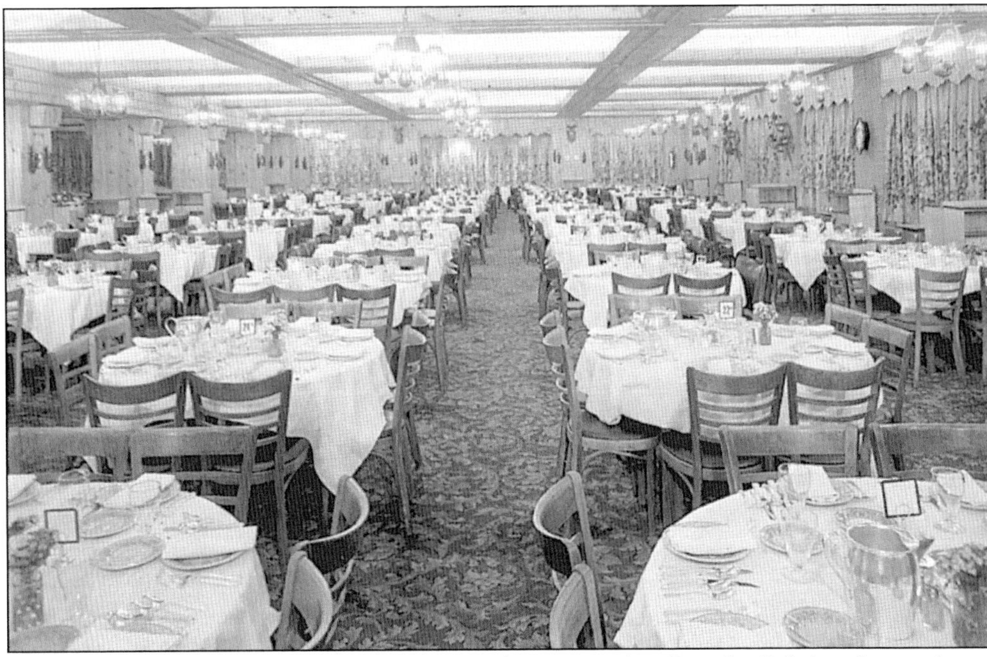

Eating was a prime pastime at Grossinger's and at most other Borscht Belt hotels, yet dining rooms were always shown empty. As one wag observed "no one wanted to show the scenes of gluttony and destruction." Mailed in 1974, this card's message includes a bit of gastronomic news: "Only accident is a cut over my eye caused by flying cork for Cold Duck bottle."

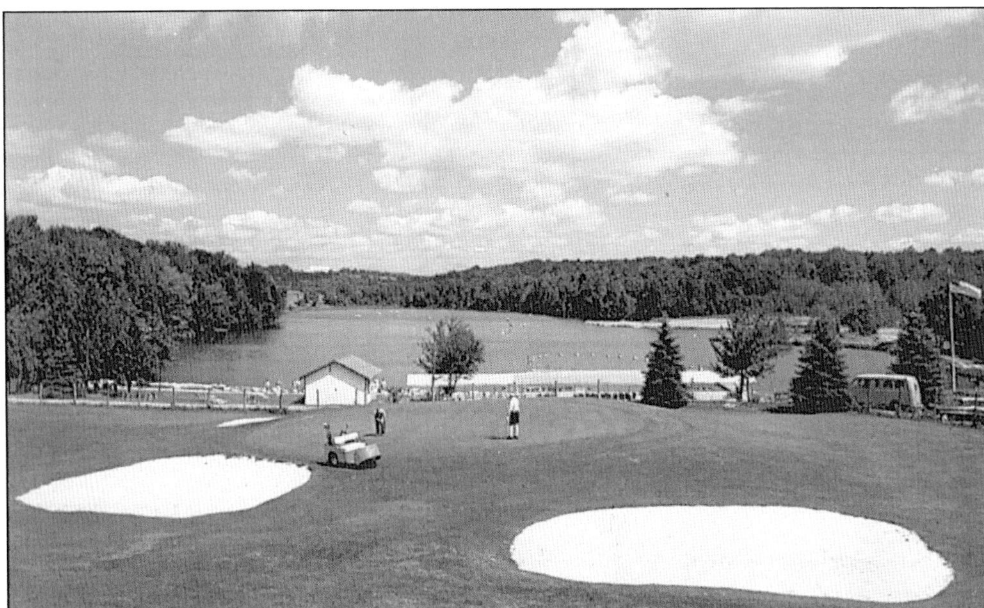

Grossinger's was justly famed for its glorious golf course on the shore of Grossinger Lake. After the hotel went into bankruptcy, Grossinger's was purchased by a Korean businessman who ran it as a golf-oriented resort for his countrymen. He, too, went bankrupt, leaving the future of Grossinger's uncertain.

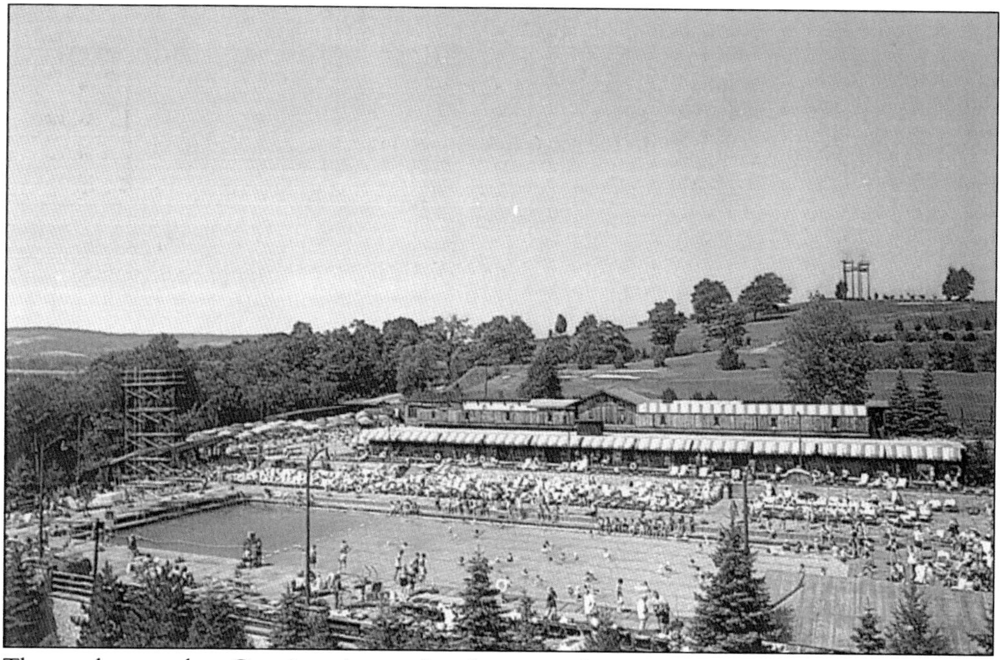

The outdoor pool at Grossinger's was the place to gather on a warm summer day. The pool had extensive cabanas and dining facilities and numerous chaise lounges and umbrella-shaded tables. As always, very few swimmers were in the huge pool.

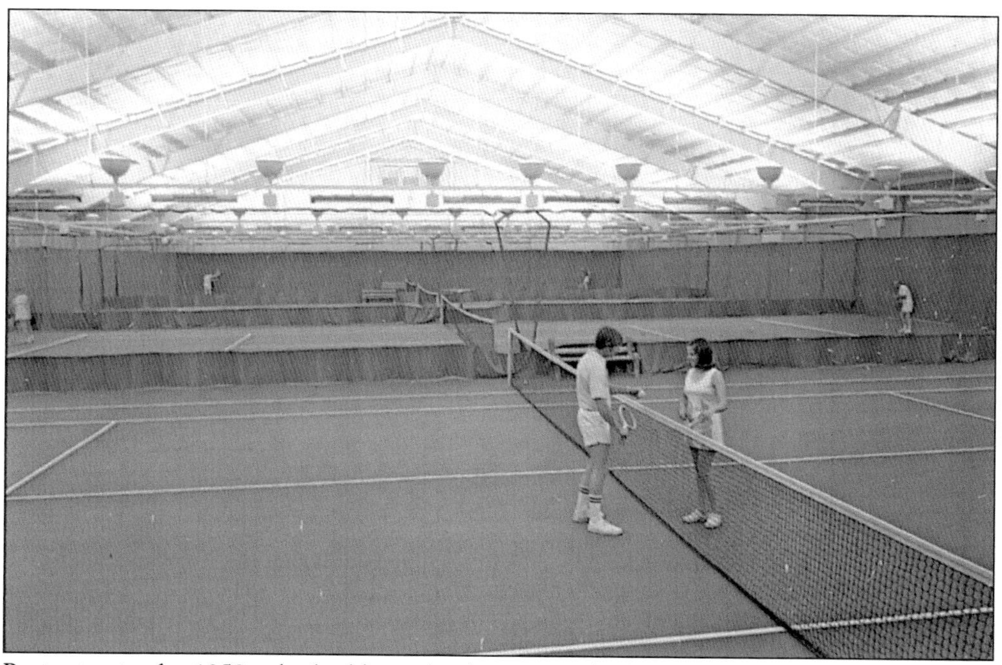

Beginning in the 1950s, the building of indoor sports facilities became especially important. Grossinger's and its chief rival, the Concord, led the way. Indoor pools, ice rinks, and tennis courts were a must. The new Grossinger motto was simple: "Grossinger's Has Everything."

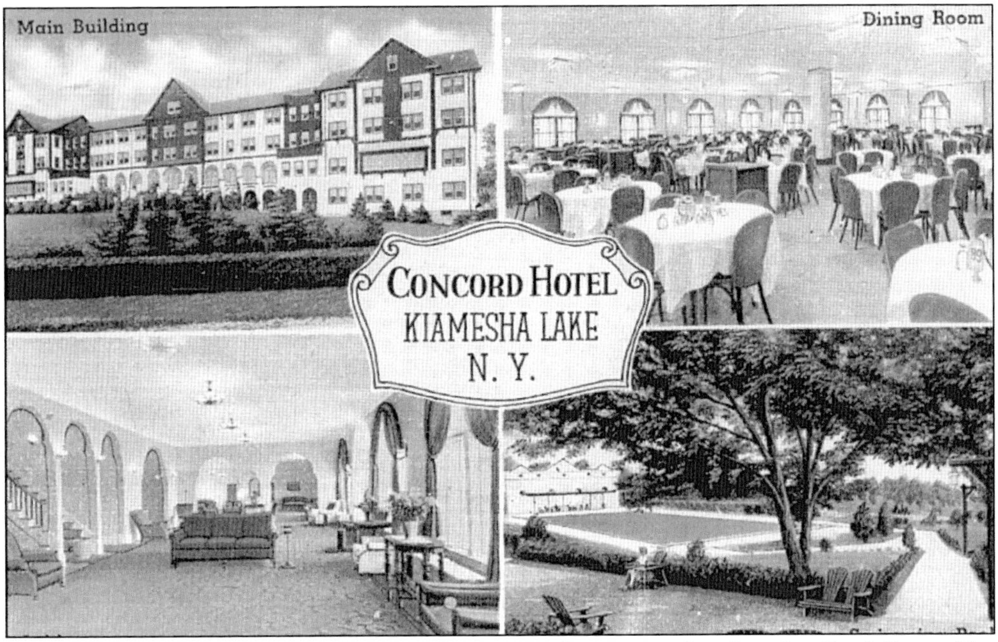

Arthur Winarick had a vision. He wanted to create the greatest hotel in the Catskills, and he did. Russian-born, he made a fortune with Jerris Hair Tonic and other toiletries and cosmetics. Buying the Kiamesha Ideal Hotel, he rebuilt it as the Concord Plaza. By 1941, it was being advertised as the Concord, with accommodations for 800 guests. The resort soon developed a loyal following. The message on this 1945 card reads, "Here we are once again & as usual having a grand time."

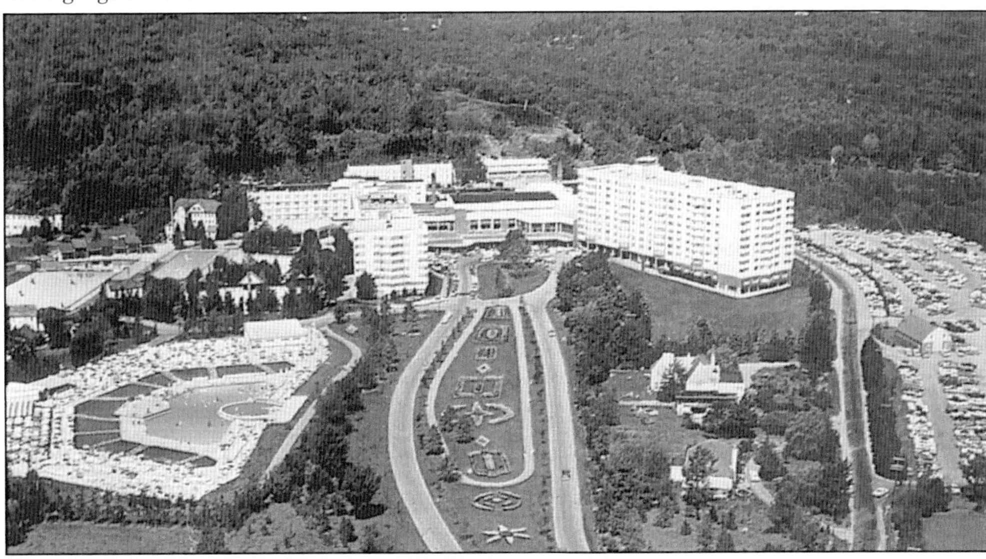

The Concord was the most ostentatious and largest Borscht Belt hotel. Originally a more modest structure in the Tudor Revival style, the hotel was transformed into a mammoth international-style extravaganza by architect Morris Lapidus, famous for Miami Beach's Fountainbleu Hotel. Slick, showy, and impersonal, it was the model for many modern resorts. The Concord went bankrupt and closed in 1998 and was then purchased by a franchise of the Sheraton Hotel Corporation, with plans for extensive remodeling and redevelopment.

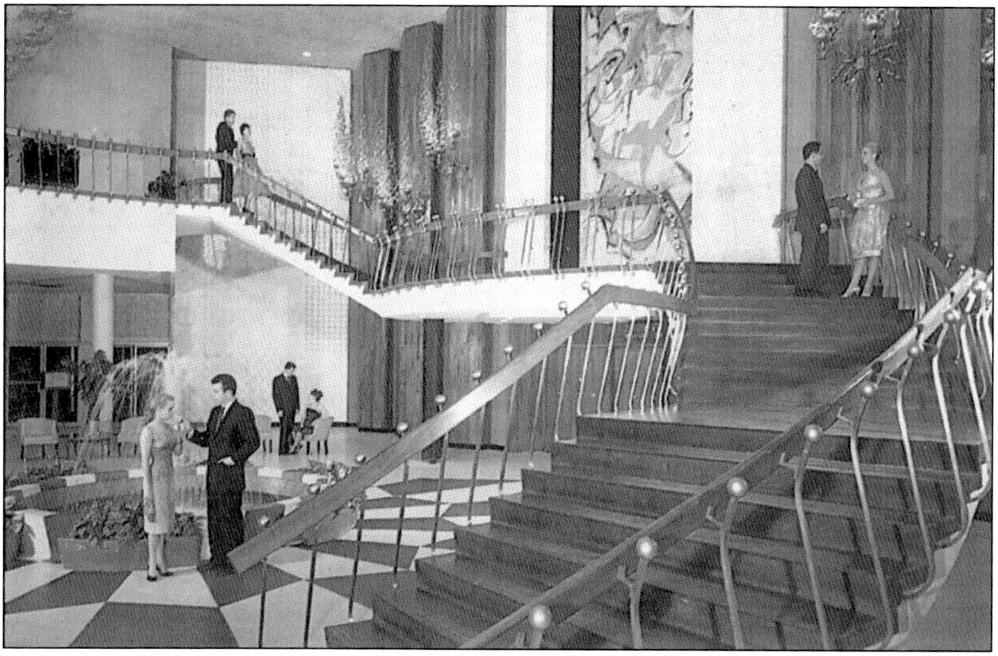

The lobby of the Concord included the famous "Stairway to Nowhere." Guests took the elevator to the mezzanine and then made their grand entrance down the stairs, always a popular exercise during the gaudy years. In the lobby, near the stairs, a jewelry kiosk sold impressive, real baubles on weekends—right in the open, where an appreciative audience could watch buyers flaunt their roll of bills and their new acquisitions.

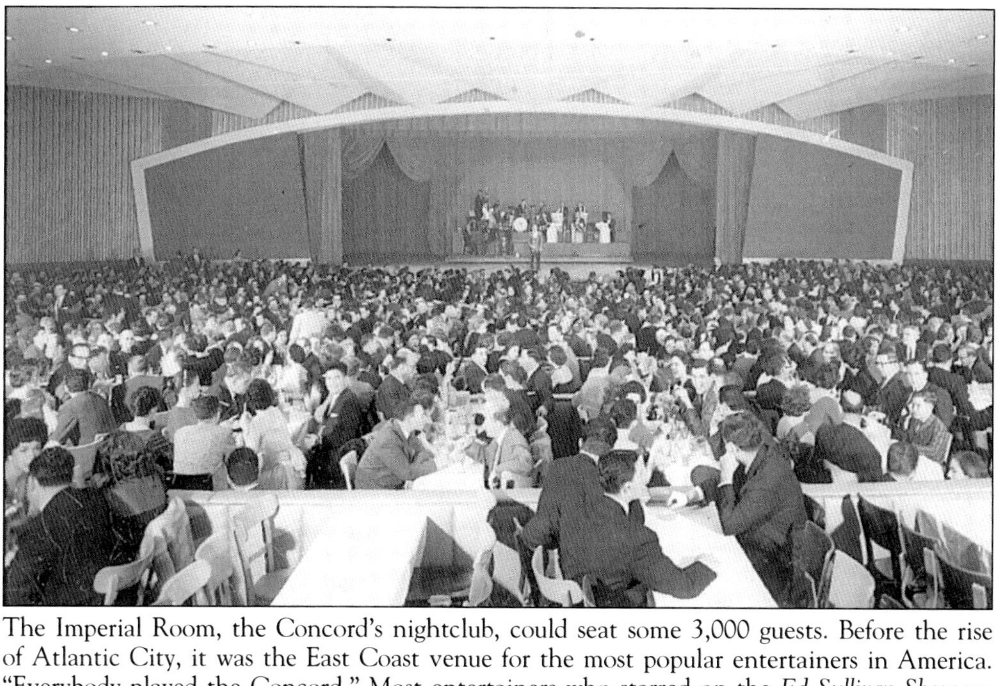

The Imperial Room, the Concord's nightclub, could seat some 3,000 guests. Before the rise of Atlantic City, it was the East Coast venue for the most popular entertainers in America. "Everybody played the Concord." Most entertainers who starred on the *Ed Sullivan Show* on television appeared at the Concord on a Saturday night.

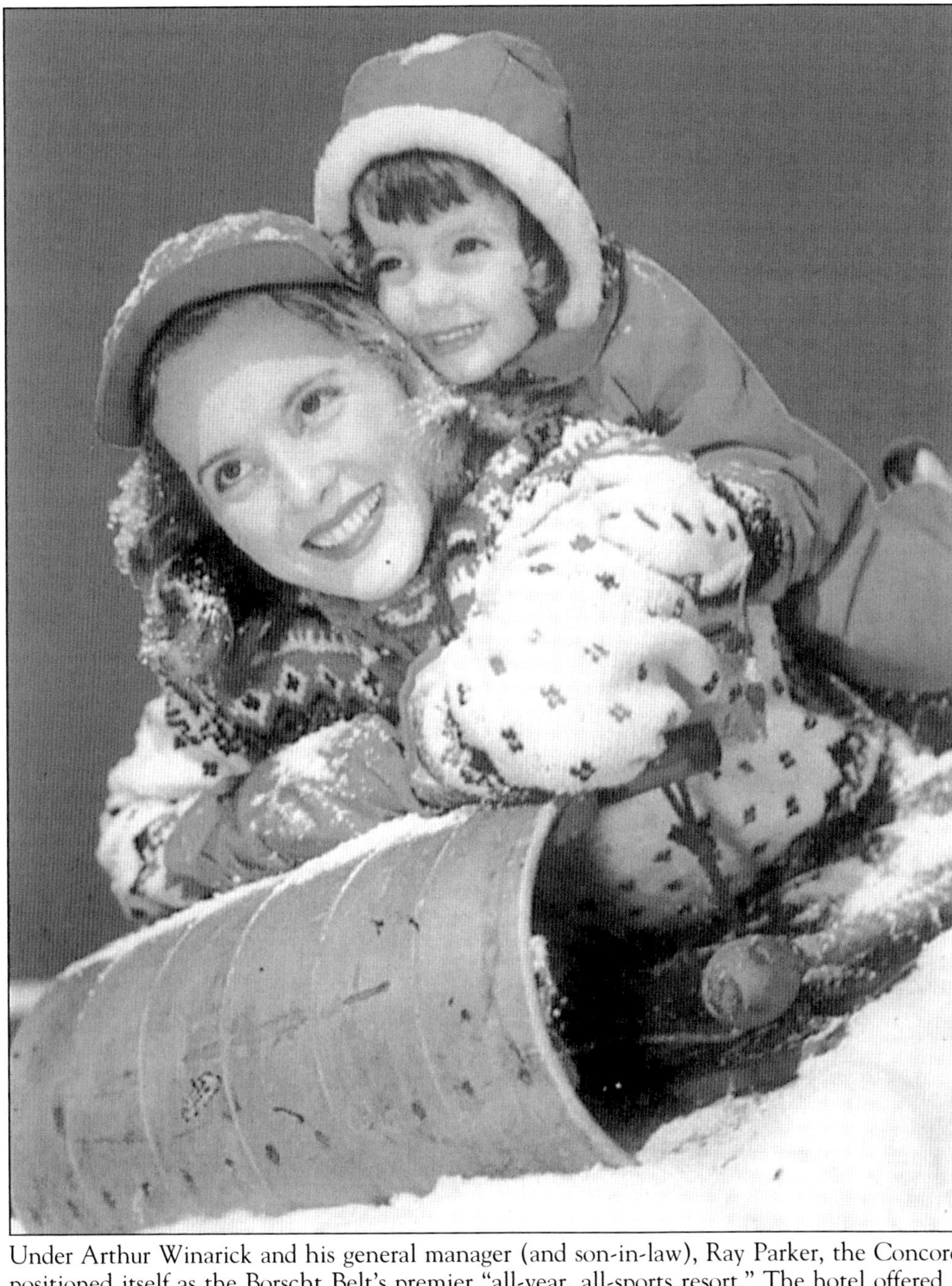

Under Arthur Winarick and his general manager (and son-in-law), Ray Parker, the Concord positioned itself as the Borscht Belt's premier "all-year, all-sports resort." The hotel offered a variety of ski slopes and a ski chalet, as well as indoor and outdoor ice rinks. From the 1960s, Borscht Belt hotels tried very hard to increase their customer base. While still kosher, resorts like the Concord emphasized their wholesome all-American image. This card, touting tobogganing and sledding, for example, could also represent Sun Valley, Idaho, or Vail, Colorado.

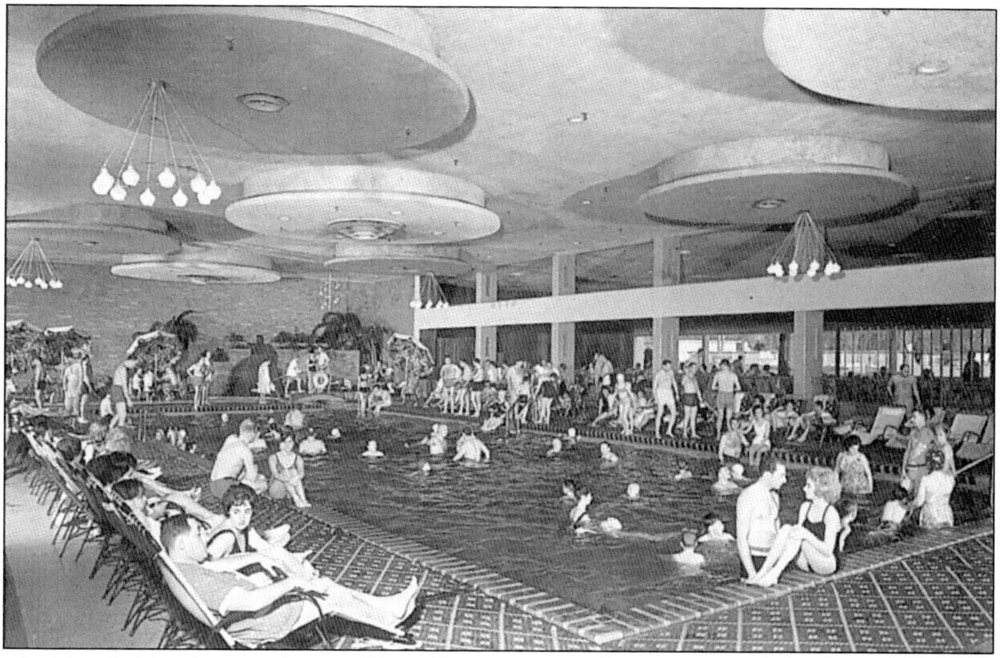

The Nevele Hotel, situated near Ellenville in a spectacular site, ignored the beautiful scenery and concentrated on lavish interiors, from a cavernous high-style 1950s lobby to an unusually busy indoor pool and a nightclub called the Stardust Room. The hotel was sold and renamed the Nevele Grande in 1998. The new owners are attempting to reposition the hotel in the market as an ethnically neutral sports resort, emphasizing its beautiful location and its championship golf courses. The Slutsky family, who owned both the Nevele and the adjacent Fallsview Hotel, and the Kutsher family of South Fallsburg are part of a very small Borscht Belt elite who were able to maintain viable resort businesses into the 1990s.

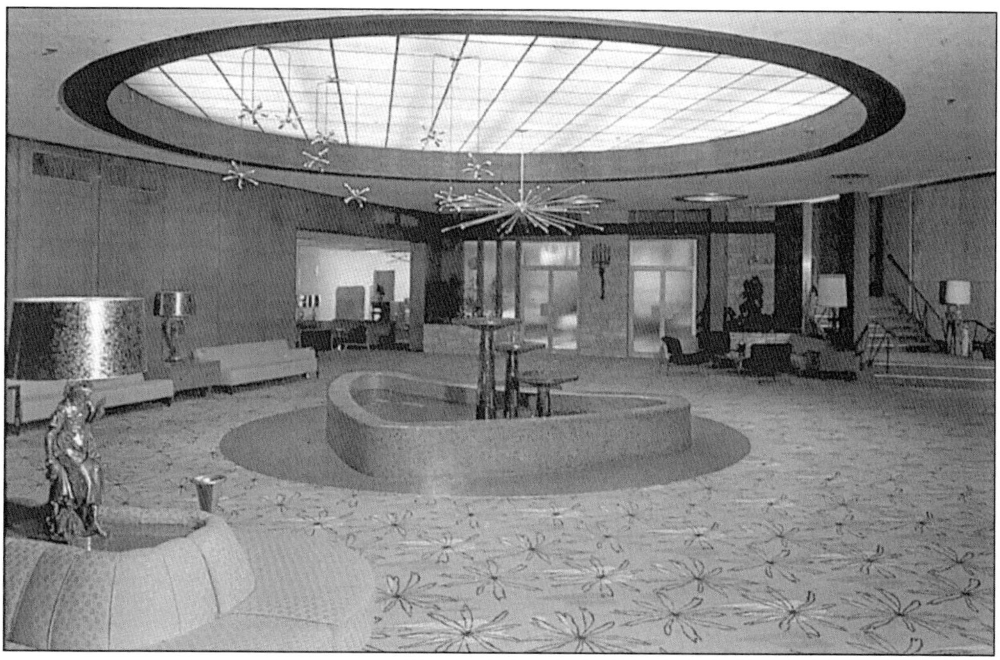

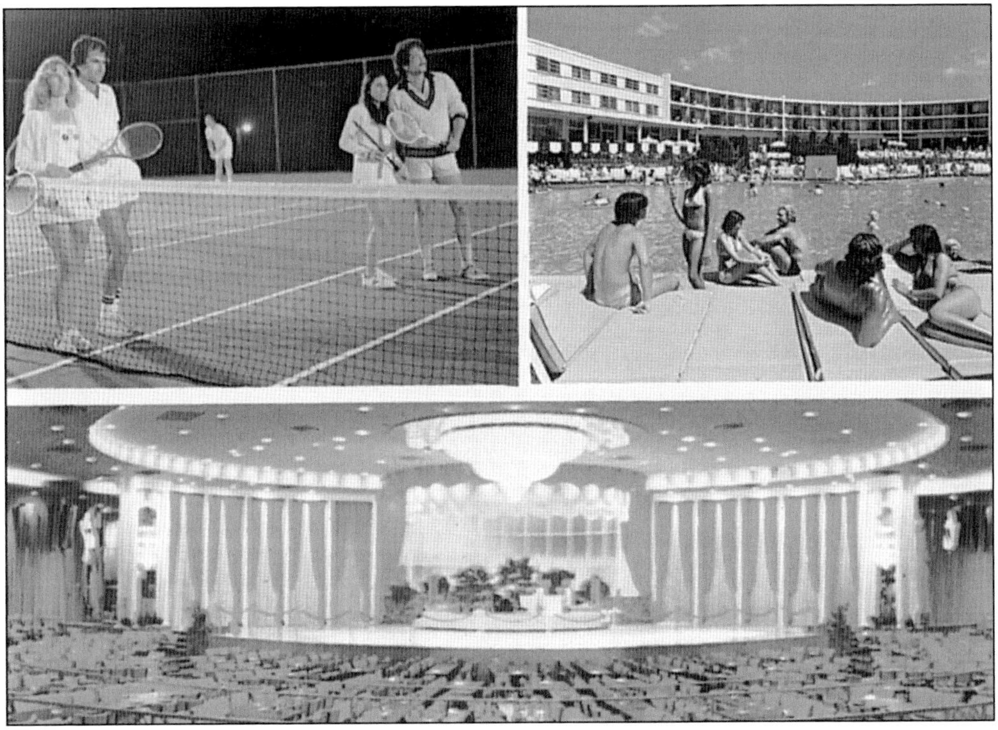

Brown's Hotel was, perhaps, the most impressive of the runner-up hotels. Lillian Brown really wanted to be Jennie Grossinger, who had become the Borscht Belt's only bona fide celebrity hotel owner. Located in a singularly unpicturesque setting, Brown's was lavish and glittery. It emerged from bankruptcy and, under new ownership, was converted into condominium apartments.

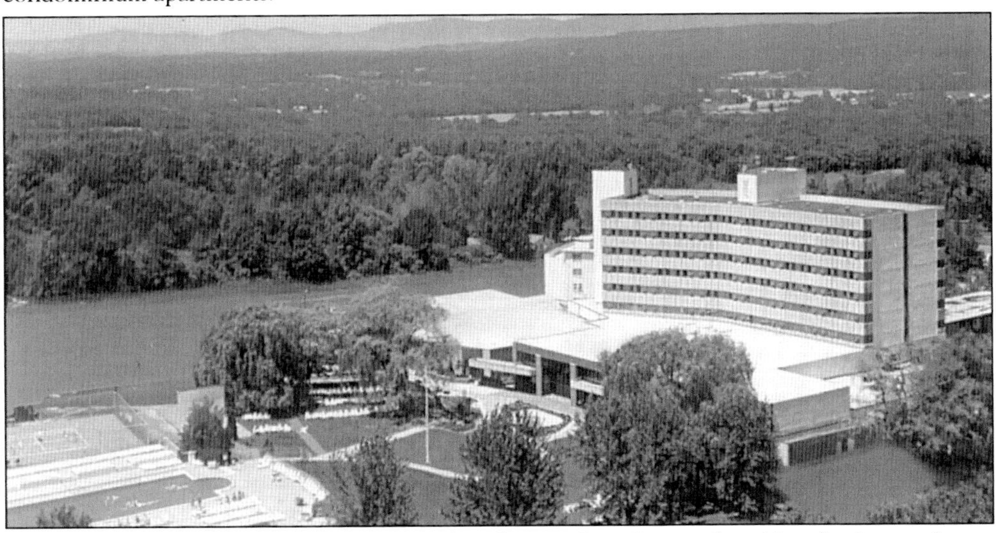

The Granit Hotel in Kerhonkson wanted to be another Concord or Nevele. Located in a beautiful setting, the Granit is visible from the Lake Mohonk Mountain House, over on one of the distant mountains. After going into bankruptcy in 1997, the Granit emerged "fresh from a $25 million renovation" as the Hudson Valley Resort Spa, "the jewel of the Catskills." Hyperbole lives on.

Seven

Tourists Welcome: What You See Is Not Always What You Get

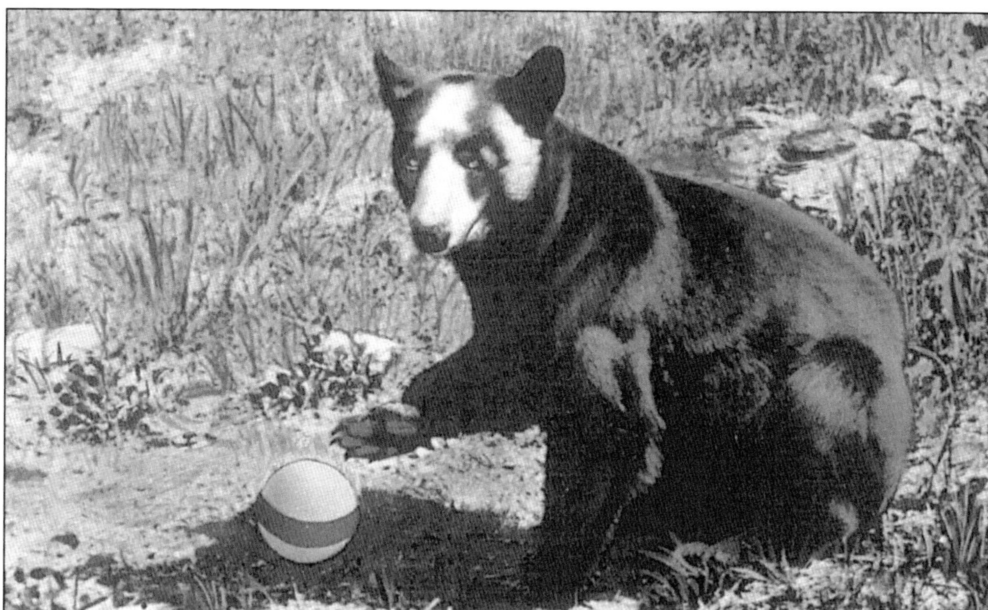

Very few Catskill summer people ever saw a bear. The photograph for this image was probably taken in the Rockies. Enhanced by the inclusion of the ball (Note there is no shadow on the top.), this card was published in Boston. Widely distributed, the same postcard, with different legends, has been sold on Skyline Drive in Virginia, and elsewhere.

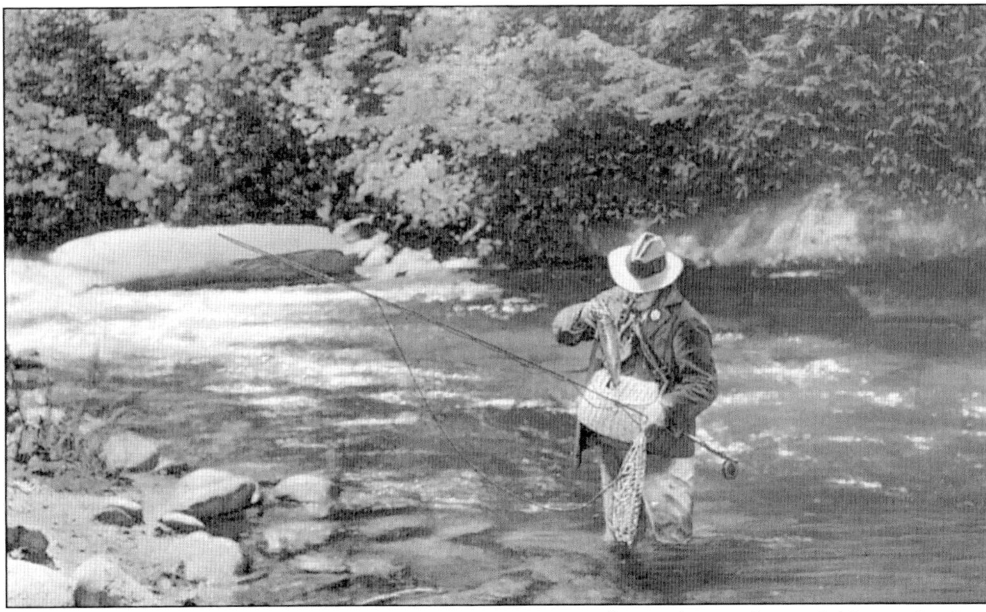

By the 1940s, the age of localism was vanishing, especially in the cards available in the less-picturesque parts of the southern Catskills. Production of these cards was often centralized in large printing plants, sometimes in distant cities. The Fisherman Card, probably showing a Rocky Mountains scene (with an illustration based on a U.S. Forest Service photograph), was published in Chicago.

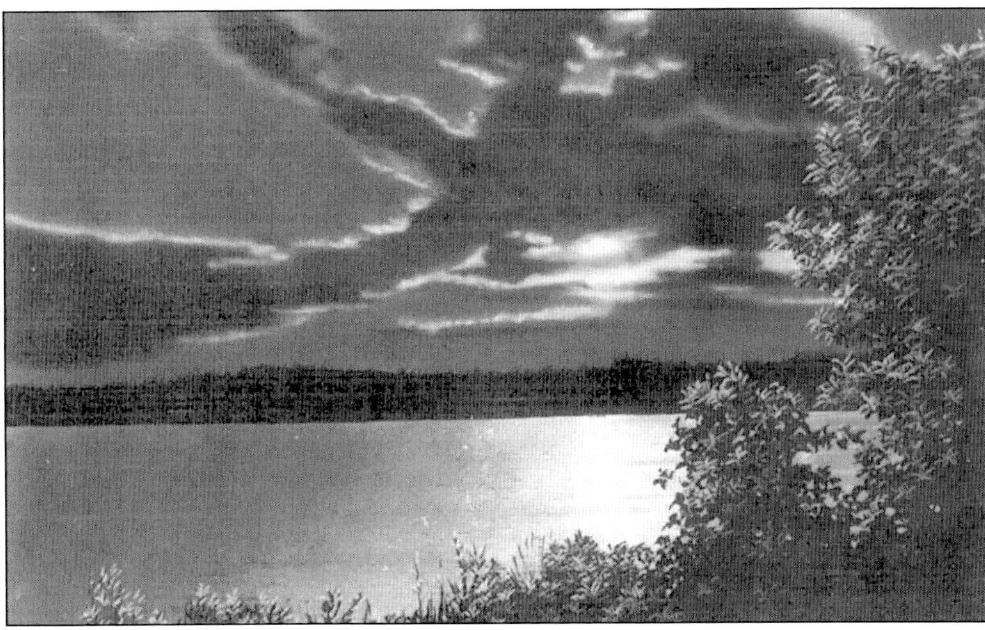

Purporting to show Kiamesha Lake, this 1940s image is a stock photograph, probably of New England origin, employed by a Boston Company. The author also owns the same card bearing the legend "Greetings from Woodbourne, N.Y." The poetic correspondent who mailed the Kiamesha card on September 5 wrote, "The trees are beginning to change color and soon this place will be a fairyland."

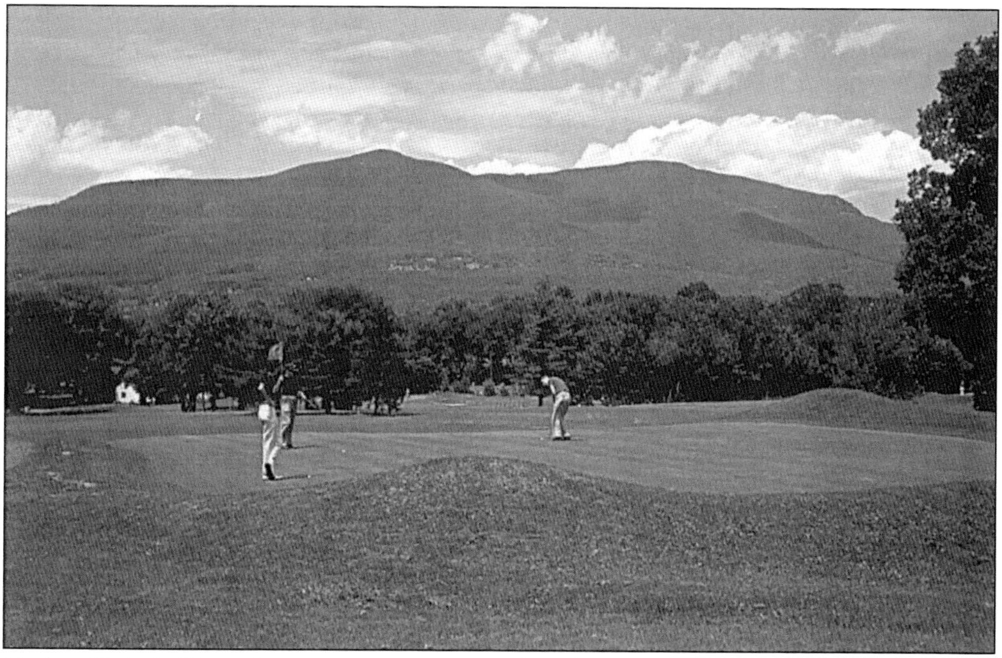

Hurleyville in Sullivan County is not very scenic, but these two cards claiming to be Hurleyville compensate for that. The golf course is, in reality, at the base of Overlook Mountain, outside of Woodstock. The Delaware River view was photographed near Pond Eddy, New York. Pennsylvania is across the river from western-most Sullivan County. Both cards were published in Delhi, New York.

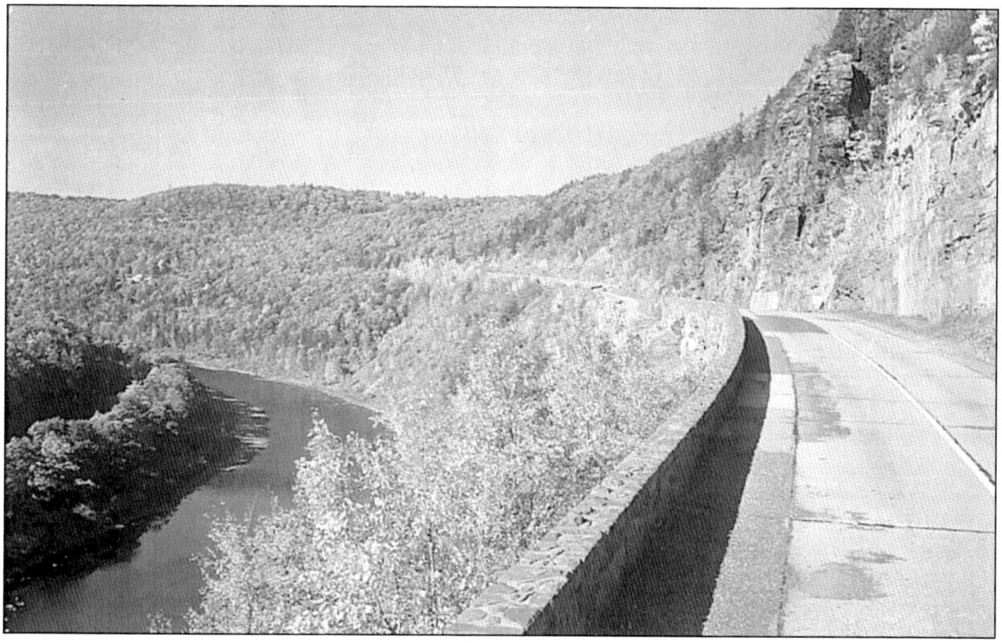

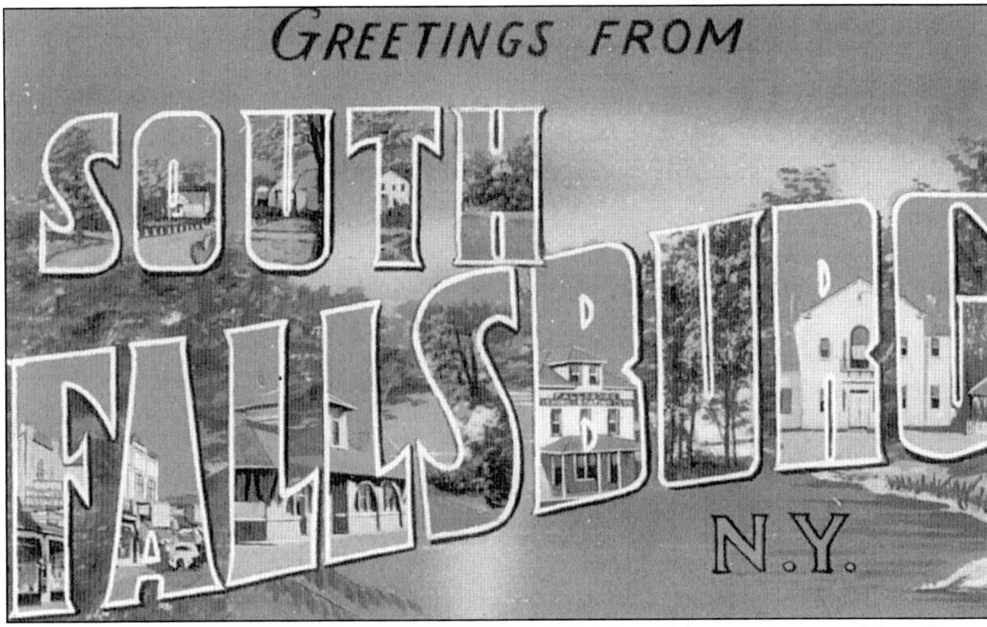

This composite card based on a series of views of South Fallsburg was created locally and published by M. Glusker and Son of Ellenville. Snippets of the railroad station are seen in the "l's" and the Community Center in "R & G."

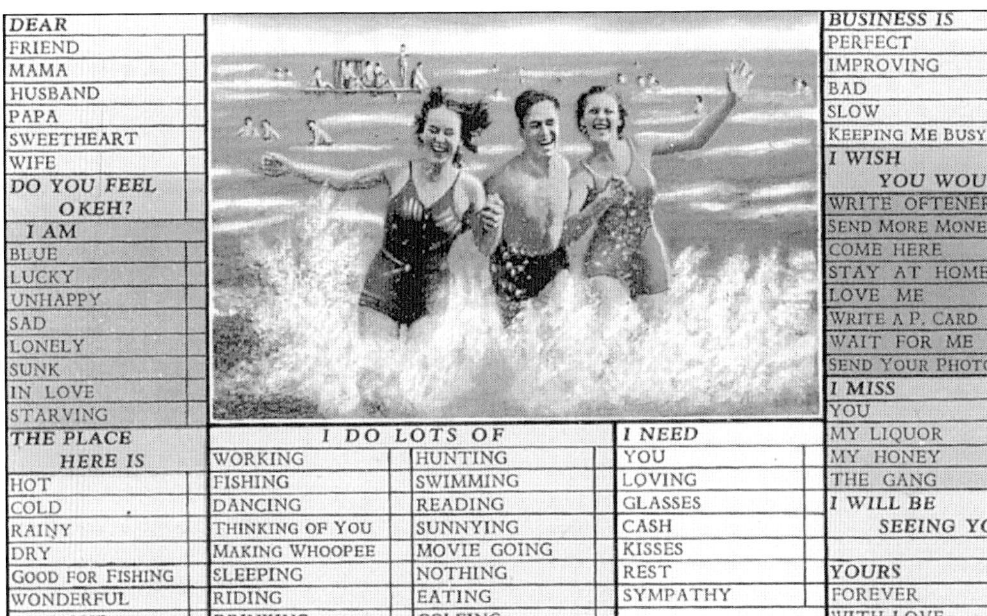

"By the Sea, By the Beautiful Sea," but tiny Hasbrouck, whose legend this card bears, is on the very modest Neversink River in Sullivan County. The card was printed in the 1940s by Curteich in Chicago and was widely distributed as originating in many resorts.

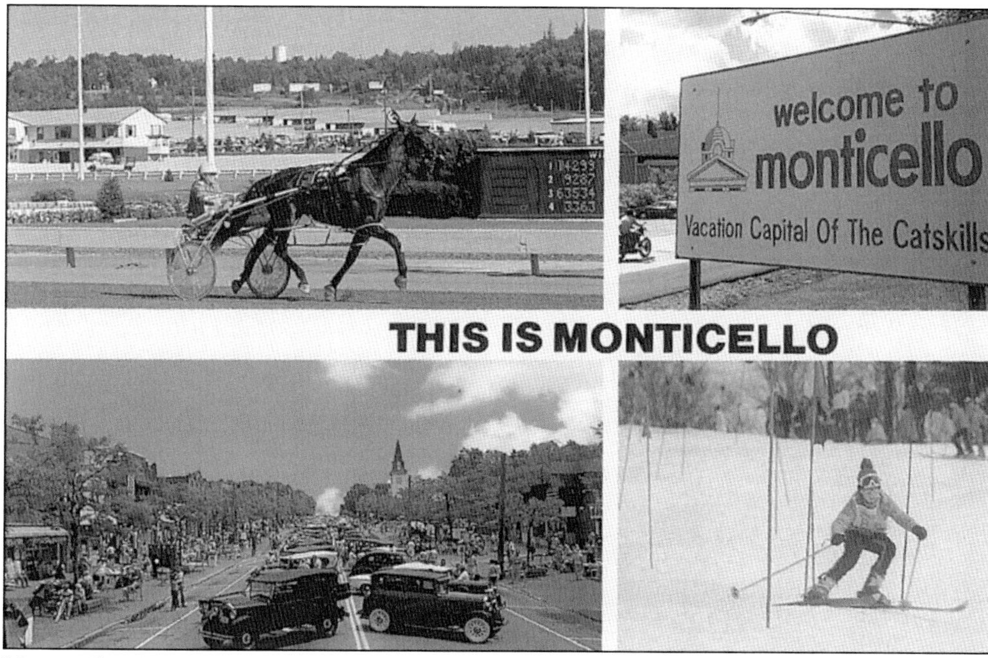

Monticello, "Vacation Capital of the Catskills," is in a perpetual state of excitement in this 1960s composite card. Feeling the effects of a declining resort industry, this card was produced as part of an advertising campaign by the Monticello Action Committee and was paid for with a grant from a local automobile agency.

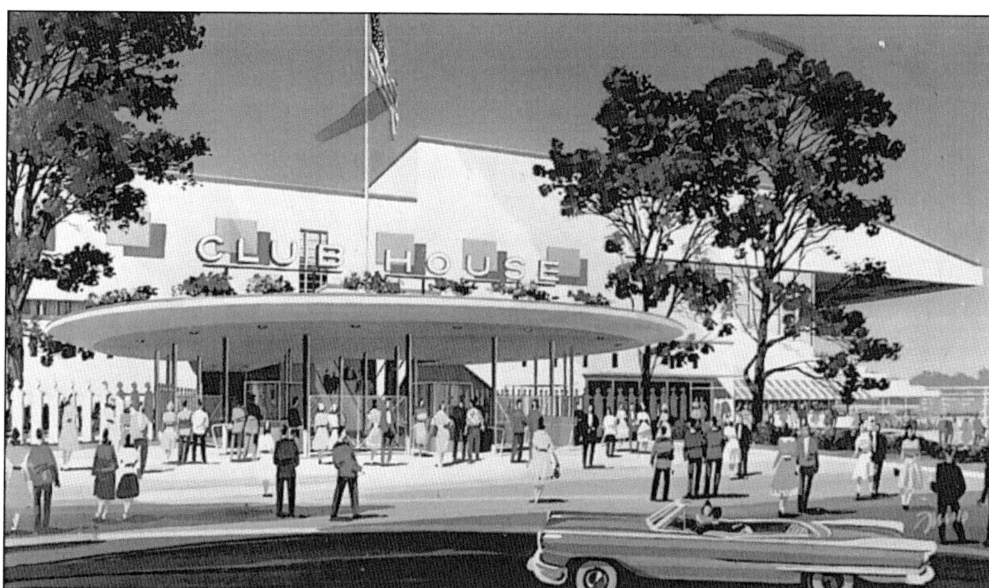

The Monticello Raceway, which opened in 1958, never looked as glamorous as it did in this card printed by "Max Schwartz, N.Y.C.—So. Fallsburg, N.Y." Enhanced with the image of a large-tail finned convertible, the card is typical of the brash advertising of the period.

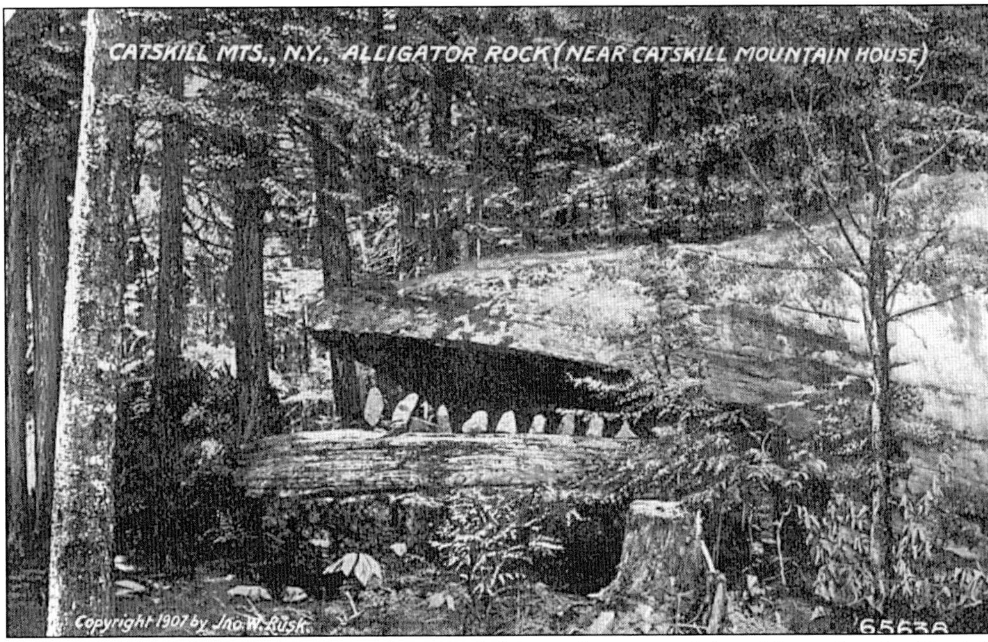

Alligator Rock is the enhancement of a natural feature that was widely celebrated in the Catskill region and was the subject of a number of postcard versions. Several earlier paintings of the rock formation are also known, but the Hudson River painters who produced them never included the "teeth" in their canvases.

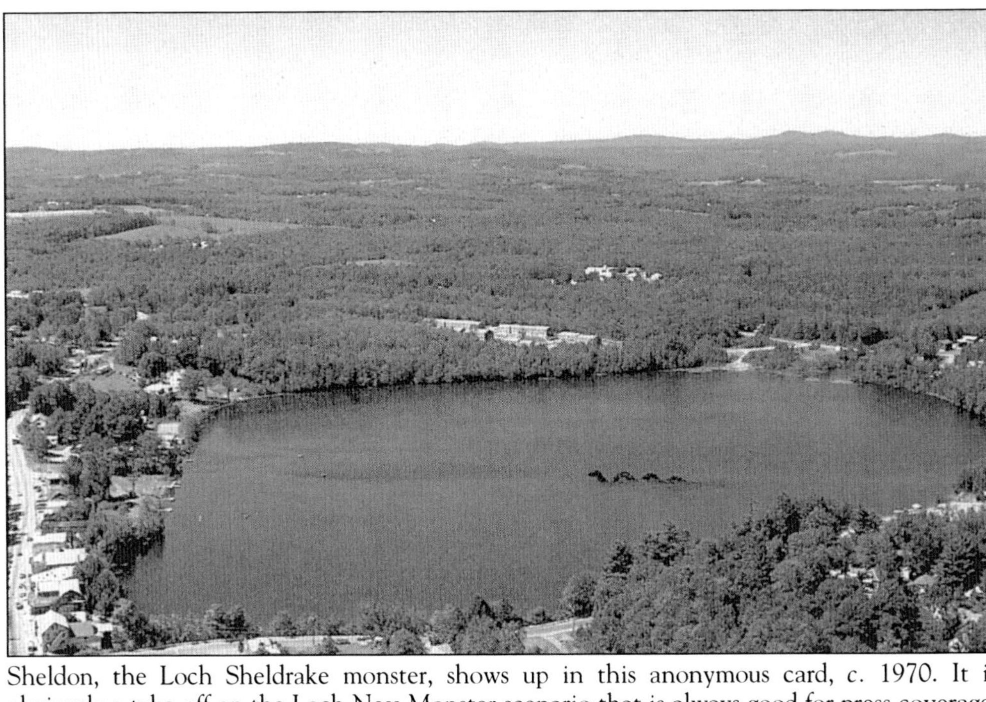

Sheldon, the Loch Sheldrake monster, shows up in this anonymous card, c. 1970. It is obviously a take-off on the Loch Ness Monster scenario that is always good for press coverage. One lakeside antique dealer claims that "Sheldon only comes out on Jewish holidays, and especially on Tish A' Bov."

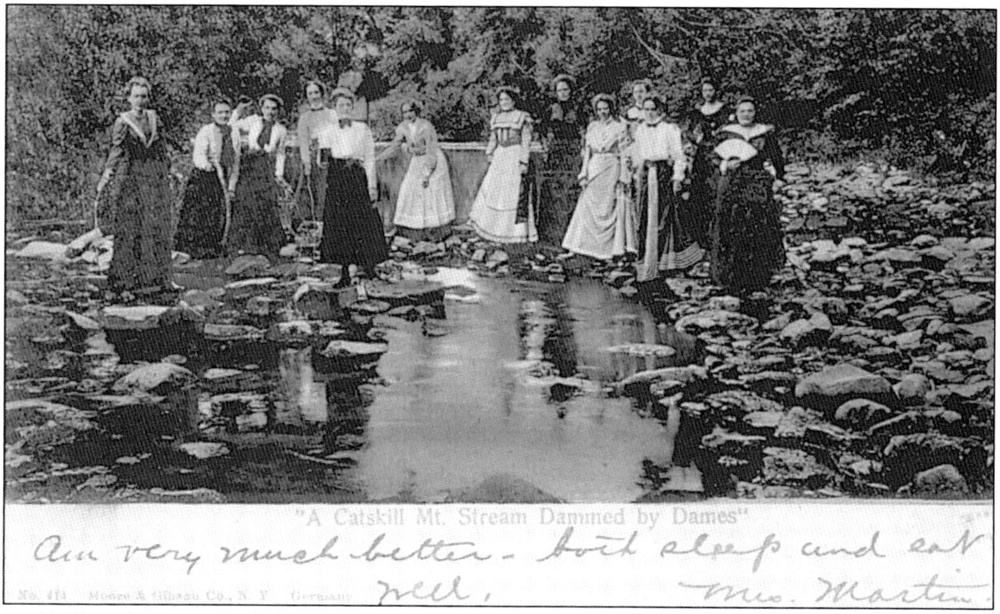

In 1905, polite people didn't say "damn," but many could laugh at the double entendre of "a Damn of Dames" that emphasized the carefree fun of a Catskill holiday. Especially note the lady with the fan. No one had to get their skirt wet.

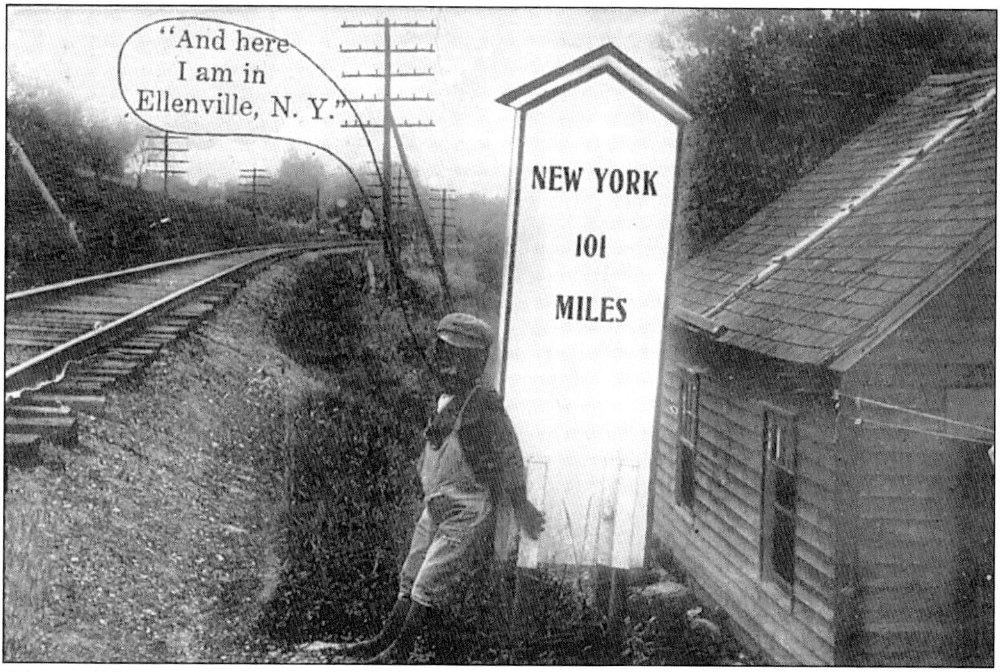

African Americans are rare in Catskill postcards. This enigmatic Ellenville card fits in with the popular, derogatory, early-20th-century "Negro" imagery. Printed in New York City, the card is obviously a composite, with the boy leaning against an outhouse, whose lines humorously double as an arrow. Many African Americans worked behind the scenes in the resort industry and there were, and are, African-American resorts in the Catskills, most notably, Peg Leg Bates Country Club in Ulster County.

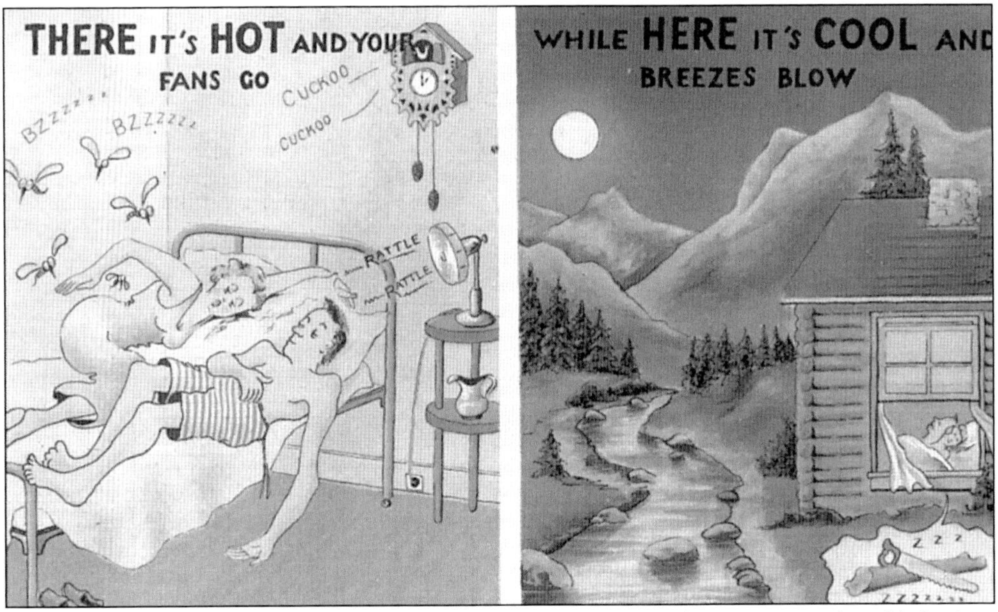

The reasons for a vacation in the mountains are shown in this 1940s card, published in Asheville, North Carolina, c. 1940. Note all the annoyances of the city: mosquitoes, heat, and noise. The mountains, again apparently the Rockies, are where you can sleep covered, with your windows unscreened.

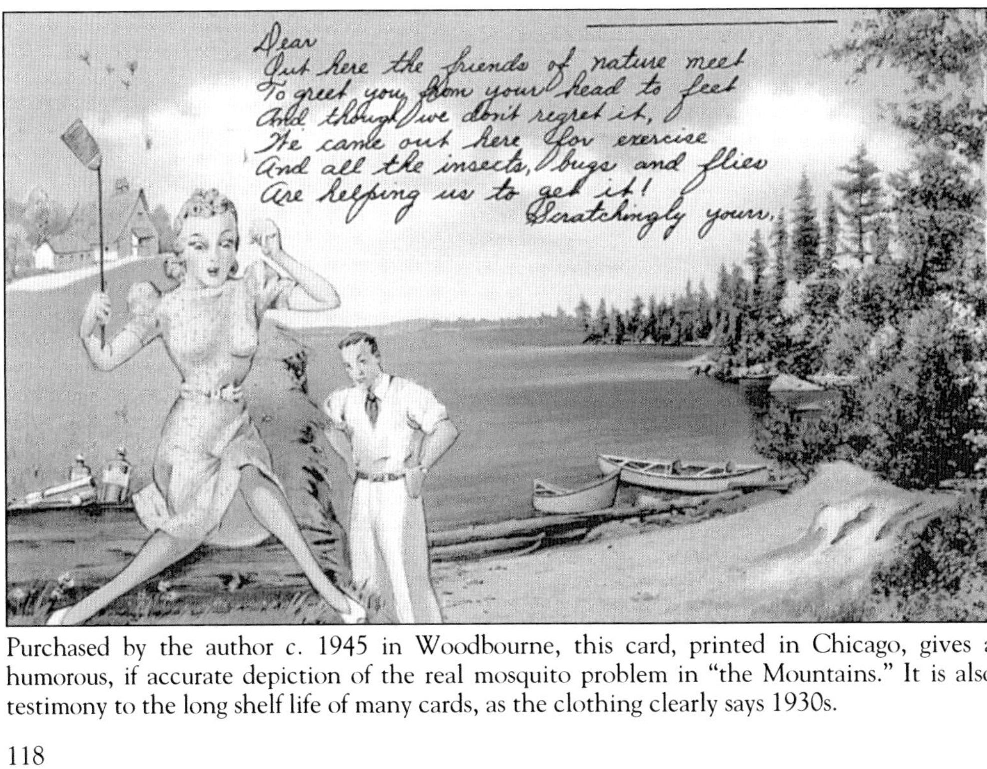

Purchased by the author c. 1945 in Woodbourne, this card, printed in Chicago, gives a humorous, if accurate depiction of the real mosquito problem in "the Mountains." It is also testimony to the long shelf life of many cards, as the clothing clearly says 1930s.

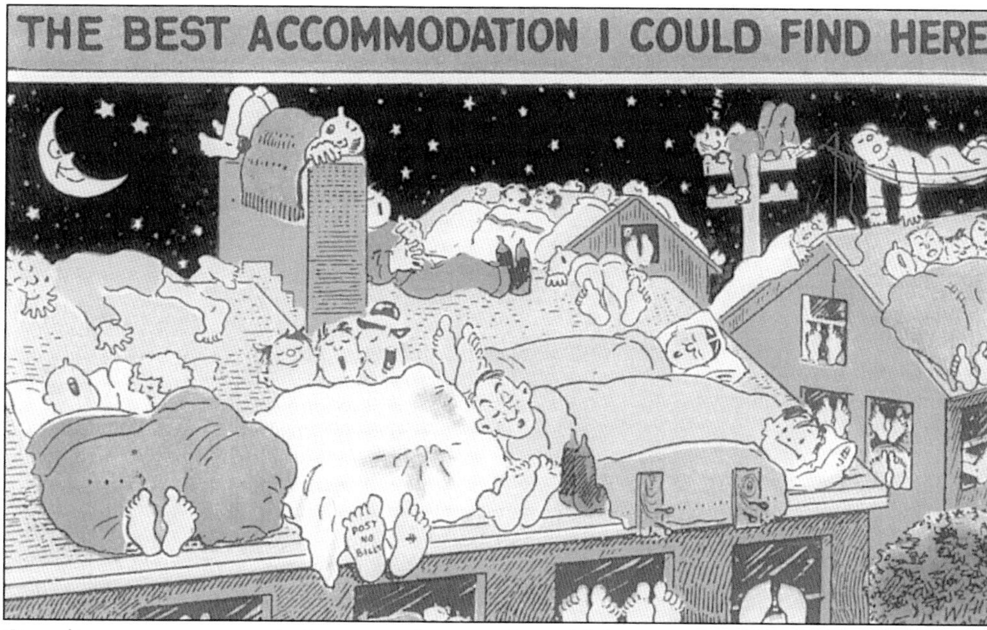

Crowding into accommodations was always a fact of life at resorts. Nowhere more than in Sullivan County, where this Asheville, North Carolina–printed card was acquired. At bungalow colonies, it was a point of honor as to how many guests could fit into accommodations. Even at plush hotels, a whole family usually shared one room.

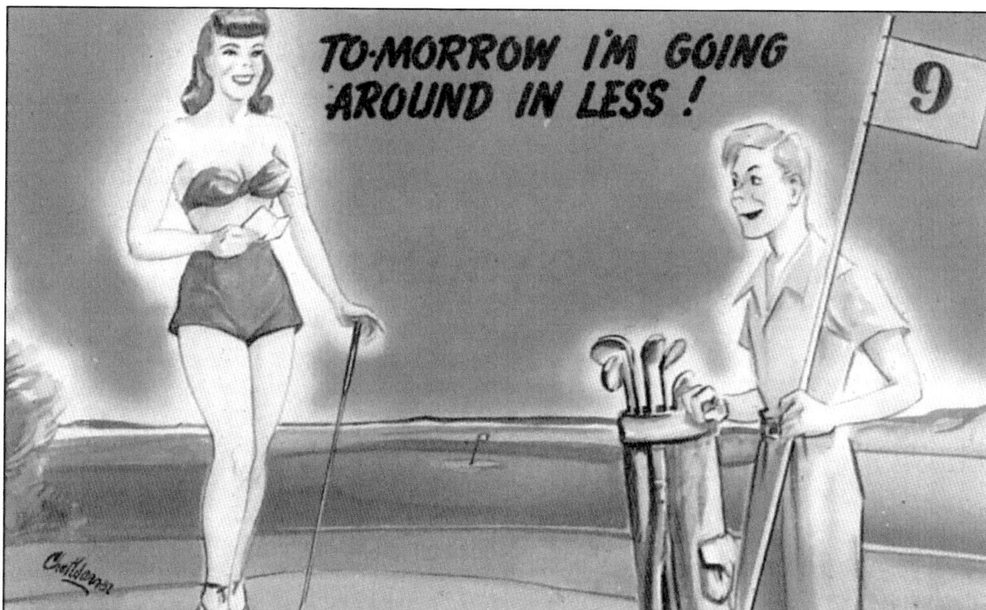

Sex and sports always sell well. This 1950s card was purchased by the author in Woodbourne, c. 1952. The female figure is inspired by the Vargas girls made popular by the magazine *Esquire*. It is one of the many risque cards sold throughout the Catskills in the boom years. Every local drugstore had racks of them.

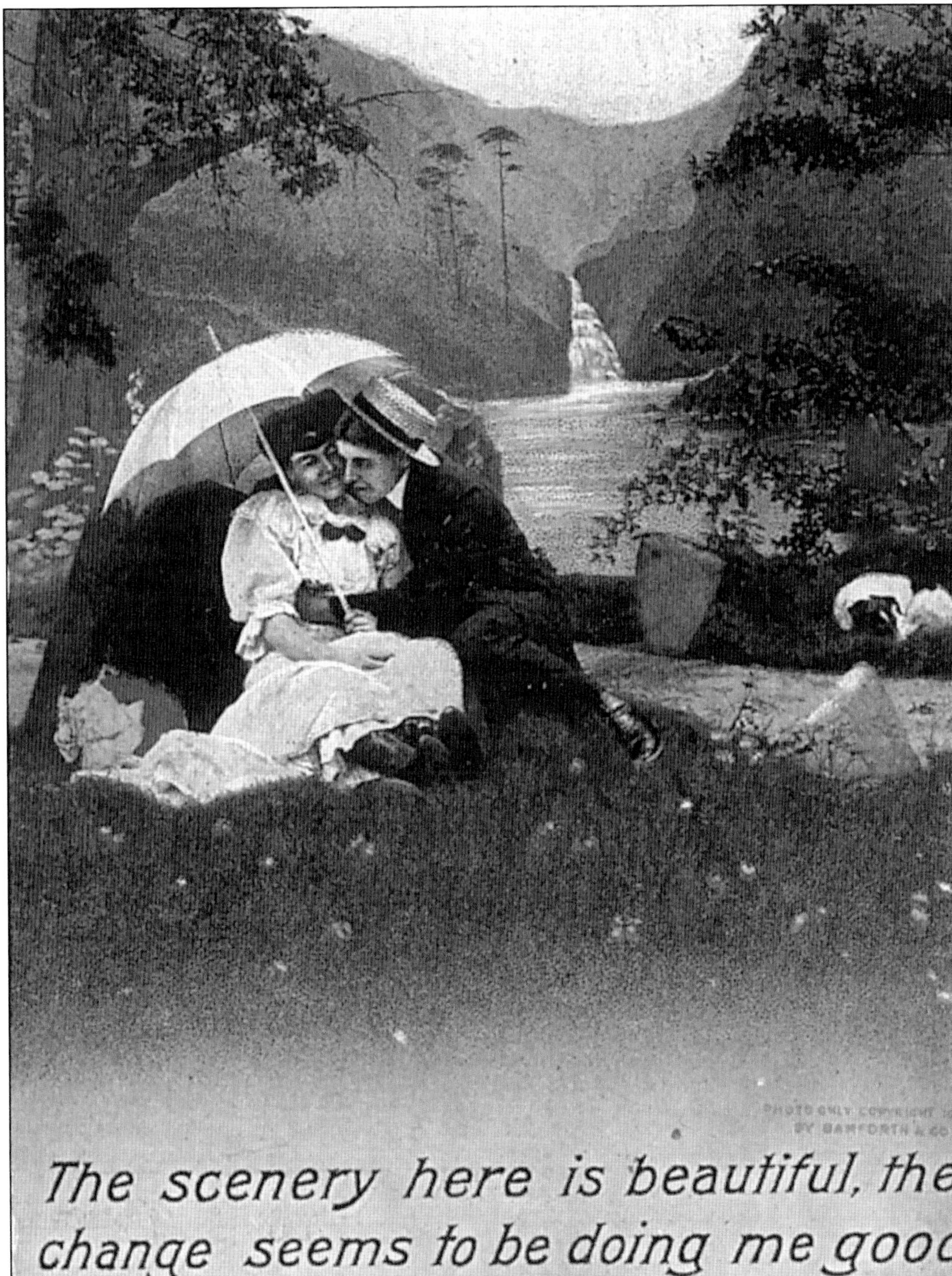

While the Catskill vacation reality was a family one, often in crowded surroundings, allusions of summer romance were always present. What more could you ask for than a flirtation under a parasol, beneath a tree, with a waterfall in the background? The year was 1908.

Eight

Postscript:
Final Thoughts After Looking Through 25,000 Postcards

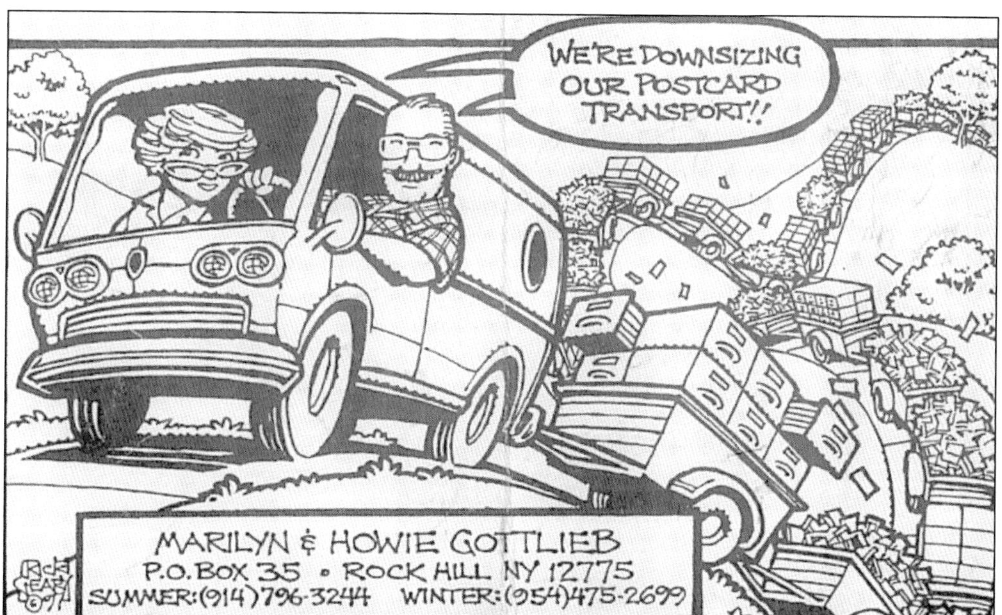

Marilyn and Howie Gottlieb may have helped create the demand for Catskill postcards. Certainly, they are premier dealers who stock thousands of Catskill cards. Representative of a Catskill trend, they are also snowbirds, wintering in Florida. Their business cards (and they have many versions) are all postcards, naturally.

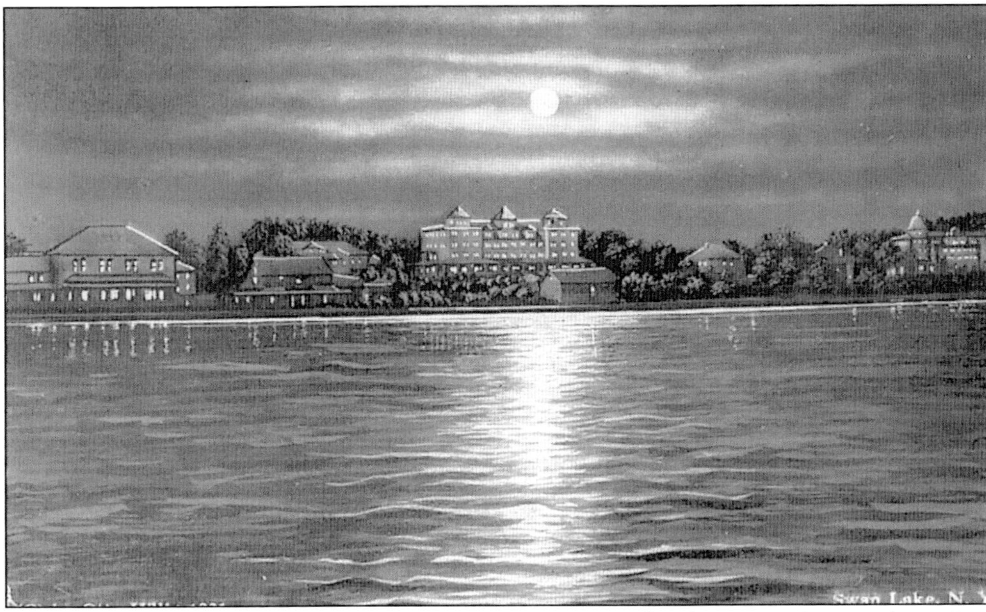

The most interesting and important Sullivan County postcard makers were German-born Otto Hillig and A.S. Landis. Hillig's night view of Swan Lake was probably photographed during the daytime and then mechanically altered, adding the moon. It is, however, romantic and evocative. Landis specialized in creating aerial views of his subjects. Both Hillig and Landis, in true Catskill fashion, enhanced their images. The Royal Inn was an example of a rather grandiloquently named hotel, and there were many: the Palace, the Grand, and the Plaza, for example. A small family hotel that failed to last long enough to install a swimming pool touted itself as "An ideal spot for summer with all modern improvements. Bathing. All sports facilities." All traces of this hotel, which stood on Route 42 between Fallsburg and Woodbourne, are gone.

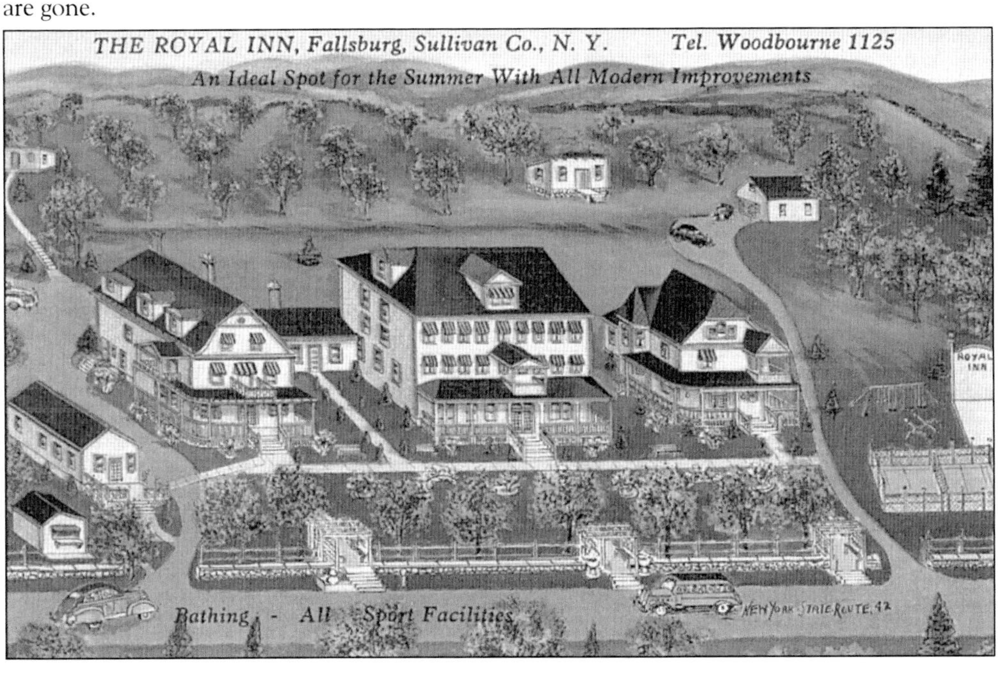

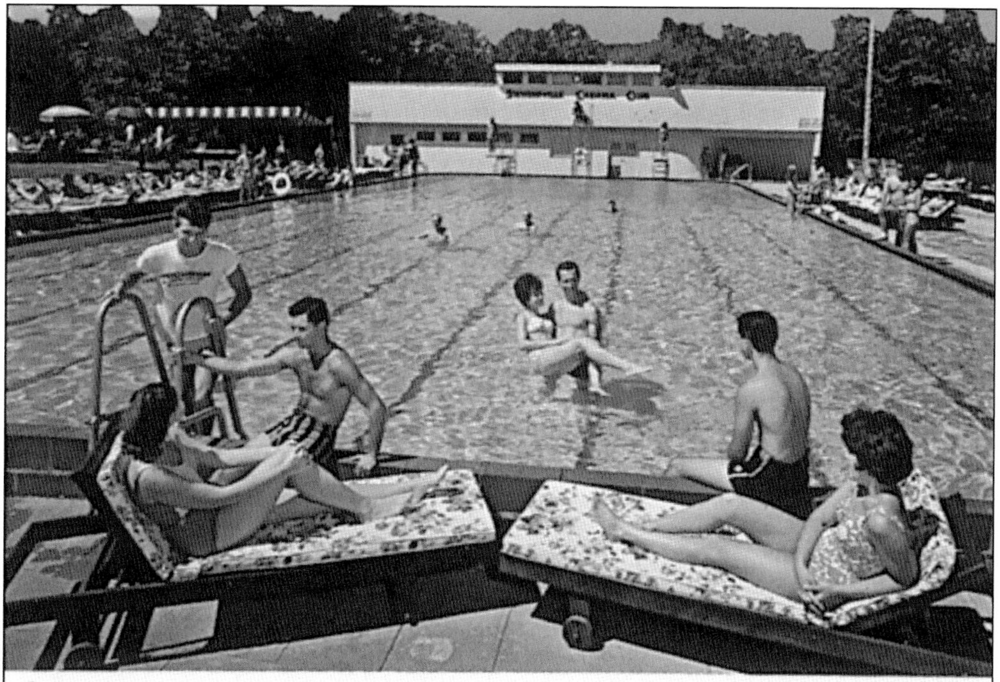

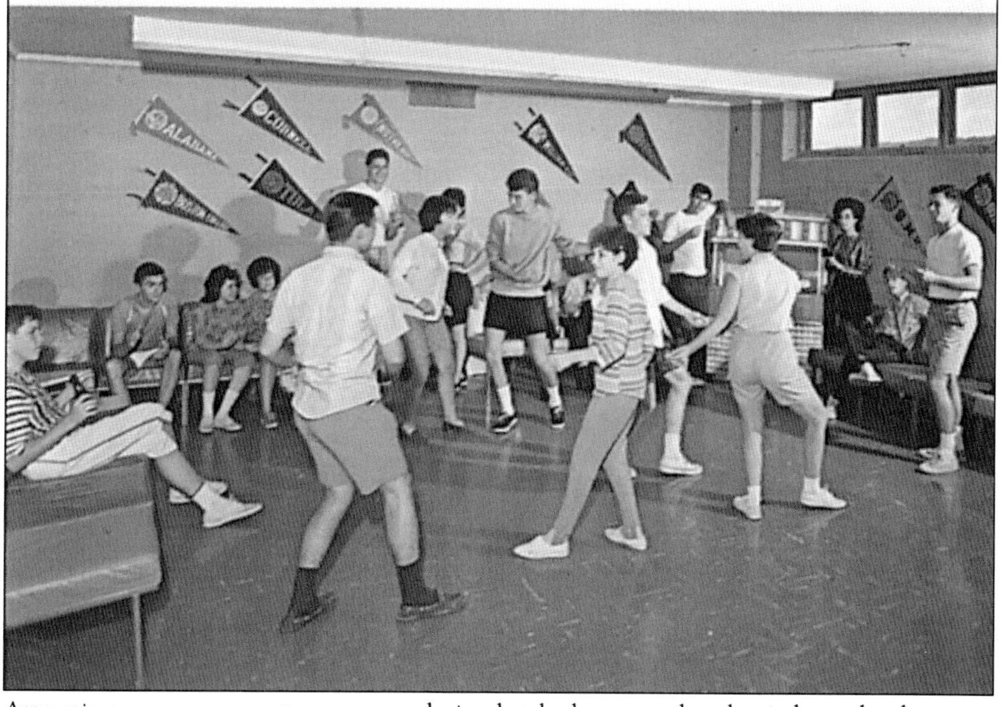

Attracting new, young customers was a losing battle, but many hotels tried very hard to cater to a "with it" crowd. At the Stevensville on Swan Lake, the couples dance the twist against a background of polyglot college pennants: Cornell, Boston College, Tulane, Notre Dame, and Alabama. (Somebody must have gotten a good deal on that batch.) Aside from Cornell, they do not represent the dream colleges of New York's Jewish middle class.

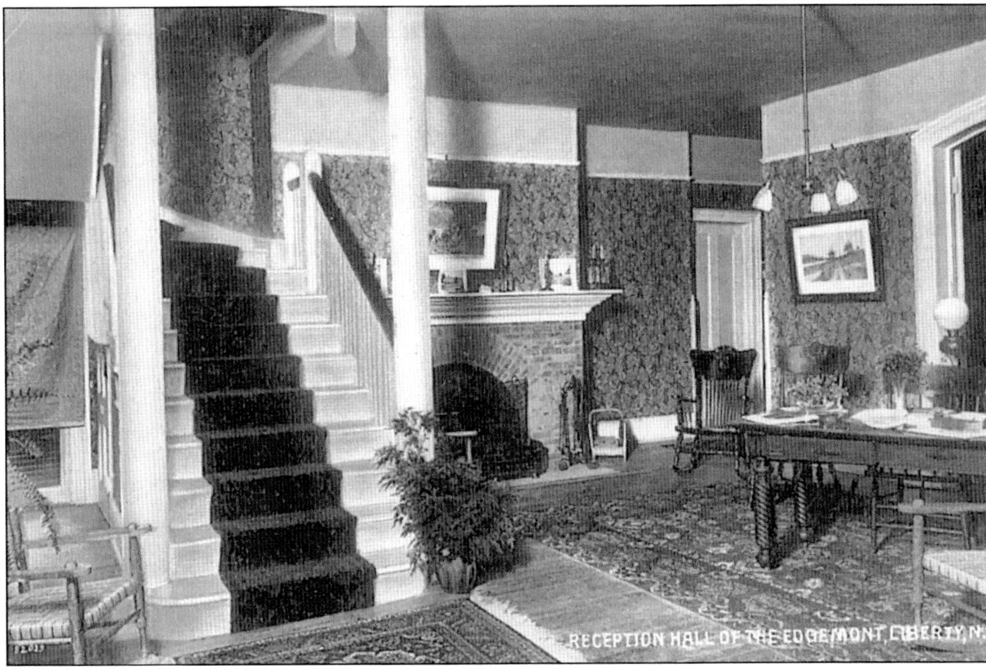

While the Catskills is best known for its glitz, another important, if lesser-known attribute was that it was homey, or *haimish*, to use the Yiddish word. The *c.* 1910 reception hall of the Edgemont Hotel in Liberty showed the same kind of Edwardian comfort that you can still find at the Mohonk Mountain House near New Paltz. While the Avon Lodge in Woodridge was very proud of its "luxurious lobby for comfort and relaxation after delicious meals or days of fun filled activity," the space looked just like an oversized, middle-class, 1950s living room. Teenaged Sid Caesar worked here as a *Tummler* and musician. The future star even married the boss's daughter. With the decline of the Catskills, show business lost one of its great training grounds for young talent.

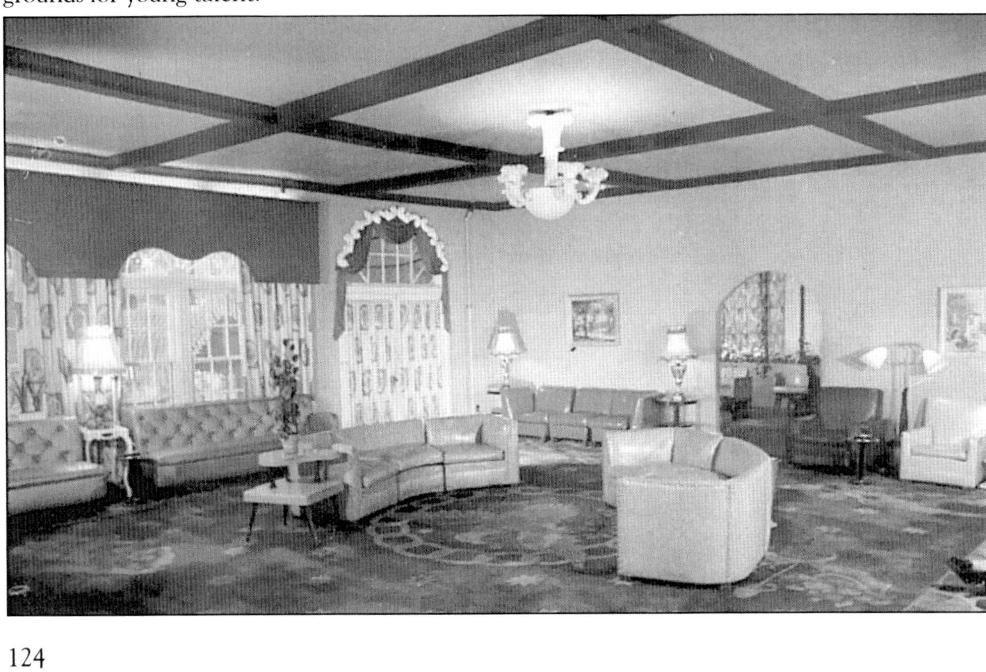

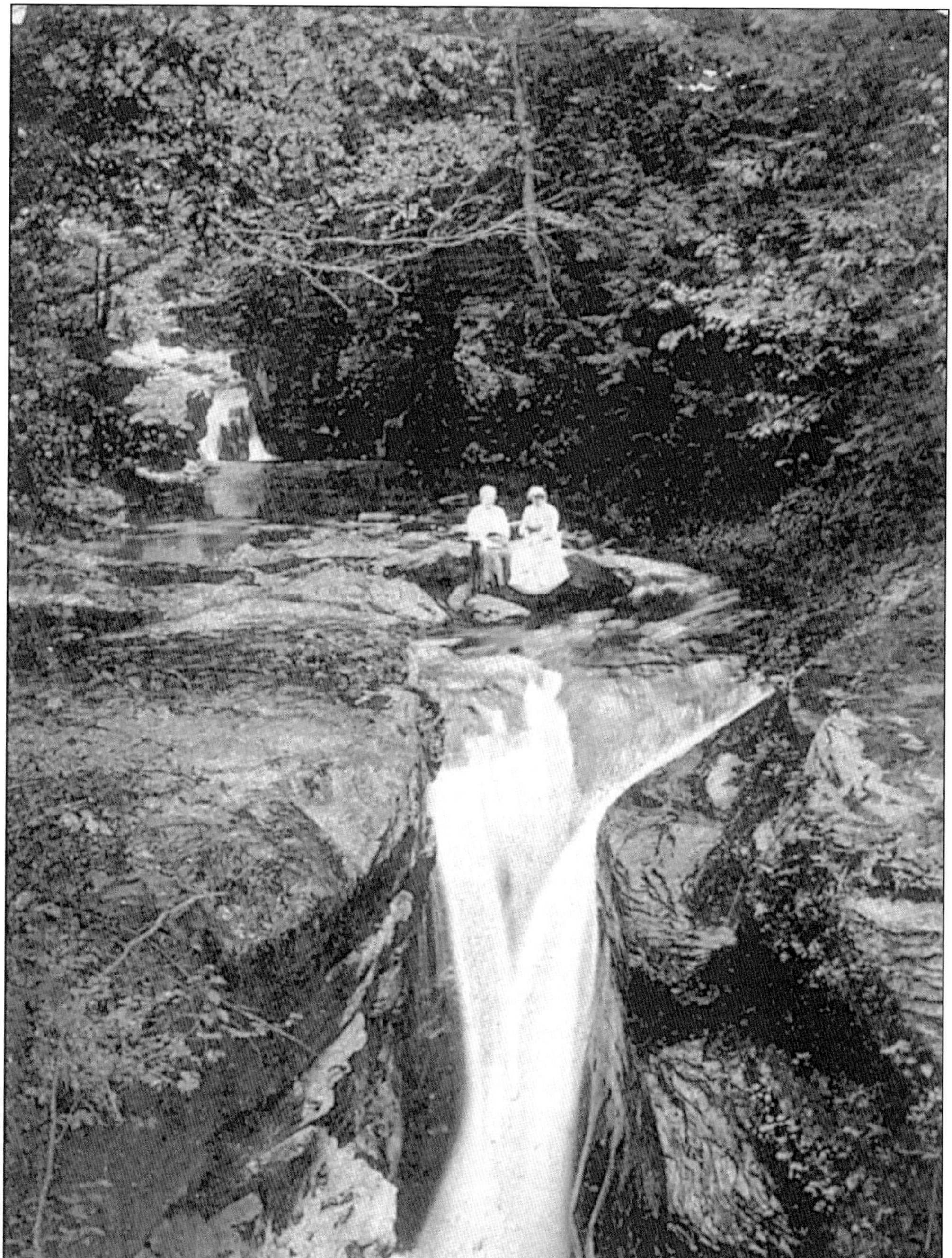

The Catskills do not always provide exactly what is expected. Names can fool. Many have been dreamed up by railroad publicists. Others are more individual and eccentric. Here, an elderly couple sit on a rock at Upper Shin Creek Falls at Lew Beach. Tourists often ask locals, "How do we get to the beach?" The answer: "There is no beach!" The place was simply named for a man named Lew Beach. Irving Berlin (1888–1989), Mister American Music, summered at Lew Beach for over 50 years. Few of his neighbors ever saw Berlin, as he always liked his privacy and always traveled by chauffeured limousine.

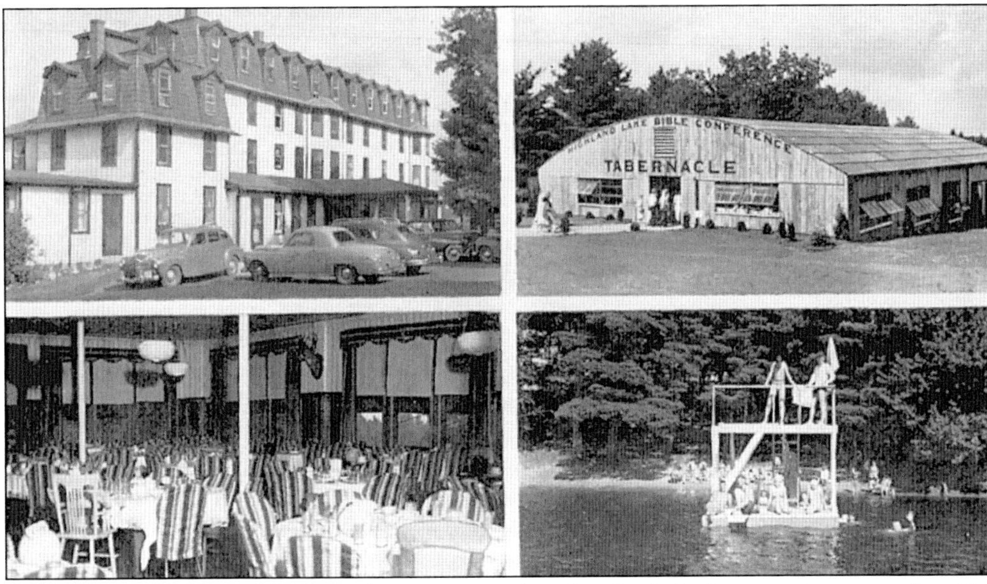

The secular and the worldly have always coexisted in the Catskills, but not always comfortably. While "Jewish" and "Catskills" are synonymous for many, the stereotype is erroneous. Most religions and ethnic and racial groups have enclaves in the Catskills. The year-round population of the entire area is overwhelmingly Christian, as it has always been. The land best known for glitzy hotels has a surprising number of church camps and conference centers, as well as several ashrams. Highland Lake Bible Conference, *c.* 1950, portrays a Christian environment with "125 hotel rooms overlooking two mountain lakes in the beautiful Catskills." A few years later, the Granit Hotel and Country Club in Kerhonkson offered a very Jewish environment with "New luxurious lobbies, Indoor Pool and Health Club," and a brown-haired goddess, posing in front a small Catskill lake, one filled with prosaic rowboats.

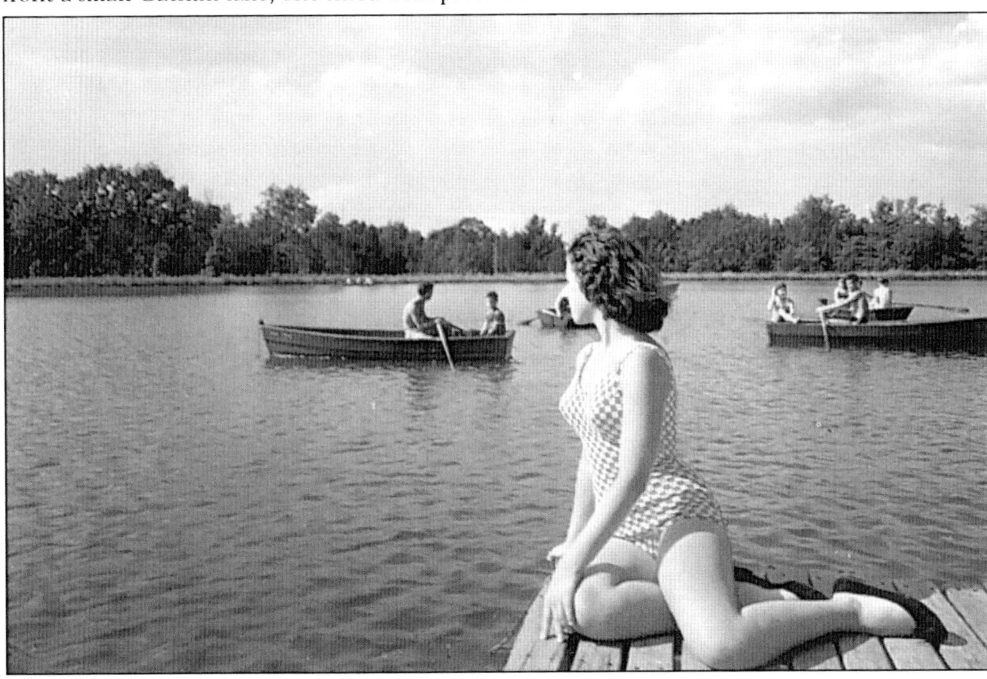

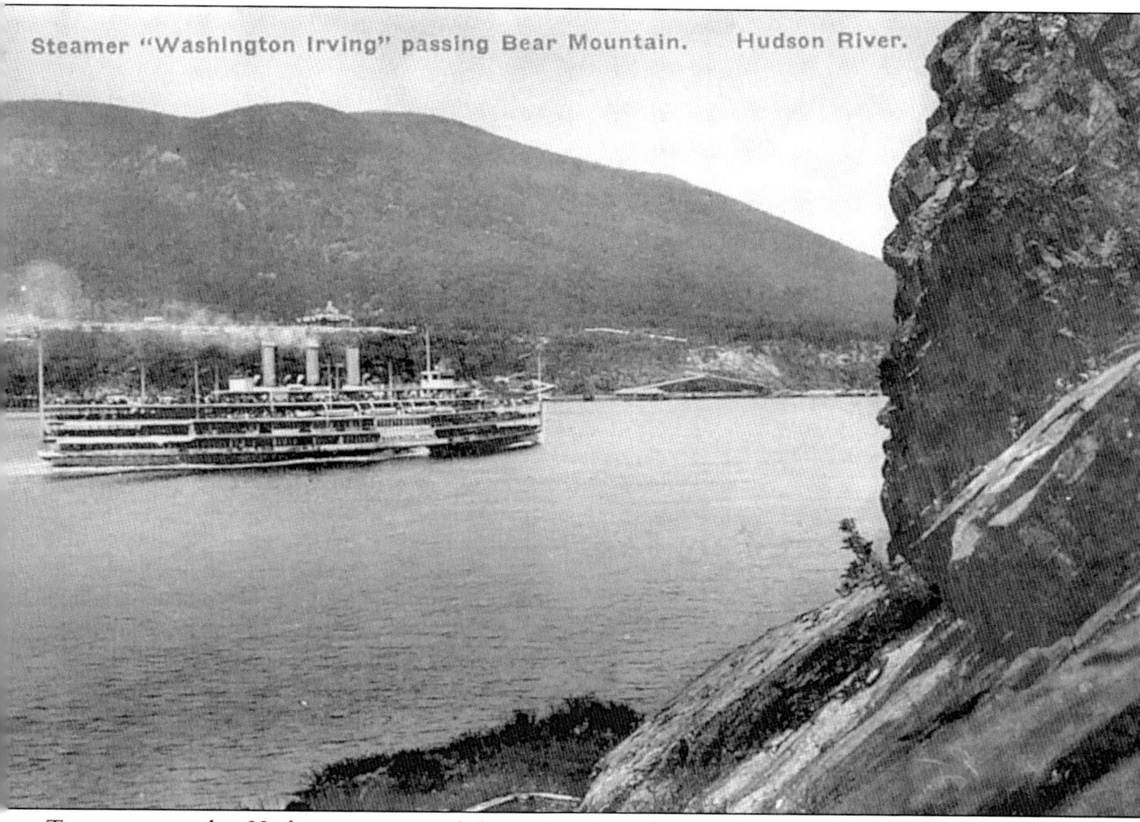

To steam up the Hudson was a modish outing as well as a scenery lover's delight. The composition of the *Washington Irving,* shown passing Bear Mountain, is very similar to the paintings by twin painters James Bard (1815–1897) and John Bard (1815–1856), who, during their careers, "recorded almost every steamer operating on or around New York . . . and the Hudson River." The author hopes that your trip up the Hudson and through the Catskills has been an enjoyable one. Call again!

Bibliography

Adams, Joey, and Henry Tobias. *The Borscht Belt*. New York: The Bobbs-Merrill Company Inc., 1959.

Brown, Phil. *Catskill Culture: A Mountain Rat's Memories of the Great Jewish Resort Area*. Philadelphia: Temple University Press, 1999.

Burgess, Larry E. *Mohonk: Its People and Spirit*. New Paltz, N.Y.: Mohonk Mountain House, 1980.

Conway, John. *Retrospect: An Anecdotal History of Sullivan County, New York*. Fleishmanns, N.Y.: Purple Mountain Press, 1996.

DuBois, Philip H. *A Catskill Boyhood: My Life Along the Hudson: 1908-1921*. Hensonville, N.Y.: Black Dome Press Corp., 1992.

Dulles, Foster Rhea. *A History of Recreation*, 2nd ed. Englewood Cliffs, N.J.: Jersey: Prentice-Hall Inc., 1965.

Evers, Alf. *The Catskills: From Wilderness to Woodstock*. Garden City, N.Y.: Doubleday & Company Inc., 1972.

Evers, Alf, et al. *Resorts of the Catskills*. New York: St. Martin's Press, 1979.

Fried, Marc B. *The Huckleberry Pickers: A Raucous History of the Shawangunk Mountains*. Hensonville, N.Y.: Black Dome Press Corp., 1995.

Frommer, Myrna Katz and Harvey Frommer. *It Happened in the Catskills: An Oral History*. New York: Harcourt Brace Jovanovich, 1991.

Gold, David M., ed. *The River and the Mountains: Readings in Sullivan County History*. South Fallsburg, N.Y.: Marielle Press, 1994.

Kanfer, Stefan. *A Summer World: The Attempt to Build a Jewish Eden in the Catskills*. New York: Farrar Straus Giroux, 1989.

Lavender, Abraham and Clarence B. Steinberg. *Jewish Farmers of the Catskills: A Century of Survival*. Gainsville: University Press of Florida, 1995.

Longstreth, T. Morris. *The Catskills*. New York: The Century Co., 1918.

Monahan, Valerie. *An American Postcard Collector's Guide*. Poole, Dorset, United Kingdom: Blanford Press, 1981.

Myers, Kenneth and Margaret Favretti. *The Catskills: Painters, Writers, and Tourists in the Mountains, 1820–1895*. Yonkers, New York: The Hudson River Museum of Westchester, 1987.

O'Neil, John P., ed. *American Paradise: The World of the Hudson River School*. New York: The Metropolitan Museum of Art, 1988.

Richman, Irwin. *Borscht Belt Bungalows: Memories of Catskill Summers*. Philadelphia: Temple University Press, 1998.

Rubin, Cynthia Elyce and Morgan Williams. *Larger Than Life: The American Tall-Tale Postcard, 1905-1915*. New York: Abbeville Press, 1990.

Ryan, Dorothy B. *Picture Postcards in the United States, 1893–1918*, updated ed. New York: Clarkson N. Potter, 1982.

Staff, Frank. *The Picture Postcard and Its Origins*. New York: Frederick A. Praeger, 1966.

VanZandt, Roland. *The Catskill Mountain House*. New Brunswick, N.J.: Rutgers University 1966.

Wakefield, Manville B. *To The Mountains by Rail*. Grahamsville, N.Y.: Wakefair Press, 1970.